Phenomenology and
Philosophical Understanding

Phenomenology and Philosophical Understanding

EDITED BY

EDO PIVČEVIĆ

Senior Lecturer in Philosophy at the
University of Bristol

CAMBRIDGE UNIVERSITY PRESS

CAMBRIDGE

LONDON · NEW YORK · MELBOURNE

Published by the Syndics of the Cambridge University Press
The Pitt Building, Trumpington Street, Cambridge CB2 1RP
Bentley House, 200 Euston Road, London NW1 2DB
32 East 57th Street, New York, NY 10022, USA
296 Beaconsfield Parade, Middle Park, Melbourne 3206, Australia

© Cambridge University Press 1975

Library of Congress Catalogue Card Number: 74-19533

ISBNs
0 521 20637 5 hard covers
0 521 09914 5 paperback

First published 1975

Photoset and printed in Malta by St Paul's Press Ltd

Contents

vi *Contents*

Editor's Introduction

Phenomenologists are not exactly renowned for their clarity. Their writings bristle with obscurities and jargon which baffle the layman and often make it difficult for him to see what problems precisely are being discussed. The purpose of this volume is to help the interested reader to identify some of these problems by removing at least some of the esoteric haze that surrounds them.

My original intention when compiling a list of topics for this volume was to include in it, in addition to new material, selected passages from the writings of well known phenomenologists to illustrate their style of approach. However it soon became apparent to me that to do this would mean to increase considerably the size of the volume without offering any great advantages from the readers' point of view. Short passages taken out of context are notoriously difficult to understand even when they originate from the books of the most lucid writers. An additional reason for abandoning my original plan was the fact that the main works of most better known continental phenomenologists are now available in English translation.

I mention all this by way of an apology to Martin Heidegger who suggested that I publish in this volume Section 7 from his book *Being and Time*, entitled 'The Phenomenological Method of Inquiry', in which he explains his own understanding of the concept of phenomenon and of phenomenology. I had originally invited him to write an entirely new paper for this collection, but he wrote back to say that because of his advanced age he felt unable to undertake this task and suggested that I publish instead the already mentioned section from his book.

Having reluctantly decided against the idea, I feel that I must report, however briefly and inadequately, Heidegger's views on phenomenology as expressed in this section. This will at once give me an opportunity to illustrate some of the difficulties involved in editing a volume of this kind. But I must begin with Husserl.

The subject-matter of phenomenological researches are *experiences* – their types and their structures; but Husserl was very anxious that a phenomenological analysis of experiences should not be confused with a psychological analysis of experiences. Psychology is an empirical science which studies experiences as empirical events in an empirical world and all its descriptions and generalizations refer to experiences in this empirical context. Phenomenology involves a different kind of attitude: it involves, in Husserl's own phrase, 'placing within brackets' the existential, the 'historical' aspect of experiences and concentrating on the 'essences' or the 'ideal types' exemplified by the experiences which we either have or can, in creative imagination, conceive ourselves as having. Phenomenology studies such essences and clarifies the various relationships between them. It investigates the essential structures of presentation, perception, judgement, feelings, etc. – in short, that which 'may be seen through a purely intuitive apprehension of essence, whether generic or specific. In a similar way pure arithmetic speaks of numbers, and pure geometry of spatial shapes, employing pure intuitions in their ideational universality' (*Logical Investigations*, Introduction to Volume Two).

Husserl is here likening phenomenology to 'pure arithmetic' and 'pure geometry'. None of them are empirical sciences. They make no pronouncements about empirical matters of fact. They are concerned, rather, with certain types of structures and their inter-relationships, and their statements articulate the characterizing features of these structures and do not involve any references to empirical particulars. They are what Husserl calls 'sciences of essences' or 'eidetic sciences' (Husserl uses 'essence' and 'eidos' interchangeably). In a sense, the relation between phenomenology (as understood by Husserl) and psychology is comparable to the relation between mathematics and physics. Psychology, like physics, is an empirical science and it depends on phenomenology for a clarification of its basic concepts in a similar way in which physics relies on mathematics for a clarification of its own basic ideas. However, this analogy should not obscure the fact that, philosophically, phenomenology stands higher than mathematics, for even mathematical concepts require a phenomenological clarification. Phenomenology also stands higher than logic in this sense: that by exploring the essential structures of the experiences of thinking and knowing it helps to bring the ideas of logic to 'epistemological clarity and definiteness'; indeed it helps to clarify the very foundations of knowledge.

Husserl's basic position might be summed up thus. We articulate knowledge in judgements, but judgements are validated by evidential experience and there are two distinct types of such experience: the evidential experience commonly referred to as 'sense-perception' which is directed to empirical matters of fact and the evidential experience which Husserl calls the 'essential' or 'eidetic' intuition *(Wesensschau)* and which (he claims) gives us access to types, structures and connections of meaning. This latter kind of evidential experience is presupposed by any 'conceptual analysis' and any 'necessary proposition'. That $a + 1 = 1 + a$, that a judgement cannot be coloured, that of every two sounds that differ in quality one is lower and the other higher, that a perception as such is a perception of something – all these and similar propositions, according to Husserl, 'bring to developed expression data of eidetic intuition' (see *Ideas*, §20).

That there exists a fundamental difference between these two kinds of evidential experience, i.e. between the 'sensory' and the 'eidetic seeing', is, Husserl claims, a *phenomenological fact*. Husserl wants to show that this is directly relevant to an analysis of experiences themselves, for experiences too can be subject to eidetic intuition; we can, he claims, abstract – in phenomenological reflection – from all existential considerations relating to experiences as empirical events and concentrate exclusively on their eidetic structure. In the case of *cognitive* experiences – the experiences Husserl is primarily interested in – this will yield us important epistemological insights and enable us to clarify the basic presuppositions of all knowledge-claims.

But let us now return to Heidegger. Although Heidegger accepts the general phenomenological distinction between 'sensory' and 'eidetic seeing' his attitude differs from that of Husserl. I do not think that he would care to compare phenomenology either with 'pure arithmetic' or 'pure geometry'. Nor is he interested in the same kind of experiences as Husserl. From his point of view, the experiences which merit greatest philosophical attention are not the experiences which find expression in statements of logic and science, but those which most frequently find expression in *poetry*. It is (he believes) only through a searching phenomenological analysis of these latter experiences that we may hope to achieve something that Husserl, from his own position, was unable to achieve, namely a clarification of the meaning of *being*. Heidegger not only regards this as the main philosophical task; he, in effect, *identifies* philosophical phenomenology with the carrying out of this task.

In this connection it is interesting to note what he has to say (in *Being and Time*) about phenomena and *being*. He distinguishes between what he calls the 'vulgar' and the 'phenomenological' concept of a phenomenon. Phenomena in the 'vulgar' sense are phenomenal entities, objects of empirical intuition (in Kant's sense), or such like. But phenomena in the 'phenomenological' sense are not entities or existents of any sort. They are not object-like; they cannot be perceived, inspected or studied in the manner of objects. They have to do with the 'how' rather than with the 'what' of objects. They are not 'neutral' items of this or that sort which call for an equally 'neutral' and 'detached' description. They have to do with modes of existing; they relate not to entities *qua* entities, but to *being*. They reveal the manner in which we are; the mode of our own being. They make themselves known through moods, feelings, emotions.

In short, the specifically phenomenological concept of a phenomenon is linked by Heidegger with *being* and the elucidation of the meaning of *being* (or perhaps we should say the meaning of *To-be*). This immediately prompts two questions: first, does this linking of the phenomenological concept of a phenomenon with *being* imply that only an analysis of the meaning of *being* (in the manner in which Heidegger himself conducts such an analysis), rather than, say, a Husserlian type of analysis of knowledge, deserves to be called 'phenomenological' in the fundamental sense of the word? Secondly, if, as Heidegger suggests (in the same section), *being* (*Sein*, To-be) is *je Sein vom Seiendem* – i.e. it is always *being* of that which exists, would it not be fair to say that we can meaningfully speak of 'being' only in the sense of the *manner-of-being* of an existent? This would immediately remove much of the mysteriousness surrounding the word 'being', for this word would no longer be associated with something above and beyond the manner-of-being of existents.

I put both these questions to Heidegger and this is what he replied:

Both your questions are important.

As far as the first question is concerned, phenomenon in the sense of philosophical phenomenology is only *being*. Here it is important to bear in mind that this phenomenon 'at first and in most cases does not show itself' (*Being and Time*, p. 35). It is made to show itself through phenomenological thought.

As for the second question, *being* is such that it is *being* of existents. All the same there is an ontological difference between the two. This difference characterizes both *being* and existents in respect of the possibility of their necessary mutual connection. It is this difference that is the actual topic of the question about the 'meaning of *being*'. This is discussed in a course of lectures on the *Fundamental Problems of Phenomenology* which I gave in Heidelberg in 1927 – the year of the publication of *Being and Time* – and which have not yet appeared in print. This topic has been also the subject of my subsequent philosophical preoccupations (comp. *Identity and Difference*, 1957, p. 59ff.).[1]

I leave these replies without comment. My purpose here is merely to draw attention to the fact that there are different views as to what course a phenomenological rescarch should pursue and what the principal objectives of such a research should be. Phenomenology does not designate a well defined body of doctrine. The word 'phenomenology' has been used in a variety of philosophical contexts. The concept of a phenomenon itself has been given different interpretations by different phenomenologists. We saw that for Heidegger 'phenomenon in the phenomenological sense is only *being*'. This was not Husserl's view. And a linguistic philosopher like Austin who at one time described his own brand of philosophical analysis as 'linguistic phenomenology' would have disagreed both with Heidegger and (in varying degrees) with Husserl, had he had read them. The phenomena which Austin considered to be of central

---

[1] 'Ihre beiden Fragen sind wichtig.

Zu 1. Phänomenon im Sinne der philosophischen Phänomenologie ist nur das Sein. Dabei bleibt zu beachten, dass dieses Phänomen sich zunächst und zumeist nicht zeigt' (*S. u. Z.* S.35). Es wird durch das phänomenologische Denken erst zum Sich-zeigen gebracht.

Zu 2. Sein ist als solches Sein des Seienden. Zwischen beiden besteht die ontologische Differenz. Dieser Unterschied bestimmt zumal Sein und Seiendes in der Möglichkeit ihres notwendigen Zusammengehörens. Er ist das eigentliche Thema der Frage nach dem "Sinn von Sein". Darüber handelt die im Jahre des Erscheinens von *Sein und Zeit* 1927 gehaltene, aber noch unveröffentlichte Marburger Vorlesung *Grundprobleme der Phänomenologie*. An diese Thematik hält sich auch mein späteres Denken (vergl. *Identität und Differenz* 1957, S. 59ff.).'

importance and which he was trying to elucidate were 'speech acts'. (See pp. 109–24 below) The disconcerting fact is that philosophers who regard themselves as 'phenomenologists' often radically differ in their handling of key philosophical issues. What unites them – and I am thinking here primarily of the 'phenomenological school' initiated by Brentano and Husserl – is their acceptance of the general principle that philosophical priority should be given to an analysis of experiences from the point of view of those who have the experiences or are able to have them.

Inevitably the differences and disagreements among phenomenologists of different denominations complicate the editorial problems involved in compiling a volume of this kind. What editorial policy should one adopt? Quite clearly, it is impossible, within the necessarily limited space, to give a hearing to every point of view that in one way or another might be characterized as 'phenomenological'. To offer a selection of exegetic articles on some of the more influential phenomenologists would perhaps make the volume attractive to some experts but boring and uninstructive to the majority of other readers. But equally to concentrate exclusively on a few selected problems while leaving out all historical references and all exegetic discussion of known views would be artificial and restrictive as well as unhelpful to many readers who wished to be enlightened about philosophical theories with which they are already partially acquainted from other sources. Obviously special attention had to be paid to Husserl's views, Husserl being the key figure in modern phenomenological philosophy. As for the other topics, I am sure that there are many more equally worthy candidates that would qualify for inclusion in a volume of this kind. But one had to draw a line somewhere and try, within the compass of the topics chosen, to satisfy as far as possible both the theoretical and historical interests of potential readers.

All the papers published here have been specially written for this collection and appear here for the first time. Although the papers can be read independently of each other, the order of topics is not entirely arbitrary and the reader might find it useful to start at the beginning. In the case of some key topics (intentionality, self-evidence, transcendental reduction, freedom) it has been possible to include papers from philosophers who are not favourably disposed to phenomenology or are sharply critical of some of its aspects as well as from those who are sympathetic to it. The contrasts in their respective treatments of these topics should, at the very least, help to throw the problems involved into clearer relief.

In the introductory paper Anthony Quinton discusses the concept of a phenomenon and the various interpretations that have been given of it. This is followed by a discussion of intentionality. David Carr explains the link between the more recent 'linguistic' treatment of intentionality and the traditional phenomenological treatment of this concept, while J. L. Mackie clarifies the distinction between intensionality and intentionality and discusses the possibility, and the difficulties, of a non-intentionalist approach to intentional phenomena. The next two papers are both concerned with self-evidence. D. M. Levin expounds Husserl's notion of self-evidence, while A. J. Ayer discusses the concept of self-evidence from a non-phenomenological point of view. R. Harrison gives a critical analysis of the phenomenologically important concept of prepredicative experience. This is followed by a paper on Austin's so-called 'linguistic phenomenology' from Anthony Manser. A discussion of the method of 'phenomenological reduction' is provided by R. M. Zaner in his paper 'On the Sense of Method in Phenomenology'. J. N. Findlay writes about phenomenology and realism and criticizes Husserl for 'capitulating to idealism' in his later philosophy. Peter Heath, in 'The Idea of a Phenomenological Ethics', discusses the possibility of a phenomenological ethics with regard to the theories of Max Scheler. Paul Ricoeur and Antony Flew both write about the problem of freedom. Ricoeur discusses the phenomenological approach to the problem of freedom and the relevance of a linguistic analysis of 'action discourse' to such an approach, while A. Flew comments on Sartre's views on freedom as expressed in Sartre's book *Being and Nothingness*. Walter Kaufmann examines in detail Hegel's conception of phenomenology. Wolfe Mays explores the link between phenomenological existentialism and Marxism under the title 'Phenomenology and Marxism' and Philip Pettit, in 'The Life-World and Role-Theory', assesses the views of Alfred Schutz.

Finally I analyse some of the difficulties arising from an analytical and a phenomenological treatment of concepts. Each paper is preceded by a short abstract written by the author himself.

Bristol *November 1974*   Edo Pivčević

The Concept of a Phenomenon

ANTHONY QUINTON

In British philosophy 'phenomenon' usually means 'sensory appearance'. Yet until Wittgenstein and Ryle standard British empiricism, following Locke and Kant in this, recognised an inner sense, coordinate with the external, physical senses. Locke is fairly, and Kant very, perfunctory about its nature and workings.
Brentano and Husserl, however, take it very seriously and I go on to consider how well they vindicate the thesis that there is, alongside the awareness of sensible appearances, a parallel awareness of mental phenomena, including the act of sensing itself.

Anthony Quinton is a Fellow of New College, Oxford.
Publications: *Political Philosophy* (ed.), (1967); *The Nature of Things* (1973); *Utilitarian Ethics* (1973); translation, with H. Skolimowski, of *Problems and Theories of Philosophy* by K. Ajdukiewicz (1973).

There are two main ways in which phenomena are contrasted with other things. The more straightforward is that in which ordinary, public, material objects of observation are contrasted with theoretical constructions or entities of various kinds. It is typically used in hard-headed, but comparatively unphilosophical, expressions of impatience with problems arising from what seem to be unnecessarily misleading hypostatisations. One who claims that science is concerned exclusively with phenomena in this sense of the word is probably trying to disembarrass himself of what he takes to be empty puzzles: what is the diameter of an electron, where in the brain is the superego located, what is the *real* measure of an increase in the cost of living?

In philosophy, however, phenomena are ordinarily private or subjective entities; impressions, sense-data, ideas; the things that really appear to, or are directly perceived by, percipients, as contrasted with the public, objective, material things which are the presumed source, in some way or other, of them.

In each case phenomena, as what is actually observed or what actually appears to a perceiver, are set against unobservable, non-appearing things which are somehow inferred, supposed or conjectured on the basis of the phenomena. It is understandable that the straightforward sense of 'phenomenon' should give way to the more extreme and philosophical interpretation. The initially straightforward distinction between what is actually perceived and what is hidden from perception turns out to be less straightforward under critical pressure. Is the wind a phenomenon? It can, after all, be felt on the skin, unlike a cold front. Is a germ, which is, in a way, visible under a microscope, a phenomenon or a theoretical construction?

In so far as the distinction between phenomena and nonphenomena is drawn between different kinds of public and material thing it is weakened to the point of evaporation by the indeterminacy of the logical constraints on the application of the verbs 'observe' and 'perceive' and their specifications, 'see', 'touch' and so on. The philosophically confined sense of 'observe' or 'perceive' removes the indeterminacy at the cost of denying that any of the ordinary objects of perception are really or directly perceived at all. According to it the only true phenomena are the things we perceive *infallibly*.

It is not always concluded that the true, philosophical,

phenomena are strictly private. If the thesis that we do not really perceive material things is mainly based on the fact that our perception of such things is always perspectival and partial, the phenomena that we do really perceive may be taken to be parts of the surfaces of objects or again to be perspective views of them. In that case they may still be conceived as public in that they are available to direct perception by different perceivers. This would seem to be true of the *sensibilia* of Russell's *Our Knowledge of the External World*. Similarly Husserl's claim in *Ideas* that we do not really perceive material things themselves because what actually appears is a perspective view of part of the surface of the object proper leaves open the possibility that the phenomena of sense-perception are inter-subjective. A material object proper could then be conceived as a whole literally composed of parts which are, or could be, or are essentially the same kind of thing as, appearances (although it would not be, as in Russell's slogan, a *class* of appearances). Nevertheless in British studies of perception in this century the dominating tendency has always been to conclude that the given phenomena of sense-perception are private. The seeming irresistibility of this conclusion is laboriously documented in Moore's essays on the topic.

In most writings on the subject the words 'phenomenon' and 'appearance' are taken to be synonymous. Kant, indeed, in a passage dropped from the second edition of the *Critique of Pure Reason* seems to distinguish them when he says 'appearances, so far as they are thought as objects according to the unity of the categories, are called *phenomena* (A249)'. For him, then, a phenomenon is an articulated system of appearances, unified by the categories in the form of an object. Appearances are ingredients of phenomena, the properties, perhaps, that enter into the constitution of a concrete individual. But the identification of the two is more usual. If the distinction Kant has in mind needs to be drawn, that can be done by speaking of apparent properties and apparent objects or of property-appearances and object-appearances.

A more insidious identification is that between appearances and *what appears*. The phrase 'what appears' is ambiguous. For it may refer either to the real object that, as it were, does the appearing, a house, for example, or to the limited perspective view that a perceiver gets of it, the appearance proper, an array of coloured patches in the perceiver's visual field that may have few properties in common with the actual house to which the array is somehow related. There is a bad argument for the existence of noumena, of non-phenomenal correlates to phenomena, which trades on the peculiarities of the word 'appear'. What we perceive is always appearances. But an appearance logically implies the existence of something that appears. It does not, of course; it implies only the *belief* by the perceiver who reports his perception in these terms that there is something real to which what he calls the appearance is somehow related.

In British philosophy the concept of the phenomenon, defined as the direct or immediate object of perception, is generally confined in its application to the objects of the *senses*. It is not denied that there is at least one other kind of perception over and above perception by the senses. Besides external, sensory perception there is internal, introspective perception or self-consciousness. Even if the *word* 'perception' tends to be appropriated to the former it is acknowledged that there is a source of empirical information which is independent of the ordinary, external senses.

But this admission has not had a very large practical effect. The detailed and minute investigation of the intellectual machinery of sense-perception to be found in the works of Russell, Moore, Broad, Price, Ayer and a host of lesser lights is nowhere paralleled by an even moderately comparable thoroughness of investigation of the nature of introspection or self-consciousness. This philosophical tradition has taken over from Locke, with his distinction of sensation and reflection, and from Kant, with his distinction of outer and inner sense, the principle that there are two coordinate and independent sources of uninferred empirical knowledge, but they have largely ignored the second of them. Their anti-dualistic critics, principally Wittgenstein and Ryle, perhaps emboldened by this uneasy silence, have, in effect, rejected the notion of introspection or internal perception, and have accounted for the knowledge we have of our own mental states either in terms of hypothetical sensory knowledge of our dispositions to behaviour or in terms of 'avowals' which they see not so much as knowledge of the mental states to which they relate but rather as expressive elements in the constitution of those states.

In the writings of phenomenologists not only is at least equal attention given to awareness of self as to awareness of the external world, if anything the balance is tilted in the opposite direction. Husserl's technique of bracketing or detachment, of suspending the 'natural standpoint', which he takes to be an indispensable methodological preliminary to the kind of inquiry that must be the foundation of any rationally acceptable philosophy, is concerned with the given of sense-perception much less in relation to external objects than in relation to other acts or states of the mind. Phenomena, of outer sensation and inner reflection, must be resolutely detached from their connections with the natural, common world so that they are available for the kind of intellectual scrutiny from which *a priori* propositions about essences and their relations can be derived. The programme of Locke and Kant, which neither they nor their modern British successors pursued in the second of its aspects, is something the phenomenologists seek to carry through. Before coming to the views of Brentano and Husserl I shall first consider the position of the two great progenitors on the two kinds of experience, with a special concern for the loose ends they both conspicuously leave.

Locke says that all ideas come from sensation and reflection; the former yielding ideas of 'external, sensible objects', the latter ideas of 'the internal operations of the mind'. Reflection, which may be called internal sense, supplies ideas of perceiving, thinking, doubting, believing, knowing, willing 'and all the different activities of our own minds'. Locke's mention in these crucial defining passages of *operations* and *activities* leaves the status of a great deal of our familiar mental furniture unclear. Are desires and emotions operations or activities in the sense he intends? Presumably they are, since he makes no other provision for the knowledge we unquestionably have of them in our own cases. Furthermore he does say at one point that 'The term *operations* here, I use in a large sense, as comprehending not barely the actions of the mind about its ideas, but some sort of passions arising sometimes from them, such as is the satisfaction or uneasiness arising from any thought.'[1]

He contends that ideas of reflection come later than ideas of sensation. He means by this that in the course of an individual's

[1] Locke, *Essay on Human Understanding*, book 2, ch. 1, section 4.

development sensation comes first, is followed by various operations carried out on these ideas (presumably sensing or having such ideas is one of these operations, the most rudimentary, no doubt, and unnoticeable except by contrast with others such as compounding), which in turn become the objects of reflection. He does not seem to hold, as some have, that every act of reflection has some sensation among its ingredients.

He says that the acts or states of mind that are the objects of reflection are weakly self-intimating. 'The operations of our minds will not let us be without at least some obscure notions of them.'[2] This returns an irresolute answer to the question whether we can be in a given mental state without being aware of the fact. If *I am in mental state x* entailed *I am aware that I am in mental state x* sensation and reflection would have to be simultaneous, not successive. As soon as I had any sensation I should have to have a reflective awareness of the sensing at the moment I was having a sensory awareness of a sensum.

Locke is even less explicit about the question of the incorrigibility of reflection which is intimately related to that of the self-intimating character of its objects. But by implication he seems committed to the view that reflection is incorrigible. The crucial point here is that sensation has two objects: external material things as its indirect objects and the appearances those things present to our senses as its direct objects. No such duality between apparent and actual mental state is provided for on the side of reflection. The idea of, say, embarrassment, which is the content of an act of reflection, seems to be identical with the actual state of embarrassment which is the object of the act.

The appearances or sensa which are the immediate objects of sensation are left in a rather puzzling position. On the one hand they are ideas of sensation. On the other they would seem to be at least essential ingredients of certain ideas of reflection, of all those, that is to say, which are or essentially involve an act of sensation. I sense (*a*) a sensum (*b*). I am reflectively aware of this fact (*c*). The reflective act *c* cannot have *a*, the sensing, alone as its object. There can be no sensing without a sensum. It must be *a* and *b* together. So every idea of sensation, where this means, as it usually does, sensum, must also be an idea of

[2] *Ibid.* section 25.

reflection, or at least an indispensable part of one, so long as the notion the mind lets itself have of its operations in this case is not too obscure.

Some of the confusion here is due to the looseness of the phrase 'idea of'. 'Idea of x', where 'x' names a faculty, may be 'idea got by x' but it may also be 'idea whose content is x'. An idea got by sensation will not be an idea whose content is an act of sensation, a sensing; its content will be an appearance of an external thing, a colour-patch or what have you. But even if this confusion were guarded against by always taking *idea of x* to mean *idea got by x* the trouble would remain. An idea of sensation in this sense would still be an indispensable ingredient of the idea of reflection whose object is that sensation.

Kant follows Locke in regarding outer and inner sense as on all fours. But his treatment of inner sense in its own right, so to speak, is even more casual than Locke's. He is most concerned with it as the source of that field of intuited entities whose form is time. In general he takes outer and inner sense to be the providers of two ranges of raw epistemic material which are accessible to synthesisation by the categories. This would appear to follow from the conclusion that the activities and states of the empirical or phenomenal self are subject to causal law. Presumably the empirical self is endowed with its measure of substantial unity by synthesisation of the immediate deliverances of inner sense by the category of substance.

Kant's way of introducing the distinction between outer and inner sense suggests that he regards their objects as wholly distinct. The outer sense represents objects as outside us and as in space. He would seem to suppose that these two criteria coincide. If 'outside us' means 'outside our bodies' they quite plainly do not. If bodily perception, the awareness we have of the states of our own bodies, is included in inner sense along with the awareness we have of thoughts and emotions, then inner sense represents some of its objects as being in space. If, more sensibly, it is not, then outer sense represents some objects as inside us, sprained ankles, for example.

If 'outside us' means something like 'outside our minds' the situation is not much improved. No doubt all and only those things we take to exist outside our minds are taken by us to be in space, but what then becomes of the appearances that are the immediate objects of sensation? These, though often *spatial* are not in space and not outside our minds either. It must follow that they are the objects not of outer but of inner sense. But in that case what is outer sense? It must be that part of inner sense whose deliverances can be categorially worked up into the conception of an objective, material, spatial world.

Kant comes near to admitting this when he says that time, as the form of inner sense, is the form of all representations, both inner and outer, on the ground that the representations of outer sense are all 'determinations of the mind'.

What the fairly perfunctory treatments of introspection given by Locke and Kant come to is that we have a direct, introspective awareness of a great many, rather heterogeneous, things that occur in and are present to our minds: among them are sensa or sensible appearances, sensings of those appearances and other mental acts exercised on sensa (such as memory, expectation and imagination in its more graphic, visualising form) and, finally, mental acts that are not essentially bound up with sensa, if there are any (examples might be emotional states such as gloom or hilarity which, though *caused* by sense-based beliefs, such as that one's car has run out of petrol or that someone's trousers have split, do not have these beliefs, or their sensory basis, as part of their essential content). Some of these introspected items are in some fashion referred to a world of objects in space existing independently of our minds, those of them perhaps which, while not in space, have spatial qualities. All the direct objects of awareness are mental and all direct awareness is therefore introspection, reflection or inner sense. But some of this awareness has indirect objects that are not mental; some introspection is also extraspection.

The difficulty is to determine which. If extraspection is confined to veridical awareness of external objects then misperception is merely introspection. If it covers any awareness which has something external as its intentional object, whether the latter really exists or not, then nearly all or absolutely all introspection is extraspection too. On this interpretation my fear of an event that is not in fact going to happen is as extraspective as my hallucinatory 'perception' of a man who isn't there. The general result is that introspection, reflection or inner sense, introduced as a modest addition to our sources of empirical information has swallowed up, and almost wholly digested, the primary source to which it was introduced as an addition.

The thesis that there are two kinds of perception, outer and inner, which are (a) analogous in structure and (b) distinct, can only be maintained if external, sensory perception is admitted to have external, physical things as its direct objects and if the internal, introspective perception of mental acts and states is allowed to be liable to error in the same sort of way as its external correlate. If the externality of sense-perception is only indirect or intentional then it gets absorbed into introspection as a special case. Kant, unlike Locke, makes some effort to preserve analogy of structure by suggesting that the empirical self stands to the states of mind that enter into its constitution as external things stand to the appearances they present to perceivers. But this stratagem is not convincing. Mental states are literally parts of empirical selves, while appearances could only be literal parts of material objects if they are conceived of as objective aspects of material things in the way that Russell's *sensibilia* are. But objective aspects so conceived are troublesome things. Since they may be qualitatively indiscriminable from hallucinations it follows that introspection is unable to determine whether the awareness of a particular coloured patch or whatever is an act of perception or introspection.

In twentieth century British philosophy the dualism of perception and introspection has either been formally acknowledged but largely ignored or else more or less comprehensively rejected. Broad is one of the few defenders of introspection who has had much to say about it. An interesting line of criticism, which falls short of the full rigour and extremity of dispositional behaviourism mitigated by the mysterious doctrine of avowals, is given by Kneale.[3] Defenders of introspection, he says, take it to be concerned with particular experiences and ignore the extent to which our knowledge of or beliefs about ourselves concern dispositions. Secondly, they take introspection to be 'a kind of experience which is itself the contemplation of another experience'.[4] Finally, they rely on an analogy which does not obtain between perception and introspection.

---

[3] Kneale, 'Experience and introspection', *Proc. Arist. Soc.* 1949–50.
[4] *Ibid.*

His first point is an entirely reasonable one but it only limits the scope of, and does not wholly undermine, the notion of introspection. When he says that belief and desire are dispositions and not occurrences he does not imply that the occurrences in which these dispositions are manifested are anything but experiences, mental phenomena, possible objects of introspection. It is not bodily utterances and bodily acts of striving-towards that he takes belief and desire to show themselves in but mental acts of thinking and wishing.

The second point is the essential matter at issue. If it is admitted, the third point, that self-knowledge is not analogous in structure to perception, immediately follows, given the hardly questionable assumption that perception is a mental occurrence in which some object is contemplated. His main argument against the view that experiences proper (as contrasted with dispositional mental states) are not possible objects of contemplation by way of other, introspective, experiences is that a person's thinking that he has an experience is a sufficient reason for the conclusion that he is having it and his having it is a sufficient reason for his thinking, truly, that he does. We can perfectly properly admit, Kneale contends, that experiences are noticed and that people come to realise what experiences they are having by asking themselves questions about their mental states without committing ourselves to the existence of a quasi-perceptual faculty of introspection. But for there to be sense to the statement that X notices the experience he is having it must be possible for X not to have noticed it, although he was actually having it. Equally for there to be any point to the putting of questions to oneself it must be the case that, prior to the answering of the question, the questioner does not know what the answer to it is. From this it follows that having an experience is *not* a logically sufficient reason for thinking truly, or realising, that one is having it. But then suppose I am in fact having an unusual experience of which I am not, in the manner Kneale seems to allow, aware. If asked whether I am having it I may say and honestly believe that I am not having it, on the grounds (a) that it is unusual anyway and (b) I have not yet become aware that I am having it. It may well be, of course, that the question may redirect my attention and so bring the unusual experience to my notice. But until that happens I may falsely believe that

I am not having it. What is more the incorrigibility thesis is now significantly changed. It must now read: if, after carefully directing my attention to my current state of mind, I believe that I am having a certain experience it follows that I am. But attention to my current state of mind is precisely the introspective 'looking' from which introspective 'seeing' may well, but, like ordinary seeing, does not have to, emerge. There is no middle way between the admission of introspection (whether by way of attentive introspective 'looking' or not) and the full rigour of the doctrine of avowals.

That there is such a thing as the careful attentive scrutiny of one's state of mind is a fact that can hardly be denied except by someone tormented by a philosophical embarrassment. Did Proust and Henry James labour in vain? Do their phenomenological exercises not bring to light a great deal of hitherto unnoticed detail in more or less familiar types of experience or states of mind?

What may underly some of the resistance to the idea that introspection is a source of knowledge about states of mind or mental phenomena, that it is an inwardly directed analogue of the perception of physical things, or, for that matter, of sensible appearances, is that its alleged objects are so very unobject-like. Things, and their appearances, are fairly determinate spatial arrays; states of mind are not. Things, although not so conspicuously their appearances, are ordinarily stable in a way that states of mind are not; the activity of scrutinising them does not seem to change them in the course of changing our ideas or beliefs about them. This may reflect the element of decision there is in the constitution of some mental states. When asked whether I believe that a certain party will win the election or whether I want some fairly important and substantial event to come about, my reflections may actually be directed to deciding whether I have good reason for thinking that the party will win or whether the event in question is worthy of being desired. But one can take a descriptive rather than critical attitude to one's states of mind, even if it is conversationally gauche to do so, and even then they may prove rather shifting and elusive.

The hostility to introspection expressed in Kneale's third point, that there is a lack of analogy between direct self-knowledge and sense-perception, is not very convincingly made out in Kneale's own discussion of it. What it may rest on is the view that supposedly introspectible experiences are not *appearances*. The word 'phenomenon' is, of course, etymologically connected with the concept of appearing and on this ground it may be felt inappropriate to suppose that non-sensory experiences are phenomena since they do not seem to be the appearances of anything. I have already mentioned the unsuccesful attempt of Kant to represent the phenomena of inner sense as phenomena or appearances of the empirical self.

If, indeed, experiences are incorrigible and self-intimating there is plainly no logical room left to contain a distinction between an experience as it actually is and as it appears to be. But if, as I have briefly argued, experiences are not of this nature it would seem possible to distinguish between the immediate objects of introspection and the real mental states of which they are the appearances. Even for Kneale there is a distinction between experiences proper and the underlying dispositions they manifest and it could be argued that the former stand to the latter as sensible appearances or sense-data do to material objects in what has until recently been the standard account of sense-perception.

Critics of that account, of whom I am one, contend that sensible appearances should not be interpreted as infallibly known private objects but in terms of beliefs, or inclinations to believe, concerned with material objects. In parallel with that view it might be held that a wish, in Kneale's sense, is really a belief about a desire, and a thought, rather less digestibly, as a belief about a belief.

Whatever the possibilities of this line of thought, those who accept the recently standard account of sense-perception are in no position to assert a lack of analogy between sense-perception and self-knowledge on the ground that some at least of the latter is incorrigible and self-intimating. In the first place, they admit that some sense-perception is of that nature too, namely the direct awareness we have in sensation of the sensible appearances of things. Secondly, they admit that some self-knowledge, and perhaps one should add 'self-belief', is *not* incorrigible and self-intimating and at the same time they admit that knowledge of the dispositional states of mind in question is based on infallible knowledge of the experiences by which it is manifested. On this set of views the parallel between perception and self-knowledge is complete. The problem they are left with, if it is one, is that of determining what sensible appearances are the objects of: perception, of which they are an indispensable ingredient, or introspection, in virtue of the fact that such appearances are, except on some such theory as Russell's account of sensibilia, logically essential ingredients of, and dependent for their existence on, a mental state, that of sensation, conceived as the act of sensing?

In the descriptive psychology of Brentano and the pheno-menology of Husserl most of the problems I have considered come up for investigation. On the whole they take mental phenomena, phenomena that are not sensa or sensible appear-ances, more seriously than either Locke or Kant or than their own British contemporaries. Husserl, of course, takes the attentive, introspective scrutiny of mental phenomena to be the fundamental discipline of philosophy, to be the first stage of the eidetic science which apprehends essences, as they are embodied in such phenomena, and discerns the *a priori* relations that hold between them.

The task which Locke and Kant fail to carry out in any but the most off-hand way is the main issue of Brentano's dis-cussion of the distinction between mental and physical phen-omena. His position is that the act of presentation in perception is mental but that the thing presented, the appearance, sensum or sensible quality, is not. In perception proper what may be called the ultimate intentional object, an independently existing material thing, whether actual or not, is plainly physical. But he seems to conclude that the sensum or appear-ance is physical too. He holds that sensory presentation is fundamental to all acts of the mind, arguing that pain is always experienced as physically located in some part of the body, but that the intensity of the feeling can sometimes obliterate the reference of the experience to a public, physical object. He rejects spatiality as a criterion of the physical on the grounds that some physical things, for example sounds, are not spatial and some mental things, emotions and even some thoughts, are located.

His conclusion is that the mental is all and only what is intentional, in that it has 'reference to a content, direction to an object'. To the objection that this does not seem to be true of feelings of pleasure and pain he replies, not, as before, by connecting them with parts of the body, but by claiming that pleasure is always the pleasure *of* something, for example of hearing. He does not deal with the objection that moods, of depression, for instance, or, for that matter, of the objectless anxiety on which Heidegger lays such stress, do not seem to have objects, even if they have causes, but are unquestionably mental, if anything is.

Inner perception, or introspection, is the awareness of a mental object thus defined. It is not to be identified with infallible perception since we have, he believes, infallible awareness of sense-contents and these, in his view, are physical phenomena. However the physical phenomena of sensation and imagination are not exclusively and virginally physical. They are part of the proper subject-matter of psychology, but only as the *contents* of the mental acts of presentation or sensation whose indispensable objects they are. This is hardly a satisfactory resolution of the problem of demarcation left by Locke and Kant. In the first place sense-contents commonly are, although they need not be, as, for example, in Husserlian bracketing, intentional, in that they ordinarily inspire, are bound up with or are essential elements of acts which have independent physical things as their objects. Secondly, sensing as a mental, because intentional, act is an infallible awareness of sensible appearances. It follows that the appearance that is the immediate object of the act of sensing is not really logically separable as a distinct object from it. The appearance or sensum is at once physical *and* a logically constitutive element of an intentional, mental phenomenon. The distinction between outer and inner perception is left in a blurred and undecided state at this crucial point.

Husserl considers and qualifies Brentano's position in his discussion of intentional experiences and their contents in Part V of his *Logical Investigations* and again in the appendix to that work that is devoted to the distinction between external and internal perception. He argues, seemingly in the manner I have criticised in Kant, that the empirical ego transcends the phenomena that are experienced just as the public material thing transcends the sensible appearances it presents. He denies, against Brentano, that all mental acts are intentional in structure, holding that sensation is not. Could this be because its content, being infallibly known, cannot be logically distinguished from the act of sensing in the way that the intentional object of an act of mind must be? Is it because he thinks of the perception proper, which is an intentional act and of which sensation is normally an ingredient, as another act, over and above sensation?

He also denies that intentional experiences are phenomena properly so called on the ground that they are not 'objects appearing as such' which is hard to square with his view that the empirical ego transcends its introspectible appearances, unless he is relying on some cavil about the object-like nature of the ego. He agrees with Brentano's view that the distinction between inner and outer perception is not the same as that between 'evident' and fallible perception (although in a tone which suggests that he is disagreeing). Certainly his reason for this conclusion is different from Brentano's. Where he cites fallible inner perception, Brentano relies on infallible outer perception, namely of the physical data of sensation.

In *Ideas* Husserl defines the realm of phenomena, of pure experience or consciousness, as what is left when the natural point of view is suspended (not doubted). He now holds that all experiences are intentional. In saying that such *parts* of experiences as whiteness need not be intentional he now seems to admit that sensations are intentional experiences, although their contents are not. Only the stream of experience is directly perceived; everything else, material things, the minds of others, numbers, transcends it. In particular the qualities that are sensibly perceived are all appearances, transcended by, and so presumably distinct from, the material thing as conceived by science. There is nothing perspectival about experiences, they are not to be thought of as things that present appearances. This fits awkwardly with his earlier notion that some intro- spection or inner perception of mental states is fallible. And he goes on to insist that outer perception of material things is not conducted through some intermediary entity; but what else are the fallibly indicative appearances on which such perception rests?

Matters are further complicated by his claim that the ex- perience I have of a feeling is always 'adequate' and yet that I can think truly or falsely about it. If, as he suggests, the experience of a feeling does not involve judgement or belief, what can it mean to describe it as either adequate or inadequate?

On the subject of bracketing or phenomenological reduction, Husserl contends that through it we suspend the carrying-out of the mental acts that 'constitute the natural world' (that is, the formation of beliefs about the existence of anything that transcends the experience itself). We can then reflect on them for purposes of study. This is a curious claim. It makes sense only if the acts in question are thought of as tools which are, as it were, still very much there and in existence even if they are not being used or exercised. But mental acts are only there if they are carried out. If suspended they are not there to be studied.

For all the resolution they bring to the task, then, it does not seem to me that Brentano and Husserl succeed in getting very far with the problem of the fundamental nature of phenomena, by which I mean that of establishing the claim that there is, alongside sense-perception of things or their appearances, a structurally analogous form of inner perception or introspection, which has experiences or mental states as its objects, and, more particularly, that of determining whether the objects of such inner perception are properly describable as phenomena, as being the appearances of something else, such as the empirical self or dispositional mental states. This fundamental problem is left by them in pretty much the condition it was left by Locke and Kant, although at least they have recognised that there is a problem and have made some effort to solve it.

To say this is not to say that the descriptive accounts they give of what they hold to be mental phenomena are undermined or that the thesis that all or most of these alleged phenomena are intentional in structure is not illuminating. Mathematics got on quite impressively before anyone had thought of set theory, after all. To report a purely personal impression, which is based on a study of their writings which does not extend beyond their discussions of what I have picked out as the fundamental problem, I must say that Brentano's wrestlings with it seem to me considerably superior to Husserl's; by the latter Brentano's insights are typically chewed, amended and returned to and an appearance of substantial philosophical work is often produced by Laocoon-like involvement with spurious issues created by pieces of cryptic verbal legislation.

Intentionality

DAVID CARR

Little has been done to relate the discussion of intentionality in
analytic philosophy (initiated primarily by R. M. Chisholm) with
the traditional phenomenological treatment of this concept. In this
paper I argue that there are more parallels than have been noticed.
Many of the problems that have been treated by Chisholm and his
successors were also seen by Husserl, and the latter has proposed
solutions to them that are surprisingly like those of some recent
analytic proposals. I try to show further how Husserl's solutions to
these problems form the basis of his phenomenological method.

David Carr is Associate Professor of Philosophy at Yale University.
He is the author of *Phenomenology and the Problem of History* (1974)
and translator of Husserl's book *The Crisis of European Sciences and
Transcendental Phenomenology* (Northwestern University Press, 1970).

Discussion among analytic philosophers of the concept of intentionality, at least under that name, dates primarily from R. M. Chisholm's paper, 'Sentences About Believing' (1955).[1] This paper evoked a wide response, and discussion and interest in the topic to date have grown to the point where an anthology was thought appropriate: one has recently appeared under the title *Intentionality, Mind and Language*, edited by A. Marras.[2] Chisholm derived his presentation of the concept from Brentano, who was the first modern thinker, as far as anyone knows, to revive this medieval term. Most of the analytic discussions of intentionality have taken their point of departure from Chisholm's reformulation of Brentano's thesis, and little attention has been paid to the fact that intentionality, as Husserl borrowed it from Brentano and also reformulated it, is one of the key concepts, if not *the* key concept, of the phenomenological tradition descended from Husserl. Even Chisholm himself, who knows the phenomenological literature well, warns readers of his article on intentionality in *The Encyclopedia of Philosophy*, after mentioning two related 'theses' of intentionality, that the term 'is also used in connection with certain other related theses of phenomenology and existentialism'.[3] This almost suggests that the two traditions share only the word, and not even the concept; or that, if the concept is the same, it is treated in very different ways.

Now there is no doubt in my mind that the concept is the same, but it is partly true that it is treated in different ways. Chisholm, following the 'linguistic turn', transforms the discussion of what is essential to psychic phenomena into a discussion of the logical properties of sentences about psychic phenomena. This, of course, is not the way phenomenologists

---

[1] An early version of Chisholm's paper appeared in the *Proceedings of the Aristotelian Society*, 56 (1955–6), pp. 125–48.

[2] Chicago, University of Illinois Press, 1972. Chisholm's paper is reprinted on pp. 31–51.

The following books are referred to by abbreviations in the notes to this paper:

IML   *Intentionality, Mind and Language*, ed. A. Marras (Chicago: University of Illinois Press, 1972).

LI   Edmund Husserl, *Logical Investigations*, trans. J. N. Findlay (New York: Humanities Press, 1970).

[3] 'Intentionality' in *The Encyclopedia of Philosophy*, ed. P. Edwards, (New York: Macmillan, 1967), Vol. 4, p. 201. Chisholm does relate the concept to phenomenology in the Editor's Introduction to *Realism and the Background of Phenomenology* (New York: The Free Press, 1960).

tend to proceed, and such a transformation was in any case foreign to Husserl. After the logical properties of certain sentences about the psychic have been delineated, the question arises as to whether such sentences are dispensable or indispensable in psychology and the philosophy of mind. This was the subject of the famous correspondence between Chisholm and Sellars, and much of the discussion in analytic philosophy has centered on this question. In phenomenology, on the other hand, this question is taken as answered – intentionality is indispensable in dealing with the mental – and the investigation goes on from there, applying the concept in its attempt to describe everything that falls under it.

In this paper I would like to suggest that despite these broad differences there are more parallels than have been noticed between the Chisholm statement, with its ensuing discussion, and the phenomenological treatment of intentionality, especially in Husserl's original introduction and elaboration of it in his *Logical Investigations*. It is true that the differences are fundamental: Husserl introduces the concept with rather different interests in mind from those even of Brentano. Still, many of the problems that have been seen by Chisholm and his successors were also seen by Husserl, and he has provided a solution to them, as I shall argue, that is surprisingly like that of certain recent analytic proposals. I shall try to show, further, that Husserl's solution to certain problems of intentionality forms the basis of his phenomenological method.

Chisholm follows Brentano in designating intentionality 'the mark of the psychological'. 'Every psychic phenomenon', says Brentano,[4] 'is characterized by what the Scholastics of the Middle Ages called the intentional (or perhaps mental) inexistence of an object, and what we, though not without some ambiguity of expression, call the relation to a content, the direction toward an object (which is not to be understood as a reality), or immanent objectivity. Each contains something as an object within itself, though not in each case in the same way. In representation something is represented, in judgment something is acknowledged or rejected, in love something is loved, [etc.] . . . This intentional inexistence is characteristic exclusive-

---

[4] *Psychologie vom empirischen Standpunkte* (Leipzig: von Duncker und Humblot, 1874), Vol. I, pp. 115f.

ly of psychic phenomena. No physical phenomenon exhibits anything similar.' Chisholm speaks of the 'intentional use' of language', which 'we need when we talk about certain psychological states and events' and which 'we can avoid when we talk about non-psychological states and events'. The claim is that all and only psychic phenomena (or sentences about psychic phenomena) are intentional.[5]

Chisholm introduces three criteria by which we can identify the intentional use of language. I shall set these out now, with some examples and comments, as a basis for further discussion.

(1)   A simple declarative sentence is intentional if it uses a substantival expression – a name or description – in such a way that neither the sentence nor its contradictory implies either that there is or that there isn't anything to which the substantival expression truly applies,[6]

Thus 'when we say that a man is thinking of the Dnieper Dam, we do not imply either that there is or that there isn't such a dam; similarly when we deny that he is thinking of it.' Chisholm has in mind sentences involving such verbs as thinking of, imagining, envisaging, wishing or hoping for, etc. Translating this back into the material mode, we should say that the existence or occurrence of such a 'psychic phenomenon', while it is necessarily *about* or *of* something, implies neither the existence nor the non-existence of that something.

Second, Chisholm turns to sentences whose principal verb takes as its object a phrase containing a subordinate verb, such as 'he believes it will rain'.

(2)   I shall say that such a simple declarative sentence is intentional if neither the sentence nor its contradictory imply either that the phrase following the principal verb is true or that it is false.[7]

Thus, if we say that he believes it will rain, it follows neither that it will or that it won't; likewise if we deny that he believes this. In material terms, claiming, asserting, supposing that something is the case implies neither that it is or is not the case.

---

[5] *IML*, p. 31. It is true that Chisholm says '*certain* psychological states and events', but he seems to argue for the 'all and only' thesis, and does not dissociate himself from this aspect of Brentano's claim.

[6] *IML*, p. 32.

[7] *IML*, p. 33.

Third, Chisholm introduces the criterion of Frege's 'indirect reference', or what is often called 'referential opacity'. 'A name (or description) of a certain thing has an indirect reference in a sentence if its replacement by a different name (or description) of that thing results in a sentence whose truth-value may differ from that of the original sentence.'[8] Thus the third criterion reads:

(3)   A simple declarative sentence is intentional if it contains a name (or description) which has an indirect reference in that sentence.[9]

Chisholm comments that this allows us to consider certain *cognitive* verbs such as 'know', 'remember', 'perceive' and 'see' – which are presumably not intentional by the first two criteria – as being intentional. Thus I may see that Jones is here and, though Jones is the chairman of the philosophy department, I cannot be said to see that the chairman of the philosophy department is here, unless I know that he is the chairman of the philosophy department.

Now it is clear that the phenomenological conception of intentionality exhibits similarities to these three criteria, provided they are translated back into non-linguistic terms. Husserl repeatedly states that the existence of an intentional reference to an object does not imply the existence of that object, just as the reference to a state of affairs does not imply that that state obtains.[10] He even hints at a version of Chisholm's third criterion when he distinguishes between '*the object as it is intended*, and the object (period) *which* is intended'. 'The idea, e.g. of the German Emperor', he says, 'presents its object as an Emperor, and as the Emperor of Germany. The man himself is the son of Emperor Frederick III, the grandson of Queen Victoria, and has many other properties neither named nor presented.'[11]

One question about intentionality is notoriously left undecided by Brentano's thesis, and also by Chisholm's reformulation of it. If we take Chisholm's first criterion, which affirms that the existence of a given mental state implies neither

---

[8] *IML*, p. 34.
[9] *Ibid.*
[10] *Logical Investigations* (*LI*), trans. J. N. Findlay (New York: Humanities Press, 1970). Cf. p. 596.
[11] *LI*, pp. 578f.

the existence nor the non-existence of the thing to which it refers, we can ask: does the existence of that mental state nevertheless imply that there is some other type of object? This would be affirmed by anyone who stated, for example, that when I think of a winged horse, there must exist, presumably in my mind, the *image* of a winged horse, even though there is in reality no such horse. Brentano seems to have expressed such a position in using such terms as 'inexistence' and 'immanent objectivity'. A second alternative would be the view of Meinong, who claims that while such items as winged horses do not exist in reality, they are also not 'merely mental' either. He says that they must be accorded some independent status, and he uses the term *ausserseiend* ('beyond being'), for this status.[12] In the first instance the mind is related to something, but instead of the thing referred to it is related to a mental entity; in the second case the mind is related to something extramental, but something which, strictly speaking, cannot be called an entity.

All this concerns the status of the intentional object, and these alternatives are clearly designed to cover such things as winged horses, round squares, present kings of France and the like. It should be pointed out that if either of them is accepted, great problems arise when we turn to more humble cases such as ordinary, existing objects. In any case, it is customary to distinguish the question of the ontological status of the intentional object from that of the 'mark of the psychological', and to deal with them separately.[13] Actually, this is not so easily done, for if the first of the above two alternatives is chosen, one is saying something about the nature of the mental by saying that it somehow contains an object or image within it. Still, for purposes of comparison with Husserl, we shall put this question aside for the moment, returning to it later.

First we must ask whether Husserl, in introducing the concept of intentionality, was interested, like Brentano and Chisholm, in discerning 'the mark of the psychological'. Did he make the claim that all and only psychic phenomena are characterized by intentionality? As for the 'all', the answer is no. Not all psychic phenomena 'in the sense of a possible definition

[12] See *Realism and the Background of Phenomenology* (note 3 above), pp. 76ff.
[13] Cf. Marras in *IML*, pp. 3f., Chisholm in 'Intentionality', *loc. cit.* (note 3 above).

of psychology' are intentional, he says.[14] Intentionality is characteristic of only 'a sharply defined class of experiences [*Erlebnisse*]',[15] not all experiences. He regards sensations – not to be confused with sense-perceptions – and certain types of feelings as being non-intentional,[16] but at the same time perfectly legitimate topics for psychology.

Are 'only' psychic phenomena intentional? A version of this question has been part of the debate following upon Chisholm's formulation. Chisholm himself recognized that comparison verbs often result in sentences that seem to satisfy his criterion (1). For example, the sentence 'Some lizards look like dragons' does not commit us to the existence or non-existence of dragons (nor does its contradictory), yet it is clearly not about the psychological.[17] It has been pointed out that sentences like 'it is probable that p' and 'this is consistent with p' satisfy criterion (2) since both they and their contradictories are indifferent to the truth-value of p.[18] It has also been noted that sentences bearing the modal prefixes 'it is necessary that . . .' and 'it is possible that . . .' often satisfy criterion (3). For example, if the governor of Alaska is the governor of the largest state in the Union, the statement 'It is necessary that the governor of Alaska is identical with the governor of Alaska' does not imply that 'It is necessary that the governor of Alaska is identical with the governor of the largest state in the Union'. In other words, here the substitution of an expression with an equivalent extension results in a sentence whose truth-value may be different from the original sentence.[19]

Here the difference between the linguistic and non-linguistic approaches is crucial. Since he did not make the shift from the psychic to sentences about the psychic, it would probably never have occurred to Husserl to ask whether some sentences about non-psychological matters share certain logical features with those about the psychic. Perhaps, even if it had occurred to him, he would have been neither troubled nor surprised. He was, after all, interested in the nature of certain experiences, not in

---

[14] *LI*, p. 552.
[15] *LI*, p. 553. He does say, however, that having intentional experiences is a necessary feature of psychic *beings*. Beings without such experiences 'would not be called "psychical" by anyone' (*ibid.*).
[16] Cf. *LI*, pp. 569ff.
[17] *IML*, p. 35, n. 5.
[18] J. N. Mohanty, *The Concept of Intentionality* (St Louis; Warren H. Green, 1972), p. 28.
[19] A. Marras, 'Intentionality and cognitive sentences', in *IML*, pp. 68f.

the features of sentences. The presence of shared logical features in psychological and non-psychological sentences does not imply that there is anything outside the mind that is 'directed upon an object' or 'of something' in the way that certain experiences are. Still, the problem cannot be disposed of so simply. If asked whether the philosophical treatment of experiences requires 'concepts' or 'categories' which, to quote Chisholm, 'we can avoid when we talk about non-psychological states and events', he probably would have answered in the affirmative. The question is really whether experiences constitute a domain that can ultimately be reduced to physical states and events and dealt with philosophically in their terms. The discovery that non-psychological sentences share some of the supposedly distinctive logical features of psychological sentences raises the question in a special way. But does this discovery really imply an affirmative answer to the question? This problem must be dealt with if the validity of the intentionalist thesis is to be decided, and Husserl clearly does not deal with it.

But perhaps the most important reason why Husserl does not look at the question this way is that his purpose is not to circumscribe the domain of psychology and distinguish it from that of other disciplines. This was Brentano's purpose, and Chisholm has taken up the problem from this point of view. What, then, is Husserl's purpose? In the *Logical Investigations*, it is to provide, as he says, for *ein erkenntniskritisches Verständnis der reinen Logik*, an understanding of pure logic from the perspective of a critique of knowledge;[20] or, as he also puts it, his task is 'to bring the Ideas of logic, the logical concepts and laws, to epistemological clarity and definiteness'.[21] In the first volume of the work, the *Prolegomena to Pure Logic*, Husserl had attacked psychologism, arguing that logic is not concerned with mental states, processes or acts of logical thinking. In the second volume, when he begins the Investigations proper, his point is to ascertain what logic *is* (or ought to be) concerned with. To this end, strangely enough, he does not turn away from mental states and processes, but turns back to them, with the idea of seeing how logical concepts and laws are related to them and

---

[20] *LI*, pp. 249f. I have translated this rather differently from Findlay.
[21] *LI*, p. 251.

how they can be disengaged from them. In a sense his purpose is still to refute psychologism, but he chooses different means; instead of advancing *reductio* and other formal arguments against psychologism and other forms of reductionism and relativism, he suggests that if we examine the mental processes of thinking, judging and the like, we will see that they must be separated from their logical content, and that the latter cannot be dealt with in terms of the former. But his purpose is also a positive one: to see how logical concepts and laws relate to mental processes in the context of a theory of knowledge and a critique of knowledge.

Thus when Husserl singles out intentional experiences as 'a sharply defined class of experiences', he does so because such experiences are relevant to his purpose of relating logic to the mental. Logical concepts and laws, he is saying, enter into mental life primarily in the knowing situation. It is the aspects of psychic life that enjoy 'mental, conscious existence in a certain *pregnant* sense of these words'[22] that interest him, and these are all intentional. Now perhaps Husserl's interest in the intentional, as distinct from Brentano's, is actually shared by Chisholm through the fact that the German word *psychisch* gets translated into English as *mental*. Chisholm, and most of those who come after him, most often speak of intentionality as the mark of the *mental*, rather than the psychic or psychological. When they refer to the mental, most English speakers usually mean precisely cognitive and related phenomena, and not necessarily everything that belongs to the domain of psychology. Though this distinction is not made as clearly as it is in Husserl, it appears that analytic philosophers, too, are interested in intentionality only as pertaining to philosophy of mind or epistemology, not as the distinguishing mark of all phenomena considered by psychology. For Husserl, of course, it is the term *consciousness* which names the focus of his interest, a term which has very much fallen out of vogue among analytic philosophers.

Now as we have seen, it did not trouble Husserl to assert that not all psychic phenomena are intentional. But it would indeed have run counter to his view if it were found that intentionality was not a feature of all those aspects of mental life deemed relevant to a theory or critique of knowledge; or, to put it in his

---

[22] *LI*, p. 553.

terms, that not all consciousness is intentional. But this is precisely one of the criticisms that have been levelled against the theory of intentionality. It appears that precisely those mental activities that one would think the most relevant of all to a theory of knowledge do not meet the most important criteria of intentionality. This claim has been made about the so-called cognitive verbs such as 'know', 'see', 'perceive', 'remember'. While the notion of intentionality seems to work well for such verbs as 'imagine', 'think of', 'suppose', 'conceive', i.e. verbs which make no claim to knowledge, it does not seem to work for verbs which do make such a claim in one form or another.

If I see or perceive *x*, *x* must really be there to see. If I remember *x*, *x* must really have happened. If I know that *p*, *p* must really be the case. Thus Chisholm's first two criteria are violated. A sentence employing 'see', 'perceive' or 'remember' implies the existence of the objects of these verbs. A sentence employing 'knows' is not indifferent to the truth value of the subordinate phrase but precisely requires its truth. Incidentally, this was one of the main criticisms levelled by Gilbert Ryle against Husserl's concept of intentionality in his report on Phenomenology to the Aristotelian Society in 1932.[23]

Now Chisholm saw this problem, too, and it is for this reason, we recall, that he introduced his third criteron. But there are serious objections that can be raised against this criterion. Chisholm states it in such a way that it applies to simple declarative sentences whose action verbs take a substantive expression as their object, but the examples he gives are of complex sentences, i.e. sentences whose verbs take a subordinate clause. Doubtless Chisholm states his third criterion in this way because he believes, as he says in a footnote,[24] that it can be made to do the work of the first two; thus he wants to cover both cases. But one may ask whether the criterion really works in the case of non-complex sentences. If I have seen the morning star, isn't it correct to say that I have seen the evening star, even though I didn't know it?[25] To use one of Dreyfus' examples, if my next-door neighbor turns out to be the murderer, it would

[23] 'Phenomenology, Goodness and Beauty', *Aristotelian Society Supplementary Vol. XI*, (London: Harrison & Sons, Ltd, 1932), pp. 8of.

[24] *IML*, p. 34, n. 3.

[25] Marras in *IML*, p. 67. Cf. A. Kenny, *Action, Emotion and Will*, (New York: Humanities Press, 1963), p. 198.

be considered not only odd but a case of perjury if I testified in court that I hadn't seen the murderer until the day his guilt was revealed.[26] Even complex sentences with verbs like 'see' raise problems. To return to our earlier example, if Jones is the chairman of the philosophy department, and I see that Jones is here, could it be the case that I don't see that the chairman of the philosophy department is here? The answer that comes most readily to mind is 'yes and no'. Thus at least some sentences employing so-called cognitive verbs seem not to be intentional by Chisholm's third criterion; and if they are not intentional by the first and second either, we must conclude that they are not intentional at all, at least not in Chisholm's sense.

How could Husserl have dealt with such an objection? Is there any sense in which the verbs in question (or the corresponding 'phenomena') are intentional? If not, then Husserl's claim, that all mental phenomena relevant to a theory of knowledge are intentional, would seem to be false precisely for those phenomena which are instances of knowledge or are very closely related to it, such as perception.

One solution to this problem has been proposed by J. W. Cornman.[27] He suggests that we need not worry if these verbs are not intentional because intentionality is meant as a characterization of verbs designating mental *activities*. Despite appearances to the contrary, he says, 'cognitive verbs are not verbs which designate certain mental activities'.[28] Then he invokes Ryle's concept of 'achievement verbs' to tell us what they do designate.[29] Rather than an activity, he says, they refer to the successful completion of a task. To know something is, according to Ryle, more like winning than running a race. In order to win, one must run, but 'winning' is not itself a term that designates merely a particular activity; its concept may involve running, but it relates it to the rules, the finishing line, etc. The non-intentionality of the cognitive verbs is not surprising because the concept of intentionality was not designed to deal with them in the first place. To use Brentano's words, these are not, strictly speaking, 'psychic phenomena'. We can

---

[26] H. Dreyfus, '*Sinn* and the intentional object', in *Phenomenology and Existentialism*, ed. R. C. Solomon (New York: Harper & Row, 1972), pp. 205f.
[27] 'Intentionality and intensionality', in *IML*, pp. 52–65.
[28] *IML*, p. 63.
[29] *IML*, p. 64. Cf. G. Ryle, *The Concept of Mind* (London: Hutchinson, 1949), pp. 149–53.

still say that all mental *activities* are intentional and that all sentences employing verbs that genuinely designate such activities are likewise intentional. And for this Chisholm's first two criteria will suffice. However, we must presumably be on the lookout for verbs that do not designate such activities. Following Ryle, we may want to assert that many terms applied to the mental designate not activities but achievements, dispositions, etc.

Now I would like to argue that Husserl not only anticipated the objection that cognitive verbs – or the corresponding phenomena – are not intentional, but that he provided an answer to it which is in some ways like Cornman's. More than this, it seems to me that Husserl's version of Cornman's solution is at the very heart of his concept of intentionality and is the key to how the full-fledged phenomenological method is derived from that concept.

Cornman's view may seem highly objectionable in its own right, and it may seem even more objectionable to attribute such a view to Husserl. Against Cornman's view our first reaction is to say that while Ryle's concept of achievement verbs may work well in the case of knowledge, how can it be applied to the other cognitive verbs mentioned, namely 'see', 'perceive', 'remember'? If any verbs at all are to designate mental activities – a question that could be debated, but is not even raised by Cornman – surely these do. As for Husserl, nothing could be more obvious than that he devotes a great deal of treatment precisely to seeing, perceiving generally and remembering, that he considers them mental activities, and that he considers them intentional. Furthermore, he is occupied in the *Logical Investigations* with such concepts as knowing, evidence and truth. In any case, as we have seen, his whole point in delineating the class of intentional experiences is to proceed to a theory of knowledge. How could he be said to be developing a theory of knowledge if precisely knowledge is now ruled out of consideration?

It is interesting to note further that if we allow for the analysis of mental terms into disposition or achievement terms, some favorite examples of intentionality seem to be affected. Brentano said: 'in representation something is represented, in judgment something is acknowledged or rejected, in love something is loved, in hate something is hated, in desire something desired'. We look in vain, I think, for a mental *activity* directly corresponding to loving, hating and desiring, and find it easy to interpret these phenomena as dispositions to say, feel, think or do certain things under certain circumstances. Once we do this, the suspicion is sure to arise that we have been misled by the grammar of certain words into inventing something that isn't there. And curiously enough, I think that no verb is more susceptible to a disposition analysis than *'believing'*, the very term which Chisholm takes as a paradigm of intentionality.

But the fact that we can easily give a dispositional or other non-action analysis of some mental verbs does not entail that all mental verbs can be so analyzed, and it can be argued, as Cornman does, that just as winning the race implies running it, so knowing implies the existence of some genuine mental activity. He suggests believing, but better candidates could perhaps be thinking, asserting, judging or claiming.[30] Now Husserl has no doubts about the existence of such activities, and it is clear that it is these that he is interested in (and not in dispositions or achievements) despite the fact that he often uses terms we would regard as expressing something other than activities. This is amply shown by the fact that Husserl's key term is *Erlebnis* (experience), which for him is clearly an episodic term. The terms 'experience' and 'content', he says, 'mean for the modern psychologist ... real occurrences [*Vorkommnisse*] (Wundt rightly calls them 'events' [*Ereignisse*]) ... In this sense, percepts, imaginative and pictorial presentations, acts of conceptual thinking, surmises and doubts, joys and griefs, hopes and fears, wishes and acts of the will etc., are, just as they flourish in our consciousness, "experiences" or "contents of consciousness"'.[31] He then goes on to distinguish the phenomenological from the psychological concept of experience, but the phenomenological refers no less to mental occurrences or events. As for Husserl's interest in a theory of knowledge, it would not be inconsistent to accept an achievement analysis of knowing itself and still insist that the class of intentional experiences is relevant to a philosophical understanding of knowledge.

---

[30] In calling the last three mental activities, I am of course distinguishing them from 'uttering' a proposition. One can utter a proposition without asserting it or claiming anything.

[31] *LI*, p. 536.

This leaves us, however, with those other verbs besides 'knowing' which are termed cognitive: 'seeing', 'perceiving', 'remembering', one of which Husserl mentions in the catalogue of experiences just quoted. These seem to refer directly to mental activities or episodes, yet they seem not to be intentional. Is there, nevertheless, an intentional analysis that can be given of them? Cornman apparently thinks so, but he does not elaborate. What could he have in mind?

One way of analyzing 'seeing' is suggested by the following example: If I am really seeing the Eiffel Tower, I am having a certain convincing visual experience, usually involving the tower as being here before me;[32] and furthermore, the tower really is here before me. I say 'convincing' in order to rule out cases like the well-known mirage of water on the road ahead: here I could be said to have a visual experience of water on the road ahead, but it is not convincing.[33] In a convincing visual experience, no reasons occur to me, from past experience or whatever, for questioning what I 'see'. However, it is also possible, of course, in the case of the sort of illusions that trouble philosophers, to have a *convincing* visual experience of the Eiffel Tower when it is not really there before me at all. In such a case, of course, I could not be said to be seeing the Eiffel Tower. Here we might be inclined to say, tentatively, that the visual experience is like that involved in the seeing of the Eiffel Tower in every detail, except that the tower is not there.

Now it may be that the analysis of seeing that I have given is not adequate. It does not rule out the far-fetched case in which I have a convincing, but hallucinatory, visual experience of the Eiffel Tower when the tower, quite by chance, happens also to be before me just as I experience it. Perhaps this is not a seeing. Is it because seeing implies a causal relation between the Tower and my experience of it? I do not intend to argue this question, for it is not important for my point. It suffices to state that having the convincing visual experience, and the tower's really being there, are necessary conditions.

What is perhaps curious about this two-part analysis is that, from the experiencer's point of view, the first part implies the

[32] I may, of course, take it to be something else.

[33] Here I am ruling out an analysis stating that what I 'really see' is the effect of heat upon the light which strikes my retina. I do not think there is any sense in which this is what I see.

second. If my visual experience is really convincing, then I am convinced that the tower is really here before me. For me, all my convincing visual experiences are seeings, at least while I'm having them. The case of illusion, however, shows that not all *are* seeings. The judgment on whether a given convincing visual experience is genuinely a seeing is rendered on the basis of another experience independent of the first, whether it is a later one of my own, that of an external observer or ultimately that of an all-*seeing* God.

This analysis permits us to apply the Ryle–Cornman distinction between achievement and activity to perception. Having a convincing visual experience can be called a mental activity with a certain goal, and the independent judgment, mentioned above, decides whether or not the goal has been reached. The analogy to running and winning a race is a good one: there, too, the decision as to whether a given case of running is a case of winning is left up to an external authority. When I have a convincing visual experience, I think I have achieved my goal. But the decision cannot be left up to the perceiver alone, any more than the runner can decide whether he has won the race; or, if he does decide, he does so in a different act, and according to standards agreed upon by all participants in the race.

Now Husserl's approach to seeing could be described in this way: he is concerned with describing convincing visual experiences as such without rendering the independent or external judgment as to whether or not they are cases of seeing. Clearly, the description of such an experience would have to include the fact that it considers itself, so to speak, a case of seeing. But Husserl is interested neither in concurring in nor in denying that judgment as an external observer. Rather, he withholds judgment. This was his approach, I would argue, in the *Logical Investigations*, though he was not explicitly aware of its peculiarity and its value. He became explicitly aware of both in the years following the publication of *Logical Investigations*, and the approach developed into a full-fledged method of philosophy in the *Ideas* of 1913 under the title of phenomenological epoché or phenomenological reduction, where it is applied to all mental activities represented by the so-called cognitive verbs.

It is to be noted especially that, in the analysis I have given, in a case of seeing, the visual experience is not something *other* than the seeing. This would seem to differ from the sort of analysis suggested by Cornman's solution to the problem. But I do not think it does. Running and winning a race are not two different activities or events. Rather, to call a case of running a case of winning is to affirm a relation between it (the running) and a certain goal. So, in the case of seeing, the visual experience is not one mental act, while the seeing is a second mental act somehow superimposed upon it. Rather, the purpose of the independent judgment I spoke about is to decide whether a given visual experience *is* or *is not* a seeing. The implication of this analysis is that a convincing visual experience must be one or the other. However, its being a convincing visual experience is not itself evidence of which one it is. Thus, as long as we consider it purely as a visual experience we are not committed to saying that it either is or is not a case of seeing, and thus are not committed to saying that its object exists. In this sense, we can say that a convincing visual experience is intentional according to Chisholm's first criterion, that is, ascribing such an experience to someone implies neither the existence nor the non-existence of the object of that experience.

Now in approaching seeing, perceiving generally and other cognitive activities such as remembering in this way (*mutatis mutandis*), Husserl obviously believes also that a description of a convincing visual experience (to stick with the same example) can be given which is indifferent to whether or not it is a case of seeing. Whatever the decision of that 'independent judgment' we spoke about, it will not change the details of the experience itself. Or, to put it in another way, given two convincing visual experiences of, say, a dancing bear, one of which is a seeing and the other an illusion (and supposing perspective, background and the like to be the same), the two would be described in just the same way.

This brings us back to the problem of the intentional object. The case of illusion has notoriously been used to argue in the following way: *ex hypothesi* the two experiences are alike in every detail, and one of the details is that they are both experiences of a dancing bear. Thus the two experiences have a like object. However, in one case there really is a dancing bear, in the other there is no such bear. Since these two details are not alike, we should not count the bear himself as one of the descriptive components of the two experiences. Rather, we should say that both experiences have something like a 'dancing-bear-appearance' which is different from the bear himself, but which in the one case corresponds to (resembles, or whatever) a real entity and in the other case does not. Now this appearance, we could say, is the *intentional object* of the experience in both cases. Whether or not the bear exists, this object must, in some sense, exist. But in what sense? This is the question of the ontological status of the intentional object. On this point, Chisholm speaks of the view that the object has a status 'that is short of actuality but more than nothingness'.[34] As we have seen, this could mean that there exists in both cases a mental entity, say, a dancing-bear-*image*. Or, accepting Meinong's doctrine of the independence of *Sosein* from *Sein*, we could point to an extra-mental non-entity, that is, something that, strictly speaking, does not *exist* (i.e., is *ausserseiend*) but still has an independent ontological status.

Husserl rejects both of these alternatives. Criticizing Brentano's presentation of intentionality, he speaks of two misunderstandings that are promoted by it. The first is 'that we are dealing with a real [*realen*] event or real [*reales*] relationship, taking place between "consciousness" or "the ego", on the one hand, and the thing of which there is consciousness, on the other'.[35] In rejecting such a real relationship, Husserl is of course affirming that the object itself need not exist; but I take him also to be stating that when it does not exist, we need not invent some other extra-mental thing, such as a Meinongian *Ausserseiendes*, to which the experience stands in a real relation. The second misunderstanding is 'that we are dealing with a relation between two things, both present in equally real fashion [*reell*] in consciousness, an act and an intentional object, or with a sort of box-within-box structure of mental contents'.[36]

In rejecting these alternatives, Husserl is affirming that the intentional object is not something *other than* the object referred to in the experience. He says explicitly, with emphasis, 'that the intentional object of a presentation is *the same* as its actual object, and on occasion as its external object, and that it is *absurd* to distinguish between them'.[37] But again, what if the object does not exist? To return to our example of the two experiences, how

---

[34] 'Intentionality', *loc. cit.* (reference in note 3 above).
[35] *LI*, p. 557.
[36] *Ibid.*
[37] *LI*, p. 595.

can we say that they have a like object, if the object exists in one case and not in the other? Is it not necessary to say that they both have a mental image, and that this is what they have in common, while the actual status of the external objects constitutes a difference between them?

Still criticizing Brentano's terminology, Husserl makes this remark: 'it will be well to avoid all talk of immanent objectivity. It is readily dispensed with, since we have the expression "intentional object" which is not exposed to similar objections'.[38] How does this help? I suggest that instead of saying 'intentional object' we say 'intended object'. If we do this we can see that the philosophical term 'intention', usually considered a technical term, is really very close to our ordinary use. We can speak of an intended object in much the same way as we speak of an intended insult. If no insult actually results from a remark, i.e. if it is not taken as an insult, it still makes perfectly good sense to speak of the intended insult. If the remark hits home, however, i.e. an actual insult does result, it is not different from the intended insult, it *is* the intended insult. Now we could say of the two experiences of a dancing bear, one veridical and one illusory, that what they have in common is an *intended* object. The intended object is not necessarily some real thing, whether internal (mental) or external, that they both have. To speak of an intended object is to refer obliquely, one might say, to a possibly real object, but not to commit oneself to its reality (or unreality). Possible equivalents for 'intended' would be 'putative' or 'alleged'. Thus one can speak of an alleged crime and describe it in great detail without at the same time affirming that such a crime took place. To speak of an alleged crime or an intended object, however, is not merely to speak of some random possibility, for one is dependent, for the content of one's description, upon a particular act of alleging or intending. Thus while Husserl denies that the intended object is other than the real object (where there is a real object), he adds that this 'does not, of course, stop us from distinguishing, as we said previously, between the object *tout court* which is intended on a given occasion, and the object *as* it is then intended . . . and in the latter case peculiar analyses and descriptions will be appropriate.'[39]

---

[38]*LI*, p. 560.
[39]*LI*, p. 596.

From these passages, one begins to get a sense of what Husserl means by phenomenological *description*. Clearly he wants to consider the intentional object as a descriptive component of an experience without thereby collapsing the two so as to make the object a real part of the experience. Furthermore, he wants to be able to characterize descriptively the different *ways* of intending. In Brentano's presentation of intentionality, he says, 'only one point has importance for us', namely that there are different ways of being intentionally related to an object – in 'mere representation', judgment, perception, etc.[40] To say more than this on the topic of phenomenological description would lead us too far afield. It should be pointed out in passing, however, that the notion of the intended object is in itself neutral with regard to the question of realism vs. idealism. Insofar as the notion I have outlined is fundamental to Husserl's phenomenological epoché, and insofar as the method of epoché remains a constant throughout Husserl's career, it could be argued that he succeeds in avoiding these two alternatives in spite of many later formulations which seem openly idealistic. I do not intend to argue this point here; suffice it to say that if these formulations are taken as being expressed within the context of the suspension of judgment that the epoché requires, they do not translate into straightforward idealistic claims.

What I hope to have shown here is how Husserl's methodological device, the epoché, was developed as a way of dealing with just the problem raised by Cornman and others, namely the problem of the intentionality of experiences or mental activities designated by the so-called cognitive verbs. And, as I have said, his solution to the problem is not unlike that of Cornman himself. While the epoché as a methodological tool is explicitly formulated only in the *Ideas*, it is already at work in the *Logical Investigations*. Only on this assumption can we make sense of what Husserl says there about perception and related topics.

A word should be said in conclusion about the relation between Husserl's approach and a theory of *knowledge*. Clearly phenomenology, as understood by both Husserl and his successors, is intended to be more than just a theory of knowledge. It wants to deal, for example, with such phenomena as thinking, imagining, and valuing outside the context of the knowing

---

[40] *LI*, p. 554.

situation. But at the same time phenomenology does claim to have epistemological import. Husserl believes that his approach is the only proper one for a theory of knowledge understood as a *critique* of knowledge. It makes it possible to deal consistently with *claims* to knowledge – or, as in the case of perception, claims to a direct contact with reality – strictly *as* claims, i.e. without having to commit oneself on the validity of those claims. One might well ask whether phenomenology, understood in this way, qualifies as a theory of knowledge at all, or even as a critique. But it must be pointed out that the epoché does not rule out a treatment of knowledge, evidence, and even truth, as *intended* (claimed) knowledge, intended evidence, intended truth. And this is, in fact, the way Husserl treats these topics. He speaks at one point of 'the "experience" of truth' (*das 'Erlebnis' der Wahrheit*).[41]

But an adequate exposition of these subjects would likewise lead us far beyond the scope of this paper. There are many aspects of the problem of intentionality I have not touched on at all. The most important of these is doubtless the question of whether this concept can be dispensed with entirely in the philosophy of mind. Like Husserl, Chisholm and Brentano, I do not think that it can. But I do not claim to have argued for this view here.

[41] *LI*, p. 194.

Problems of Intentionality

J. L. MACKIE

Some 'problems of intentionality' can be solved by distinguishing this psychological feature ('tee-ality') from the logical feature intensionality ('ess-ality'). We can explain why ess-ality, which arises from an interest in properties and propositions, often accompanies tee-ality, but also why either can occur without the other. These clarifications, however, uncover a deeper problem. Intentional objects are contents of experience masquerading as separable objects. But how can there be one (psychological) state of affairs which is adequately described only through a (partial) description of a different, merely possible, state of affairs?

John Mackie is a Fellow of University College, Oxford. His publications include articles on logic, moral philosophy, philosophy of religion, and philosophy of science, and two books, *Truth, Probability, and Paradox – Studies in Philosophical Logic* (Oxford, 1973), and *The Cement of the Universe – A Study of Causation* (Oxford, 1974).

It seems to me that some of the problems that have been raised
about intentionality, and some of the disputes about it in which
philosophers have engaged, can be resolved fairly easily; but it
has other aspects which I find puzzling, though I may or may
not be able to persuade others to share my embarrassment.

But first, if we are to achieve any clarity we must distinguish
intentionality from intensionality (tee-ality, perhaps, from
ess-ality) and also several senses of 'intentional' from one
another. The essential work has been done, and set on a firm
historical foundation, by Kneale.[1] An *intentio* in, for example,
Aquinas is something whose being consists in its being thought,
rather like a Berkeleian idea. Following this, Brentano speaks
of intentional inexistence meaning existence as an object of
thought. But to intend is also, etymologically, to aim or shoot at
something,[2] and Husserl for one calls a state of mind or a mental
event intentional meaning that it is directed on an object.
(Kneale suggests that Husserl's development is due to a misunderstanding of Brentano: certainly – as we shall see – he
takes 'direction upon an object' in a sense stronger than
Brentano's.) Intensionality, on the other hand, is a logical, or
perhaps grammatical, feature or cluster of related features,
contrasting with extensionality. A context is intensional if
coextensive predicates cannot in general be substituted for one
another in it *salva veritate* – for example, since I may know that
X is ϕ without knowing that X is ψ, even if everything that is
ϕ is in fact ψ and *vice versa*, 'I know that X is . . .' is an intensional
context. Again, a context is intensional if co-referring sub-
stantival terms cannot be so substituted: 'The vicar is *ex officio*
chairman of the school board' may be true but 'The headmistress's lover is *ex officio* chairman of the school board' false even
if the vicar is the headmistress's lover: so '. . . is *ex officio* the
Y' is also intensional. Again, a context is intensional if truth-
functionally equivalent clauses – clauses which as statements on
their own would have the same truth-value – cannot be so
substituted: since even if 'q' and 'r' are both true, 'p because q'
may be true while 'p because r' is false, 'p because . . .' is an
intensional context. Again, a statement or a sentence in use is

[1] W. Kneale, 'Intentionality and intensionality', *Aristotelian Society Supplementary Vol.
XLII* (1968), pp. 73–90.
[2] G. E. M. Anscombe, 'The Intentionality of sensation: a grammatical feature', in
R. J. Butler (ed.), *Analytical Philosophy*, Second Series (1965), pp. 158–80.

intensional if it does not imply the existence (or the non-existence) of items apparently referred to by substantival terms, or if it gives such items a kind of indeterminacy – as 'I want a cup of tea' does not imply that there are any cups of tea, or that there is a particular cup of tea that I want, or even that there is some specific kind of tea, Indian, China, or Ceylon, say, that I want: lots of questions which can be asked and answered about any actual cup of tea do not arise with regard to the cup of tea which is the object of my want, and to ask them would be to display a failure to understand the meaning-structure of this sentence. Similarly a sentence in use is intensional if it does not imply the truth (or the falsity) of embedded clauses as '*A* believes that *p*' does not imply either the truth or the falsity of '*p*'.[3] Chisholm has suggested two further criteria of the same general sort, but since he proposed them especially in order to mark out intentionality as an exclusively psychological feature, and since Cohen has shown that they fail to do so, they seem to be of little importance.[4]

But tee-ality and ess-ality come together in, for example, some uses of such verbs as 'look for', 'worship', 'see', and of course 'intend'. An atheist can describe a theist as worshipping God, and Diogenes did not compromise his cynicism when he said that he was looking for an honest man. An action may be intended under one description but not under another which also truly applies to it. And many people have seen ghosts, though there are none. In such cases it is plausible to speak of an object of thought or of a directing of the mind on some object, perhaps linked with some overt behaviour. Something in them, therefore, is intentional; but the sentences we naturally use to describe them are intensional by one or other of the logical criteria.

It is such facts as these that have encouraged Chisholm, following Brentano's suggestion that intentional inexistence is the mark of the mental or of the psychic, to try to formulate logical criteria for the intentional use of language such that

---

[3] R.M. Chisholm, *Perceiving* (1957), chapter 11, and 'Intentionality' in *Encyclopedia of Philosophy* (1967), ed. Paul Edwards, Vol. 4, p. 203; A. N. Prior, 'Intentionality and intensionality', *Aristotelian Society Supplementary Volume XLII* (1968), pp. 91–106; L. Jonathan Cohen, 'Criteria of intensionality', same volume, pp. 123–42; G. E. M. Anscombe, *op. cit.* (reference in note 2 above).

[4] Chisholm, 'Intentionality'; and Cohen *op. cit.* (references in note 3 above).

psychic phenomena, and these only, require intentional sentences to describe them adequately; he is trying to find some
variety of ess-ality which is coextensive with tee-ality and hence
with mentality also. But this project seems misguided. I would
not, indeed, accept Husserl's view that sensations and certain
types of feelings are psychic but non-intentional.[5] They need
not involve anything that we can call in a strong sense the
directing of the mind on an object. There may be no mental act
which deals in any further way with the content of the experience, so that Husserl is rightly reluctant to call these items
intentional in his sense. Yet a sensation of pain or of pricking, or
a feeling of lassitude, has something that we can call its content
but that is not existentially separable from the experience; it
exists in and by being the content of the experience and so is an
intentional object in Brentano's sense. On the other hand, it
does not seem that the description of these experiences calls for
intensional sentences. Whereas ghosts can be seen without
existing, pain and lassitude exist if they are felt, and unlike
wanted cups of tea or imagined castles in Spain, they have no
indeterminacy about them: there are no further descriptions of
them that we might first think of enquiring for, and then realise
that they did not allow. But this is surely because the language
that we use to describe such sensations and feelings belongs to
them alone, whereas the language that we use to describe wants,
imaginings, and so on is borrowed from that whose primary use
is to describe concrete objects and states of affairs. The description of a desire for a cup of tea is parasitic upon the description
of cups of tea, but the indeterminacy in the former results from a
mismatch between the two: real cups of tea have far more
features than are mirrored in desires for cups of tea. There is no
room for any such mismatch in the description of the sensations
and feelings mentioned. Here already, therefore, we find tee-
ality without ess-ality. But equally we can find ess-ality
without tee-ality. It does not seem that intensionality, or any
variety of it, will prove to be a sufficient criterion of the mental
or psychic. The literature is full of examples of intensional but
non-psychological statements. 'Lizards are like dragons' does
not entail that there are, or that there are not, any dragons.

---

[5] Carr, this volume, pp. 17–36; E. Husserl, *Logical Investigations*, trans. J. N. Findlay
(1970), pp. 552–3, 569ff.

'Any offspring of a white rat and a white mouse must be a barren albino' is similarly non-committal about barren albinos. 'Possibly what caused the power-cut was that a swan flew into the wires' does not imply either the truth or the falsity of the embedded clause about a swan. Even if the predicates '. . . has atomic number 10' and '. . . has atomic weight 20' are co-extensive, the statement that some property of neon is due to its atomic weight does not entail that the property is due to its atomic number. 'It is contingent that grass is green' does not have the same truth-value as 'It is contingent that if grass is green then grass is green', the first being true and the second false, though the two that-clauses have the same truth-value, being equally true. 'This blackcurrant bush needs an extra supply of nitrogen' does not entail that there *is* an extra supply of nitrogen or that there is any particular form which the needed supply takes or is to take. And in general Cohen's examination of Chisholm's successive proposals justifies his conclusion : 'Only by question-begging definitions of intensionality and/or psycho-logicalness shall we ever demonstrate, it seems, that the logical property of intensionality affords a sufficient and/or necessary condition of a proposition's constituting a psychological description.'[6] It is better to say, with Prior (and in agreement also with Kneale) that 'intensionality' is a rather general phenomenon of which 'intentionality' provides some of the most interesting examples.[7]

If we consider what in general would give rise to ess-ality, it is in no way surprising that there should be non-psychological as well as psychological examples of it. Intensional constructions contrast with extensional ones; extensional ones are those in which we are concerned only with picking out certain things or sets of things or perhaps certain truth-values; but wherever an expression is used not just to pick out things, to identify exten-sions, but to say something about one or more properties or propositions, so that the connotation or sense of the expression plays some special role, the construction to which it belongs will be intensional. There are some properties that something would need to have if it were to count as a dragon; as well as these, there

[6] Cohen, *op. cit.* (reference in note 3 above) ; J. O. Urmson, 'Criteria of intensionality', same volume pp. 107–22.
[7] Prior, *op. cit.* (reference in note 3 above), p. 91.

are further properties which are frequently ascribed to dragons in stories or given to them in pictures. To say 'Lizards are like dragons' is to say that lizards have some of these properties, especially some of the more striking or distinctive ones. The word 'dragons' is here used to indicate a somewhat vague cluster of properties, not to pick out a set of things, and it is irrelevant whether this cluster is instantiated or not. Yet on the surface the sentence is constructed on the same model as 'Zebras are like horses', which is most naturally construed as presupposing the existence of both kinds of animal and stating a relation of resemblance between them. Similarly the sentence about lizards speaks as if there were dragons: there is a conflict between its surface form and its underlying structure, the truth-conditions to which someone who uses it is ultimately committed. Causal statements like those about a barren albino, neon's atomic weight, and the blackcurrant bush's need for nitrogen are again intensional because they assert relations between properties. Both parents' being albino would result in any offspring's being albino; the parents' being of different species would result in any offspring's being barren. It is the absence or shortage of nitrogen in any assimilable form that has caused this bush's poor condition, and it is the supply of anything of that *sort* that would bring about an improvement. The necessity of 'If grass is green then grass is green' and the contingency of 'Grass is green' belong to these respective propositions, they are features that result from their internal propositional structure, and there is no reason why either should survive the substitution of another proposition of the same truth-value.

In saying this we are not, of course, committed to reifying intensions – properties or propositions. To talk about the property of ϕ-ing is just to talk in some, possibly complicated, way about actual or possible cases where something ϕs or does not ϕ; talking about properties is merely (in some circumstances) more expeditious and facilitates generalisation. And the same goes for talking about propositions.[8] For example, to say that it is one rather than the other of two coextensive properties that enters into some causal relation is just to say that

---

[8] Cf. A. N. Prior, *Objects of Thought*, chapters 1, 3, and 4; W. Kneale 'Propositions and truth in natural languages', *Mind*, Vol. LXXXI (1972), pp. 225–43.

it is A's being ϕ, not A's being ψ, that caused B's being χ, and the central part of what this says is that if, in the circumstances, A had not been ϕ, B would not have been χ, but that even if A, in those circumstances, had not been ψ, B might still have been χ; there is perhaps also a suggestion that A's being ϕ led on in some continuous way to B's being χ, whereas A's being ψ did not.[9] Similarly to say that a certain proposition, for example that grass is green, is contingent is just to say that grass might not have been green; however this is to be further analysed, it is quite clear that to say this is to say something different from what one gets by substituting any other equally true proposition, for example that gold is malleable, for the proposition that grass is green, and so saying that gold might not have been malleable. Yet to realise this difference it is not necessary to recognise propositions as entities.

(Reference to properties or propositions is not, indeed, the only source of intensionality or referential opacity. In 'Giorgione was so called etc.' references to the man Giorgione and to the name 'Giorgione' are run together, and that is why '. . . was so called etc.' is a non-extensional context. Similarly 'The vicar is *ex officio* etc.' condenses references to the vicar and to the office of vicar. But reference to properties and propositions is of far more interest and importance.)

Once we have this general understanding of what gives rise to ess-ality, it is easy to see why so many psychological statements are intensional. Statements about kinds of overt action that are guided by thought are rather like causal statements. To look for an honest man is at least to do things that seem likely to put one in touch with something that is both human and honest, if such there be in the neighbourhood, and to do them because they seem likely to have this result. (It is probably more than this – it may indeed include say, wondering whether and if so where there is an honest man, but the more will be covered by one or other of the following kinds of example.) If I see a ghost, then I have a visual experience (associated perhaps with a belief) which is most adequately described by describing the content of each, that is, by indicating the set of properties that I take (in part at least wrongly), or am inclined to take, to be coinstantiated at a certain place and time. Thinking often

---

[9] I discuss the analysis of causal statements in detail in *The Cement of the Universe* (1974).

(Kneale suggests 'always') involves the entertaining of propositions; consequently sentences used to describe thinking commonly express propositions about propositions.[10] Referentially opaque belief-statements fit into the same pattern. If Tom believes that Cicero denounced Catiline, the content of his belief is appropriately expressed by some such sentence as 'There was someone who was called "Cicero", and who was famous for this and that, and who denounced someone called "Catiline".'[11] We need to mention some such proposition in order to give the content of Tom's belief, and if we change the proposition, say by using expressions with different senses, or by using condensed formulations which surreptitiously introduce names other than 'Cicero' or 'Catiline', we shall of course misrepresent the belief. Referentially transparent belief-statements are in fact more puzzling than opaque ones, though their logical structure is only different, not more obscure. Formally, a referentially-transparent belief-statement is one in which the name or definite description of the thing or person that the belief is about is given larger scope: it may say, in effect, 'As for Cicero and Catiline, Tom believes that the former denounced the latter.'[12] The identifications of the two characters stand outside the scope of the belief-operator, and consequently any co-referring expressions will achieve the same identifications and yield equally true statements. But if I say this, I am saying that Tom has somehow succeeded in directing his thought towards the very same individual men that I am talking about, and this may well seem to be a more remarkable achievement, and one for which more of a further explanation is required, than merely to have, among the contents of his thoughts, certain clusters of properties which are ascribed, with the help of existential quantifiers, to external reality.

But why, then, do some psychological verbs such as 'know' and 'see' (in its most natural sense, as distinct from that in which people have seen ghosts) fail to obey the logical criteria of ess-ality? I think that Carr, following Cornman, is right to explain this by distinguishing, within the meaning of such verbs,

---

[10] Kneale, 'Intentionality and intensionality', p. 86 (reference in note 1 above).

[11] Prior, 'Intentionality and intensionality', p. 99 (reference in note 3 above).

[12] Cf. R. Sharvy, 'Truth-functionality and referential opacity', *Philosophical Studies*, Vol. 21 (1970), pp. 5–9; A. Smullyan 'Modality and description', *Journal of Symbolic Logic*, Vol. 13 (1948), pp. 31–7.

achievement-claims from descriptions of 'genuine mental activity' or 'experience'.[13] If I say, in the most usual sense, that Tom is seeing the Eiffel Tower, I am saying that Tom is having an appropriate visual experience, and is himself taking it as the seeing of something real and external (and this much, in itself, does not require the real existence of the Eiffel Tower within Tom's range of vision, or indeed anywhere); but I am also saying that the Eiffel Tower is there, that Tom has got it more or less right, and that this appropriate visual experience of Tom's is causally dependent in some suitable way on the tower's being there. The visual experience, then, involves intentional inexistence, and any adequate description in terms of a tower, or anything similar, would be intensional for that reason. Again, Tom's taking it as the seeing of an externally real object, the fact that his seeing points towards a supposedly actual tower, although there might not have been one, calls for an intensional description. But my claim that the tower is there and has helped to produce his more or less correct visual experience will refer extensionally to the actual tower.

'Know' works similarly. Knowledge generally involves belief – though there are marginal cases where we would ascribe knowledge, in the absence of belief, on the strength of an ability or disposition to give correct answers, and so on[14] – and such belief on its own will be described by the use of intensional sentences, whereas the success entailed by 'know' will be described by ones which are in some respects extensional: for example, 'Tom knows that the Eiffel Tower is made of steel' entails the truth of the embedded that-clause.

It seems to me that the points made so far are straightforward and should be relatively uncontroversial: but from here on the subject becomes more difficult. I have accepted Brentano's terminology of intentional objects and inexistence; but just what does this represent, and how is it related to the other kinds of intentionality that are indicated by the metaphors of pointing and aiming? It is useless to think of the intentional object as an internal picture, a real object which actually exists somewhere inside one's head and which is inspected there. For this would force us to make another move of the same kind, to introduce a

---

[13] Carr, this volume pp. 17–36.
[14] Cf. D. M. Armstrong, *Belief, Truth and Knowledge* (1973), chapter 10.

further intentional object as the content of the experience which is the inspecting of this one.

Again, it will not do to say that where there is an intentional object there is an experience E which is its own object, or even part of its own object, though Brentano seems to have taken inexistence to imply this. The supposition that E is (part of) the object of E leads at once, as I have argued elsewhere, to a vicious infinite regress.[15] One bit of experiencing could not be part of what it was itself an experiencing of, though it could presumably be the object of some other piece of experiencing. We cannot explain inexistence by the use of a relational model, even by making the relation reflexive.

Similarly it will not do to postulate propositions as entities, of which that-clauses are the names, to be real objects of belief and other propositional attitudes. Apart from the stock objections to uneconomical postulation, this move only creates further difficulties. It is quite obscure how believing, fearing, hoping and so on could be analysed as real relations to such entities. It is equally obscure how such proposition-entities, when true, would be related to the concrete states of affairs that made them true. Consequently if belief, for example, were so analysed, it is obscure how Tom's believing-relation to the proposition that-it-will-rain-tomorrow would have anything to do with the actual falling of rain on the next day.

In contrast with all these unhelpful moves, we must insist that the only entity involved is, for example, Tom's having an experience of a certain sort. Talk about its intentional object can be no more than a way of characterizing it, of saying what sort of an experience it is by indicating its content. But what gives rise to the difficulties and to the mistakes we are constantly tempted to make in this area is that this content, though it is really only a feature of the experience, though it really only makes it the particular sort of experience it is, presents itself as if it were a more or less distinct object to which the subject is related, this whole relational situation then being the experience. I feel a pain in my leg almost, and yet not quite, as if it were something in my leg apart from my feeling of it, and this

---

[15] In my 'Are there any incorrigible empirical statements?', *Australasian Journal of Philosophy*, Vol. 41 (1963). pp 12–28.

applies even more to my hearing a sound or my seeing a patch of colour.

This truth, that a content which masquerades as a separable object really only makes an experience the sort of experience it is, holds for beliefs, fears, and so on as well as for sensations. In consequence, it is more illuminating to punctuate a belief sentence in the way Prior recommends, '*A* believes-that *p*', than in the more usual way, '*A* believes that-*p*'.[16] Grammatically we can, of course, admit that prefixing the word 'that' to any sentence represented by '*p*' yields a noun-equivalent: this is a device of nominalization. But this bit of grammar is misleading or at least useless with regard to ontology: there is no entity for this noun equivalent to name. Prior's punctuation, on the other hand, brings out that we are ourselves using the sentence '*p*' to characterize, by presenting its content, *A*'s belief-condition which is reported by the larger sentence in which '*p*' is embedded.

It is therefore tempting to accept Husserl's thesis, quoted and endorsed by Carr,[17] that the intentional object is merely the intended object, and hence that it is none other than the real object: 'the intentional object of a presentation is the same as its actual object, and on occasion its external object . . . I mean the transcendent object named in each case.'[18] This would mean, presumably, that the intentional object of Tom's belief that it will rain tomorrow is just rain actually falling tomorrow, which, if it rains, will be a fully objective, external, state of affairs. But this is no more than a half-truth. It is true that what Tom believes (or hopes, fears, and so on: we might say 'intends' in a sense that covers all these) is just that rain falls tomorrow; it is with this possible state of affairs itself that he is concerned, and not with any image or counterpart of it or substitute for it. Yet this object as intended lacks many of the features that the actual external object, if it occurs, will have. This was, of course, our starting point. As intended, it is somewhat indeterminate: rain some time tomorrow, but not for any precise period and not in any exact quantity. And it is no less an intended object if the actual rain should not occur at all. In presenting Tom's state of

---

[16] Prior, *Objects of Thought*, pp. 19–21.
[17] Carr, this volume pp. 17–36.
[18] Husserl, *op. cit.* pp. 595–6 (reference in note 5 above).

belief (hope, fear, and so on) we have to speak about the object-as-intended, as distinct from the object as it (perhaps) will be. And the object-as-intended has just those features that distinguish a proposition from a concrete occurrence or state of affairs and tempt us into what we have already noted as the error of postulating proposition-entities. Admittedly Husserl also notes these distinctions. But they entail that it is false to say that the intended object is identical with the real object, except as a way of emphasizing that Tom's belief (and so on) is about actual rain tomorrow, and nothing short of this.

At last we are beginning to get into focus the real puzzle about intentionality. Is it not strange that there should be one state of affairs (Tom's state of believing, hoping, fearing, or whatever it may be) that requires for its adequate description the partial, incomplete, selective, indeterminate description of a quite different and so far merely possible state of affairs? Some remarks of Wittgenstein's about expecting an explosion may help to bring this out,[19] 'Here my thought is: If someone could see the expectation itself – he would have to see *what* is being expected. (But in such a way that it doesn't further require a method of projection, a method of comparison, in order to pass from what he sees to the fact that is expected.)' This presents the problem, but Wittgenstein's surrounding remarks do nothing to resolve it. He says 'The statement "I am expecting a bang at any moment" is an *expression* of expectation' and 'if you see the expression of expectation you see "what is expected"', and he offers the dictum 'Like everything metaphysical the harmony between thought and reality is to be found in the grammar of the language'. This looks profound, but it is shallow. What the grammar of the language, even with Prior's construal, shows is simply that a clause governed, for example, by 'believes that' is used, with just the meaning it would have as a sentence on its own, to describe a state of believing (and so on) : but this constitutes the problem and does not solve it. After we have understood the logical structure, we still want to know what psychological (or other) reality underlies it and is represented by it.

We might think that since ess-ality is found in other, non-psychological and non-puzzling, cases, notably causal ones, we could make tee-ality less puzzling by assimilating it to such

---

[19] L. Wittgenstein, *Zettel*, 53–6; cf. *Philosophical Investigations*, 444–5.

causal relationships. Perhaps what makes a certain state of strain the expectation of an explosion is just the fact that hearing an explosion would relieve it, while nothing else would. Or, if this alone is not enough, perhaps it is this combined with the fact that this tense state has causal antecedents which are themselves somehow connected with an explosion. Perhaps it has been induced by hearing talk about a possible explosion, or by observations of things that are known or believed to be causes of explosions, and so on. If an explosion comes in only at one or more places in a network of causal relationships surrounding the tense state, then there will indeed be true statements about that state in which expressions that seem to refer to an explosion occur intensionally; but this will be no more puzzling than similar intensional occurrences in our causal statements about the blackcurrant bush, the albino rats and mice, and so on.

But let us see just why this would not be puzzling; I suggest that what makes it non-puzzling also makes it inadequate as an account of intentionality. We can distinguish intrinsic from relational descriptions. When a naive realist says that a rose is red, he takes himself to be describing it intrinsically: the being red, he thinks, is right there in the rose. But when a sophisticated realist says that a rose is red, meaning only that it looks red to normal observers in normal conditions, he is offering a relational description of the rose. Again if I say that a hole is round, I have described it intrinsically, as it is in itself. But if I say that it is such that a square peg would not fit it, though a round peg would, I have described the hole relationally: an adequate intrinsic description of the hole could have been given without mentioning the pegs. Similarly if I say that a state of strain is such that only the hearing of a loud bang will relieve it, I have described it relationally, and so also if I say that it was produced by the observation of something that was thought likely to lead to an explosion. But we can apply the notion of intrinsic description to mental states, though not so simply as to roses and round holes. If I say that this state is one of expecting an explosion, I seem to be describing it intrinsically. That is how it is in itself, how it would be no matter what the rest of the world was like. And yet I cannot adequately describe how it is in itself without mentioning a possible explosion. This is what is puzzling: that the reference to another, merely possible, and in this case future, event should be required for an intrinsic description of the tense state. The assimilation of this sort of case to merely causal examples of ess-ality does away with their difficulty but at the cost of denying something that seems to be significantly characteristic of them.

This problem occurs equally with believing, hoping, fearing, supposing, wondering whether, and so on. It may seem, indeed, to be less acute with believing, just because some cases of believing lend themselves to a dispositional analysis. But it is hard to deny that there are also cases of occurrent belief, as well as of the other propositional attitudes.

There is a well known argument that someone's intending to do *X* is so logically connected with his doing *X* that the former cannot cause the latter. This is a fallacy: the kind of logical connection involved here, the need to describe the intending in terms of the action intended, is no obstacle to their being distinct existences in the sense in which a cause and an effect must be.[20] But the widespread reluctance to admit this, and the prevalence of attempts to make all intending adverbial, all just a matter of doing *X* intentionally, may reflect some awareness of our difficulty about there being two distinct states of affairs such that an adequate intrinsic description of the one is parasitic upon a (partial) description of the other.

Berkeley said firmly that an idea can be like nothing but an idea.[21] It would have been better if he had merely raised the problem, *How* can an idea be so like something else as to call for a description that is parasitic on the description of that something else? It is, of course, this problem that suggests a theory of images or mental pictures, for a picture can be like what it is a picture of, and we can describe a picture by describing the scene it portrays. Yet, as we have seen, this is a trap, a dead end. Anything that was literally a picture would raise the same problem all over again. The notion of a picture seems helpful if we think of the picture not just as another physical object that in some respects resembles the scene, but as a picture *of* that scene, as pointing beyond itself to an independent (possible) reality. But this feature belongs not to the picture as a physical object,

[20] Cf. A. I. Melden *Free Action*, p. 53; G. H. von Wright, *Explanation and Understanding*, pp. 94–5 and 115–16; F. M. Stoutland *The Logical Connection Argument, American Philosophical Quarterly Monograph no.* 4 (1970), pp. 117–30; I have discussed this issue in *The Cement of the Universe*, chapter 11.

[21] G. Berkeley, *Principles*, section 8.

but to the picture as interpreted by us. It is our thinking that points to this reality, not the picture on its own. Pictures taken thus provide us only with another mental example of intentionality, not with a non-mental analogue of it.

It might be objected that my puzzle is a spurious one which disappears as soon as it is clearly formulated. If Jane, say, describes Tom as believing that it rained yesterday, her description of Tom's belief-state is parasitic upon her way of describing the concrete state of affairs, 'It rained yesterday'. But if she can describe this state of affairs, why should Tom not be able to do so too? And why should not Jane's describing of how Tom might describe it be related to her own describing of the same state of affairs?

But this objection misses the point. I am not saying that indirect speech is puzzling whereas direct speech is not, or that there is anything surprising about the relation between them. The real problem is about a capacity which even direct speech expresses. Since Jane can say, and mean, 'It rained yesterday' there is already in her a mental state which points beyond itself to yesterday's rain.

Someone might resort to a transcendental argument here. Anyone who raises the sort of difficulty that I am raising must himself be exercising the capacity that he professes to find strange. This is true, but what does it show? This sort of argument might be effective against someone who went beyond puzzlement to scepticism, who professed to doubt or deny that we have the capacity in question. But it does nothing to resolve the difficulty for someone who does not for a moment doubt that we have this capacity, but who finds it hard to understand *how* we have it.

One way of highlighting the problem is to consider whether, and how, a physicalist theory could cope with intentionality. It would have to give some kind of reductive analysis, aiming eventually, perhaps, at micro-reduction. If the assimilation to causal cases of ess-ality, discussed above, were satisfactory, then there would be no serious obstacle to a materialist account; but if, as I have suggested, such an assimilation is unsatisfactory, it is hard to see how the physicalist could even begin. Irreducible intentionality would be fatal to physicalism. To this extent Brentano was right after all in calling intentionality a mark of the mental. But it would be a rather hollow victory for the anti-physicalist if he could defeat his opponent only at the cost of admitting something of which he was equally incapable of giving any satisfactory explanation.

But it is in this unsatisfactory state that I must leave the question. I have tried to show that some problems about intentionality and its relation to intensionality can be cleared up, but that their removal uncovers a deeper problem. I have not solved this problem, but have merely argued that some initially attractive ways of resolving or avoiding it will not do.

Husserl's Notion of Self-evidence

DAVID MICHAEL LEVIN

This paper investigates Husserl's notion of self-evidence: its nature, methodological importance and its role in Husserl's phenomenological humanism. The first section of the paper contrasts Husserl's notion with other notions erroneously attributed to Husserl. In the second section, the analysis moves from a primary dimension (self-evidence as the lived unquestionableness of act and intention) to a secondary dimension (self-evidence as an unquestionableness whose features correspond to the internal structure of the *noema*). When self-evidence is thus understood, it becomes possible to examine the function of self-evidence in perception and knowledge. The next section shows just how and why a genetic logic must supplement the method of self-evidence.

Professor Levin, formerly on the faculty of the Massachusetts Institute of Technology, is now teaching in the Department of Philosophy at Northwestern University, Evanston, Illinois. He is the author of *Reason and Evidence in Husserl's Phenomenology*, and also of numerous shorter studies in phenomenology and phenomenological aesthetics.

54   *David M. Levin*

'Some make the world believe that they believe what they do not
believe. Others, in greater number, make themselves believe it,
being unable to penetrate what it means to believe.'

Montaigne, *Essays*, Book II: 12.

Clearing away the thicket of misunderstandings

Like all devices of interpretation, 'rationalism' is a construct
which assembles the thinking of some very divergent philosophers.* Nevertheless, it is a striking fact, I think, that, in one
guise or another, self-evidence played a decisive role in the
thought of each philosopher so interpreted. As a school of
thought opposed to rationalism on many fronts, empiricism has
stubbornly contested the notion of self-evidence. Of course,
many things can be said in support of rationalism. But it has
always seemed to me that the empiricist arguments against
self-evidence were strong and compelling. In his paper,[1] Professor Ayer has staked out the positions on this muddied field of
battle between rationalism and empiricism. With great accuracy, I think, he defines the theme of self-evidence which
orchestrates the many voices of rationalism; and he carefully
unfolds, in lucid argumentation, the various empiricist objections. If self-evidence must be construed as Ayer proposes, little
can be said on its behalf.

Now, the notion of self-evidence is of central importance in
Husserl's phenomenology. Does Husserl's notion significantly
differ, then, from the one Ayer finds in rationalism? Or does it,
on the other hand, resume and embrace the features of the
older notion so fully that it, too, must fall under the empiricist
axe Ayer has wielded? Limited space prevents much direct and
explicit contrast between Husserl's position and the position of
an older rationalism. It is hoped, however, that a faithful,

* The following works by Husserl are referred to by abbreviations or short titles in the
notes to this paper:

Crisis   *The Crisis of European Sciences and Transcendental Phenomenology*, trans., with an
          introduction, David Carr (Evanston: Northwestern University Press, 1970).
Ideas   *Ideas: General Introduction to Pure Phenomenology*, trans. W. R. Boyce Gibson
          (Collier Books Edition, 1962).
FTL   *Formal and Transcendental Logic*, trans. Dorion Cairns (The Hague: Martinus
          Nijhoff, 1969).

The *Logical Investigations* referred to in the notes is Husserl's *Logical Investigations*,
trans., with an introduction, J. N. Findlay (London: Routledge and Kegan Paul;
New York: Humanities Press, 1970).
[1] See A. J. Ayer, 'Self-evidence', following this paper.

detailed account of Husserlian self-evidence will suffice by itself
to demonstrate the numerous and, indeed, profound differences
which establish Husserl's deliberate distance from the tradition
of rationalism out of which he emerged.

And yet, it might be helpful to outline, here, some of these
points of difference, so that it will be feasible, ultimately, to
determine whether or not Husserlian self-evidence is vulnerable
to the empiricist arguments (or, at least, to those which
Professor Ayer, who does countenance propositions, has
advanced). (1) For rationalism, self-evidence is a matter of
conviction or psychological intuition. For Husserl, however,
it is a matter of transcendental apperception and explication,
whose function and authority are rigorously defined by the
phenomenological reduction. (2) For rationalism, self-evidence
distinguishes those propositions which, as the objects of such
conviction or intuition, can stand self-sufficiently by themselves
as the absolute foundation of a domain of knowledge (the true
propositions of logic and mathematics, for example, and even,
according to some philosophers, the true propositions of
metaphysics and the fundamental principles of morality). But
Husserl explicitly denies that self-evidence can be used to single
out some *fixed* domain of fundamental, self-sufficient knowledge.
In fact, it is his contention, which he supports by a phenomenological analysis of inner time-consciousness, that there are no
propositions which can be possessed in this way. (3) For
rationalism, self-evidence always presents an apodictic knowledge of absolute truths. For Husserl, on the contrary, self-
evidence not only admits the possibility of error and revision,
but indeed constitutes the veritable ground of this possibility.
(4) For rationalism, self-evidence simply exhibits either the
givenness of truth or the givenness of falsehood; whereas, for
Husserl, it shows forth much more of meaning: epistemic
modes and styles, for example, and degrees and intensities of
givenness. (5) For rationalism, self-evidence functions solely
in propositional knowledge, or judgement; whereas, for Husserl,
it functions also in the immediacy of perception, imagination,
memory, volition, and sentiment. (6) Finally, for rationalism,
self-evidence must establish a foundation for knowledge *within*
the structure of knowledge. For Husserl, however, self-evidence
founds knowledge by preceding it and, as it were, shadowing it
forth. (So you might say that phenomenological self-evidence is

not the basement, or ground-floor, of the temple of knowledge, but is, rather, the supportive earth which the temple normally conceals.)

To be sure, there are affinities as profound as these various differences. But affinities are not identities; and they, too, can be easily misunderstood. Here are four points to consider. (1) Like the rationalists, Husserl sought the ground of knowledge. Unlike them, however, he found this ground in the simply *lived* moment of consciousness. (2) Like the rationalists, Husserl aspired to disclose an absolute Archimedean point. But, unlike them, he found this absolute, not in some forever-fixed propositions of knowledge whose truth follows from their being the objects of singular conviction, but rather in a passing moment of lived unquestionableness. (3) Like the rationalists, Husserl located an *experience* of self-evidence. Unlike them, however, he located it, not in the mundane, but in the transcendental. Moreover, he insisted on the fact that this experience is a noetic–noematic structure: a correlation of the intentional act and its *Sinn*. (4) Like the rationalists, Husserl understood the need for a moment of epistemic presence.[2] Unlike them, however, he recognized that such presence not only requires, but indeed itself discloses, the immediate absence of fully determinate sense.

Let us consider in detail, now, the role of self-evidence in Husserlian phenomenology. To begin with, we should note that the function of self-evidence is strictly limited to the domain of meaning (what Husserl calls 'noematic sense'), not the domain of existence (reference) itself. In other words, to secure the self-evidence of a state of affairs (*Gegenständlichkeit*) is not, as such, to verify its existence, or in any sense to prove its being. The phenomenological notion of self-evidence is thus altogether different from the everyday, juridical, and scientific notions of objective evidence. This is not to deny, however, that in phenomenology too self-evidence plays a role in existential, or empirical, verification. On the contrary. Self-evidence is, as we shall see, the logical foundation for the very possibility of verification. My point is simply that Husserlian self-evidence must be located in transcendental space, rather than in empirical space.

---

[2] Is not skepticism the only alternative? Ayer himself seems to acknowledge this in the penultimate paragraph of his paper.

Thus, the so-called phenomenological *epoché* – the transcendental suspension, or bracketing, of the domain of accepted existence – must *precede* the logical investigation of phenomenological self-evidence. This methodological condition should serve to illuminate Husserl's contention that phenomenological self-evidence is not at all like the self-evidence which philosophers were wont to attribute, for so many centuries, to the axioms of mathematics and geometry. It may well be fitting to say, for example, that the concluding proposition of a certain proof is valid and is indeed known to be valid; but insofar as the preceding steps of the deduction have not been brought explicitly to mind, or insofar as the relevant rules of inference have not been fully grasped in their employment, or insofar as there is some primitive, undefined element in the proof whose original sense, as a formation of certain theorizing operations, still remains obscure and, so to speak, in the background, Husserl would not want to say that the proposition is fully and properly self-evident.[3]

Nor is self-evidence in any way a problem for empirical psychology to handle. Phenomenological self-evidence is solely a function of noematic sense, not human sensibility. The transcendental reduction was designed to suspend precisely this sensibility insofar as it should belong in the domain of psychological facts. Self-evidence, therefore, is not the same as certainty, for certainty (at least, in its ordinary, mundane sense) can attach to matters which do not at all meet the technical, and very special requirements Husserl has set for phenomenological self-evidence.[4]

In search of self-evidence

I. Unquestionableness as the primary dimension of self-evidence.

In *Ideas* (§24, p. 83), Husserl enunciates what he calls his 'principle of all principles': 'that very primordial dator intuition is a source of authority (*Rechtsquelle*)

[3] See Edmund Husserl, *The Crisis of European Sciences and Transcendental Phenomenology*, (trans., with an introduction, David Carr (Evanston: Northwestern University Press, 1970), pp. 72, 78 and 365.

[4] See Husserl, *Ideas: General Introduction to Pure Phenomenology*, trans. W. R. Boyce Gibson (collier Books Edition, 1962), §21, p. 79 and §145, p. 369. Also see Husserl's *Logical Investigations*, trans., with an introduction, J. N. Findlay (London: Routledge & Kegan Paul; New York: Humanities Press, 1970), Vol. II, Sixth Study, §§3 and 45.

for knowledge, that whatever presents itself in [genuine pheno-
menological] "intuition" and in primordial form (as it were,
in its bodily reality) is simply to be accepted as it gives itself
out to be, though only within the limits in which it then
presents itself'. Let us see just what this statement amounts to,
and how far it takes us into the inner structure of self-evidence.

Consider the following sentences, each of which is to be
construed as phenomenological description of an intentional
act and the noematic sense in virtue of which that act intends,
or refers to, its object.

(1) I am imagining the terrible wrath of Achilles.

(2) I cannot remember the date of Newton's death.

(3) I am claiming to know that Prague is the capital of
France.

(4) I think it true that the sum of the angles of a triangle
is equal to 180 degrees.

As a result of our methodological shift of focus (our transcendental reduction), these sentences will be describing (albeit
crudely) only what Husserl calls the 'thetic character' of my
intentional act and the logical content (the noematic sense,
or the *Sinn*) of my act. Thus we are not concerned whether in
fact there is a character in the *Iliad* called 'Achilles'; whether
or not Homer's Achilles withdrew to his tent to brood over and
nurse his wrath; whether or not there ever existed (and died)
a person named Isaac Newton; whether or not Prague is the
capital of France; and whether or not the angles of a triangle
invariably add up to 180 degrees. These are referential, or existential, issues; and our method has turned us away from them.

Considering, then, solely the intentional acts and their
corresponding logical contents, just as I 'immediately' live
them in simple awareness (and thus, just as I 'inhabit' them
prior to any phenomenological reflection upon them which
would make them, for me, the 'immanent' intentional objects of
such special reflection), we find that both the intentional act
itself and its logical content are lived by the person having them
in a dimension of self-evidence that we may characterize as
an 'unquestionable givenness'. In other words, what, in each
of the five cases, is unquestionable will be:

(i) exactly what mode of consciousness is involved
and (ii) precisely what, or precisely which, noematic *Sinn*

it is that the subject is entertaining in respect of the object intended.[5]

Thus example (1) is unquestionably lived as an act of imagining (and not, say, an act of doubting, seeing, or hypothesizing); and what I unquestionably imagine is unquestionably the terrible wrath of Achilles (and not, say, the death of Hector).

(2) is unquestionably a failure of remembering (and not, say, a failure to see clearly or a failure to imagine or a successful remembrance); and what I unquestionably cannot remember is unquestionably the date of Newton's death (and not, say, the date of John Quincy Adams's inauguration as President). And so forth, *mutatis mutandis*, for the other examples.

It is crucial to appreciate the nature and limits of this unquestionableness. Husserl calls it only a '*Rechtsquelle*', signaling thereby that its logical function is at once fundamental and also extremely limited; it is no more than the *founding moment* in the movement toward knowledge, but is not as such a moment of knowledge. If it is true that, as Husserl says, 'every evidence "sets up" or "institutes" for me an *abiding possession*', it is equally true that it is of the essence of *this* abiding possession that 'I can "always return" to the itself-beheld actuality, in a series of new evidences as restitutions of the first evidence.'[6]

---

[5] See my review of the Findlay translation of Husserl's Logische Untersuchungen (*Journal of Philosophy*, Vol. LXIX, no. 13: 13 July 1972, pp. 395–6). Perception, however, poses a special, indeed a unique, problem for the transcendental reduction. It alone, among the various kinds of consciousness, maintains its transcendental irreducibility; it stubbornly resists the Husserlian method. Perhaps we should say that precisely *this* is its ownmost essence, transcendentally considered; and that, moreover, it is only in attempting to 'reduce' perception in this manner that we apprehend, for the first time, its transcendental essence. In any event, why is it so elusive? Every perception is, as the German word *Wahr-nehmung* makes quite plain, a giving of something itself; in every perception, the thing is given as itself there. Thus, the act of perception is in its essence a moment of existential commitment. As Maurice Merleau-Ponty put it: 'Perceiving is pinning one's faith, at a stroke, in a whole future of experiences, and doing so in a present which never strictly guarantees the future; it is pinning one's belief in a world.' See his *Phenomenology of Perception*, Trans. Colin Smith (New York: Humanities Press, 1962), p. 297. Elsewhere, he argues that 'Perception is precisely that kind of act in which there can be no question of setting the act itself apart from the evidence to which it is directed.' It is 'inseparable from the consciousness which it has, or rather is, of reaching the thing itself' (*ibid.*, p. 374). If this be so, then the possibility of a methodological suspension of the existential belief-component of the perceptual act becomes problematic. (Would it not annul the very *sense* of the intentional act?) Still, insofar as we bear this point in mind, we can proceed faithfully to explicate perceptual sense by a transcendental method.

[6] See Husserl, *Cartesian Meditations*, trans. Dorion Cairns (The Hague: Martinus Nijhoff, 1970), p. 60.

In its 'first evidence', the intended object is already inserted into a partially determinate, partially indeterminate *field* of evidences: in this sense, then, 'the particular evidence does *not* as yet produce for us any abiding being'.[7] For, 'after the living evidence of clarity has passed, the effect of this evidence produced in the realm of habit persists [as a sedimented, founding evidence merely], along with the possibility of a restoration [or, a confirmation], which at first is empty, but contains, in empty form, the determinate sense-predelineation.'[8] Elsewhere, Husserl notes that

the original being-itself-there, in the immediacy [*Aktualität*] of its first production, i.e., in original self-evidence, results in no persisting acquisition at all that could have objective existence. Vivid self-evidence passes – though in such a way that the activity immediately turns into the passivity of the flowingly fading consciousness of what-has-just-now-been. Finally, this 'retention' itself disappears, but the 'disappeared' passing and being past has not become nothing for the subject in question: it can always be reawakened.[9]

It is a logical, or conceptual, truth (and not merely a contingent fact of empirical psychology) that intentional acts and the particular noematic *Sinne* they sustain are 'inhabited' by the subject, at the time they are actually lived, in the mode of founding self-evidence, or unquestionableness. For if, or insofar as, they were not so lived, we should have to say that the subject was (in some sense) unconscious. (This is perhaps the root of the issue whether '*S* knows that *p*' entails '*S* knows that he knows that *p*'.) What Husserl says, here, is that there is 'an original transparency' in 'the make-up of the noema'.[10] And what he means is that it is of the essence of consciousness that it be, during the time it is lived, unquestionable and founding *for that time*. Such unquestionableness does not exclude cases of absent-mindedness and inadvertence. But insofar as there is no unquestionableness in the intentional act and no unquestionably lived noematic *Sinn*, we should have to say, as a purely logical matter, that the behaviour of the

[7] *Ibid.* p. 61 (My italics).
[8] Husserl, *Formal and Transcendental Logic* (*FTL*), trans. Dorion Cairns (The Hague: Martinus Nijhoff, 1969), Part I, Introduction, p. 10.
[9] *Crisis*, p. 359.
[10] *Ideas*, §145, p. 369.

subject was 'blind', 'automatic', or 'unconscious'. In this sense, and this sense only, 'there "must" be', as Husserl says, 'an absolute experience'.[11]

Now, this unquestionableness no more entails that the subject is in possession of a full self-knowledge than it entails that he is in possession of a full objective knowledge (i.e., a full knowledge of the intended object). Indeed, this self-evidence is neither an evidence whose *origin* lies in the subject's reflection upon his intentional act and its *Sinn*, nor an evidence establishing its truth through progressive confirmation; so it is not at all an issue of knowledge. Since such self-evidence pertains, rather, to the intentional act and its *Sinn* only as (and only while) lived, it does not exclude the possibility that, at some later time, the subject may see fit to revise, amend, or fill out – but this time, too, on the ground of such self-evidence – what he claims to *know* about that act, its noematic *Sinn*, and *a fortiori*, in virtue of that *Sinn*, the object intended by the act. Thus, I may indeed be imagining Achille's wrath, but only its most general characteristics. (I cannot imagine this wrath, for instance, in accordance with the exact words Homer used to portray it.) And, while I do indeed think it true that the angles of a triangle add up to 180 degrees, I could not now prove this or reconstruct the steps of the formal demonstration which I once knew. To this extent, my thinking is wanting in fullness and clarity. Self-evidence never 'guarantees that the judicative believing is not mere believing, but rather a believing that makes the truth itself actually given'.[12]

Montaigne, for whom the exercise of writing was an attempt to create a meaningful self that he had somehow lost (or perhaps, had never had), described the problem with exquisite accuracy: 'It is a thorny undertaking, and more so than it seems, to follow a movement so wandering as that of our mind, to penetrate the opaque depths of its innermost folds, to pick out and immobilize the unnumerable flutterings that agitate it.' And he followed this with the comment that, 'it is a new and extraordinary amusement, which withdraws us from the ordinary occupations of the world, yes, even from those most recommended.' (Essays, Book II: 6.) He learned, as he says, that, 'Even in my own writings, I do not always find again the sense of my first thought; I do not know what I meant to say ...' (Book II: 12). Elsewhere, he explains: 'The occasion, the company, the very sound of my voice, draws more from my mind than I find in it when I sound it and use it by myself.' (Book I: 11).[13]

II: Further dimensions of self-evidence.

Thus far, our analysis of self-evidence has exposed only its primary dimension, or function, viz., a simply lived unquestionableness of act and *Sinn* that grounds the possibility of knowledge. Now we must articulate its 'inner structure', so that we can see in detail just *what* this unquestionableness 'founds' in respect of the intended object toward which our knowledge moves and also just *how* it functions in this movement toward knowledge.

Consider the following formulations of the notion of self-evidence:

(1) 'Self-evidence means nothing more than grasping an entity with the consciousness of its original being-itself-there [*Selbst-da*].'[14]

(2) 'We therefore designate as evident a consciousness of any sort that, with regard to its object, is characterized as giving it-itself, without inquiring whether this giving of it-itself is adequate of not.'[15]

(3) '*The concept of any intentionality whatever* – any life-process of consciousness-of something or other – *and the concept of evidence, the intentionality that is the giving of something-itself, are essentially correlative.*'[16]

These formulations add a certain dimension to the primary one in that they say something both about the object referred to and about the referring itself. We learn that, in terms of an act and its *Sinn*, the intended object is always unquestionably given, unquestionably in evidence, either *as itself-there* or *as itself not-there* (i.e. when there is an empty intention devoid of evidence).

---

[13] See Husserl's exquisitely refined discussion of these matters in *FTL*, Part I, ch. I, §16, pp. 56–62.

[14] *Crisis*, p. 356. See also *FTL*, Part II, ch. I, §59, pp. 157–8.

[15] Husserl, *Erfahrung und Urteil*, ed. Ludwig Landgrebe (Hamburg, 1954), p. 12. In the *Cartesian Meditations*, Husserl makes it clear that his phrase 'a consciousness of any sort' includes experience 'in the ordinary sense'. See, for example, p. 57.

[16] *FTL*, Part II, ch. I, §60, p. 160. Also note Part II, ch. I, §59, pp. 157–8.

Now consider these formulations:

(4) To explicate (i.e., to make explicit *and also*, at the same time, to clarify) the self-evidence of some object is to explicate 'how an object . . . exhibits itself as being and being-such'.[17]

(5) 'Everything stands in correlation with its own [actual and possible] manners of givenness . . . within [actual and] possible experience; and everything has its modes of validity and its particular manners of synthesis.'[18]

(6) '*Category of objectivity and category of evidence are perfect correlates. To every fundamental species of objectivities* – as intentional unities maintainable throughout an intentional synthesis and, ultimately, as unities belonging to a possible "experience" – *a fundamental species of "experience," of evidence, corresponds*, and likewise a fundamental species of intentionally indicated evidential style in the possible enhancement of the perfection of the having of an objectivity itself.'[19]

The fourth formulation brings out not only the fact that the intended object is always given unquestionably as itself present or itself absent for the act but also the fact that the object, in being either itself-there or itself not-there, is given unquestionably as *being-such*, being *something with some properties* that determine it in a field of evidence as an object of a certain ontological kind.

As we have noted, the unquestionableness of the intentional act and its referring *Sinn* is an 'abiding possession' only in the sense that it founds the possibility of knowledge; but it is not itself an 'abiding possession' *of knowledge*. Thus, formulations (5) and (6) point to the possibility, the path, of such knowledge. And they show that, whereas the dimension of self-evidence that we have called 'unquestionableness' is a clarity we enjoy passively, simply in virtue of the fact that we are conscious beings and not (say) mere automata, the dimension of self-evidence we must ultimately be concerned with is an accomplishment, a 'creation', so to speak, of an active, self-conscious, profoundly rational being.[20]

---

[17] *Crisis*, p. 159.

[18] *Ibid.* p. 166.

[19] *FTL*, Part II, ch. 1, §60, p. 161.

[20] *Ibid.* p. 10 (My italics). Consider, on this same theme, Samuel J. Todes, 'Knowledge and the ego: Kant's three stages of self-evidence', in Robert Paul Wolff (ed.), *Kant: A Collection of Critical Essays* (New York: Doubleday Anchor Books, 1967), pp. 156–71.

In his late manuscript, 'The Origin of Geometry', Husserl argues that the explication of meaning involves

> extracting one by one, in separation from what has been vaguely, passively received as a unity, the elements of meaning, thus bringing the total validity to active performance in a new way on the basis of individual validities. What was a passive meaning-pattern has now become one *constructed* through active production. This activity, then, is a special sort of self-evidence. . .[21]

Explication (*Sinnesauslegung*) is always *more* than a securing or restoring of meaning: it is always also a deepening and enriching of meaning. For man is not a passively conscious being; he is, rather, a being whose consciousness is rooted in an active discovery of his world (mainly, though not exclusively, through the powers of his perception) and whose self-consciousness, guided as it is by the desire to understand, is therefore an active creation, or bestowal, of sense.

Now, phenomenology, as we know, is meant to be a science of essences. As such, its special contribution to ontology lies in the fact that it works out a phenomenologically grounded logic of evidence for every essentially different kind of object, and thus a logic of evidence for every particular object as an object of a certain kind. In so doing, its makes possible many further determinations and clarifications of our noematic *Sinne* and, *a fortiori*, many further determinations of the (kind of) object itself. For obviously, an eidetic understanding of the nature and limits of evidence, with regard to some (kind of) object, provides precise rules of verification – transcendental rules of intentional 'fulfillment', to use Husserl's own preferred terminology.

Let us now consider one other formulation of self-evidence, since it makes the verification-(fulfillment-) function of self-evidence especially clear:

(7) 'Sense-investigation [*Besinnung*] signifies nothing but the attempt actually to produce the sense "itself", which, in the mere meaning, is a meant, a presupposed, sense; or, equivalently, it is the attempt to convert the "intentive sense" ["*intendierenden Sinn*"], . . . the sense "vaguely floating before us" in our unclear aiming, into the fulfilled, the clear, sense, and thus to procure for it the evidence of its clear possibility. Precisely this possibility is

---

[21] *Crisis*, p. 364.

genuineness of sense and is, accordingly, the aim of our investigative search and discovery. Sense-investigation, we may also say, is radically conceived *original sense-explication*, which converts, or at first strives to convert, the sense in the mode of an unclear meaning into the sense in the mode of full clarity or essential possibility.'[22]

In this formulation, Husserl unpacks his point about the limits and horizons of evidence that are unquestionably present in the unquestionable moment of self-evidence; and he connects this moment to other such moments in terms of the problem of fulfilling, or clarifying, the self-evidenced *Sinn*. This formulation introduces, therefore, a new depth in Husserl's investigations: that of reflectively guided explication. We can now see that (and to some extent, how) we must go *beyond* the self-evidence which gives a noematic *Sinn* just as it is lived, at the time it is lived, in its reference to some intended object. We can see that self-evidence, in its primary function, secures a 'brute', or simple *Sinn*, but also that it is precisely within this evidence that the possibilities of a richer, or more refined, *Sinn* are disclosed. However, until we have specifically analyzed this simple *Sinn* in regard to its different logical components, we are not in a position to understand how self-evidence functions as the mode of givenness and fulfillment *of the object*. For this position *presupposes* that we see *just how the noema* (*but especially, the noematic Sinn*), properly differentiated in its components, *is related to the intended object*.

Now, I have argued that, in order to move from the original, simply lived clarity of unquestionableness to the reflectively accomplished, rational clarity of a *Selbstbesinnung*, we must focus on the inner logical structure of the *noema*. For if it is *in virtue of the noema* that an intentional act is directed to its object, then we can not understand how self-evidence functions in the clarification of meaning, nor can we investigate the various *objects* of consciousness in regard to their modes of self-evidence, without first getting a hold on the structure and function of the *noema*.[23]

---

[22] *FTL*, Part I, Introduction, p. 9.

[23] If I am thinking of a unicorn, of course, no object exists. My thinking does have a direction, though; hence it has a *noema*. The unicorn itself, as something to which a multiplicity of intentional acts, each with its own peculiar noema, can be directed, is just a systematic unity of *noemata*: what we might call a *merely* intentional object.

According to Husserl, a *noema* has two components, which Dagfinn Føllesdal has described as follows:[24]

(1) one which is common to all acts that have the same object, with exactly the same properties, oriented in the same way, etc., regardless of the 'thetic' character of the act, i.e., whether it be perception, remembering, imagining, etc. and (2) one which is different in acts with different thetic character.

The first component is the sense (*'Sinn'*) proper (also called the *'noematischer Sinn'*). The second is the correlate in the *noema* of the thetic character of the intentional act; as such, it is the noematic correlate of the mode of givenness (*'Gegebenheitsweise'*) of the object: the way in which the object is cognized (*'die Weise, wie der Gegenstand bewusst ist'*). Sometimes, though, Husserl refers to the *noema* as a *whole* as the *'Sinn'*, since the second component also necessarily characterizes every intentional access to the object.

It is the noema uniquely borne by an intentional act, then, which prescribes *what* the particular object (the object may be a 'state of affairs') of the act is. Now, the first component of the *noema*, namely, the noematic *Sinn* (or, more briefly, the *Sinn*), can itself be further analyzed into two constituents:

(i) a constituent which prescribes (picks out, individuates) exactly *which* object is being referred to, or intended: it correlates with the object *simpliciter*, the indeterminate but variously determinable 'substratum' (call it '*X*') in abstraction from its manifold properties;[25]
and (ii) a constituent which prescribes the particular configuration of properties (aspects) of the object (some of them will be 'actual', or 'directly' intended as present, such as the side of the tree now facing me, while others will be experienced as dispositional properties of the object, such as the properties of the far side of this tree, properties actually lived as co-present, but still, for this act at this particular time, somewhat indeterminate and only potentially accessible for subsequent acts),

---

[24] Dagfinn Føllesdal, 'Husserl's notion of noema', *Journal of Philosophy*, Vol. LXVI, no. 20: 16 October 1969, p. 682. See also Husserl's *Ideas*, §§87–92, 97–9, 103–4, 114, 124–6 and 129–32.
[25] See *Ideas*, §131.

just as, and only insofar as, this configuration is livingly intended by the act.

What accordingly becomes the *third* component of the *full noema* – the one which, as (2) above indicates, is different in acts with different thetic character – reflects the *evidence* of the object intended by the act: not the 'what' of the object in its evidence but the 'how', the object's unique mode of givenness (e.g., whether the properties of the object are given in perception, memory, imagination, etc.; whether the properties are given in certainty, dubiety, supposition, etc.; whether they are given clearly, dimly, in shadow, etc.; and whether and to what extent they are given fully or incompletely.)

In light of this analysis, we can see that, since intentionality (or reference) is accounted for by the *noema*, we have the makings of a *procedure* for establishing, with regard to every object (or every object as an object of a certain kind), its epistemological place on the ontological map of our human world.[26] For if we scan the system of *noemata* which are unified into a system in virtue of the fact that, one and all, they refer to, or designate, one and the same object (the 'determinable X'), we shall be able to establish, for that (kind of) object:

(a) in a further specification of (i) above, the essential (necessary), the possible but contingent, and the impossible properties peculiar to it,

and (b) in accordance with (2) above (i.e., the noematic correlate of the thetic character of the acts), the essential nature and limits of the *self-evidence* peculiar to, and prescriptive of, that (kind of) object.

Ultimately, therefore, the issue of self-evidence involves Føllesdal's second component (*our* third component) of the full *noema*. *Given* a reference to some object – given, that is, a reference to some determinable substratum X in accordance with (i) above – we can explicate and supplement the properties belonging in (ii) above only by understanding, as a matter of essence, the nature of that object's correlative self-evidence (i.e., component three). This means, in effect, that it is only insofar as we understand the essential nature and

---

[26] Compare: 'If I know an object, then I also know all the possibilities of its occurrence in atomic facts. (Every such possibility must lie in the nature of the object.)' Wittgenstein, *Tractatus Logico-Philosophicus*, 2. 0123.

limits of *self-evidence* (component three) with regard to some (kind of) object, that we can grasp the rules (requirements) prescribing how (and how far) it would be possible to explicate the relevant system of noematic *Sinne* (component two, in particular) and bring it to further distinctness and clarity.[27]

The more we understand the self-evidence conditions for objects, the more we shall understand how to proceed with the task of *Selbstbesinnung*. And, *a fortiori*, of course, insofar as we do follow these rules in our intentional contacts with objects, we shall succeed not only in clarifying our meanings, but also, through these meanings, our objective reference. And this, indeed, would greatly enrich our contact with the objects of our concern in the surrounding world.

We can now notice an interesting and by no means accidental correspondence between the elements in Husserl's various formulations of self-evidence and the components which make up the full noematic description. To the first component of the *noema* (the determinable sub-stratum X) there corresponds, as the '*distinctness*' of evidence, the fact of an unquestionable giving of the thing itself: as Husserl's formulations (1)-(3) assert, a distinct substratum is unquestionably itself there (*Selbst-da*) as, in Husserl's phrase, an 'abiding being'.[28] To the second component of the noema there corresponds, as the clarity[29] (or *unclarity*) of evidence, the fact that some *definite* configuration of properties or aspects is given: the thing is itself there, given, indeed, as *a something which is* . . . (See formulations (4)-(6), but especially the first of this set.) This configuration may, however, consist of nothing more than

---

[27] The percipient's movement toward fulfillment of evidence (i.e., a richer intentional contact with the object) is in accordance with *a priori* rules. Some of these rules prescribe the requisite movement for perception in general (e.g., that further fulfillment must be perceptual, and not, say, a mere recollection of past perception), while others prescribe the requisite movement for the perceptual encompassing of precisely *this* (and no other) object (as an object of a certain at least *somewhat* familiar kind). In regard to the evidence-conditions for the objects of visual perception, see Samuel J. Todes, 'Shadows in knowledge: Plato's misunderstanding of shadows, and of knowledge as shadow-free', in Don Ihde and James Edie (eds.), *Dialogues in Phenomenology* (The Hague: Martinus Nijhoff).

[28] This holds true even for the spatio-temporal objects of transcendent perception: 'The spatial thing which we see is, despite all its transcendence, perceived . . . we are not given an image or a sign in its place.' *Ideas*, §43, p. 123.

[29] For Husserl's distinction between 'distinctness' of evidence and 'clarity' of evidence, see *FTL*, Part I, ch. 1, §16, pp. 60–2.

some extremely indeterminate, vague or dim predelincation of properties. (See formulations (5) and (6) above.) Consider, for example, the configuration of properties I have in mind when I refer to the Taj Mahal. It happens to be the case not only that, when I now refer to this perceptual object, I am not actually perceiving it, but also that, when referring to it thus, I am referring to something I have never seen and of which I have little information, but not so little that I don't know that it is the Taj Mahal, and not something else, to which I am referring; nor so little that I would not be able to recognize it if I were to see it, and so forth.

So, to the third component of the *noema* (the noematic correlate of the act's thetic qualities, or character), there correspond, as the (originally somewhat limited) clarity of an unquestionable lived evidence, first, *the kind of consciousness* in terms of which the properties of the object are present (e.g., perception, apperception, memory, etc.); second, what Husserl calls *the 'thetic positionality' of this consciousness*, in terms of which the properties of the object are intended (e.g., 'doxic positionalities' such as apodicticity, the supposition of possibility or of impossibility, simple belief, the stronger claim to knowledge, disbelief and mere hunch, and such other positionalities as wishing, hoping, loving and admiring);[30] and third, *the various styles, intensities, degrees and other 'qualities' of this consciousness*, which have to do with the intentional fulfillment (or lacks and failures of fulfillment) peculiar to the givenness of the intended object, and which obviously also tell us, when we reflect on the matter, how (and also how far) it would be possible to obtain, in respect of the object, a fulfilled, or anyway more complete, 'possession'.[31]

Perhaps, as Husserl suspects, an absolute perfection of evidence (the perfection he calls 'adequation') and, correlatively, a total encompassing of the object, amount to no more than an ideal limit. Still, we *can* move closer to an evidence of 'abiding being'. For we *can* know the nature of this limit for each ontological region, hence for every object within a region, insofar as our knowing this limit and our knowing, on this

---

[30] See Husserl's *Crisis*, p. 166 and *Ideas*, §101.
[31] See Husserl's formulations (above, notes 5–7) in this regard. And consider *Ideas*, §§82–4, 87–93, 97–127 and 129–32.

transcendental ground, just how to proceed *toward* this limit must be a question of knowing our own minds – knowing exactly what we mean and how we mean.

Ultimately, as Husserl says, this task requires a completed phenomenology of essences.[32] More specifically, we must apply *the method of eidetic variation* to the third component of a rather large number of the noemata unified into a system in virtue of the fact that all these *noemata* refer to one and the same kind of object. The reflective method of eidetic variation always presupposes a certain pre-reflective, 'passively constituted', rough-and-ready intuition that has already predelineated the ontological region in question. In other words, the eidetic variation cannot get off the ground unless it proceeds from an antecedent fund of experience. It is designed to give clarity to a sense which we already possess, but only in a somewhat crude and less than optimally clear way. Thus, for example, everybody knows, roughly, what it is for something to be a pumpkin or an elf. This fund of rough-and-ready knowledge then serves as the point of departure for a reflective eidetic variation, aimed at giving this knowledge a greater clarity, a greater definition, and a more complete phenomenological grounding.

So we must scan this unified system of *noemata*, concentrating on the third component, in order to explicate what is invariant among the noemata we consider. Given some ontological region, we attempt to establish:

(i) possible, impossible and essential *kinds of consciousness* (for example, pumpkins are accessible to acts of perception, acts of imagination, and acts of memory, whereas elves are accessible to acts of imagination and acts of remembering these imaginings, but are not accessible to acts of perception);

---

[32] See Husserl's *Cartesian Meditations*, p. 12; *Ideas*, §§19 and 83; and *FTL*, p. 62n and Part II, ch. 7, §§105–6, pp. 277–82. Here, too, completeness seems to lie at infinity. As Husserl says: 'it would be going too far to say that all self-evident apprehension of the essence demands that the subsumed particulars in their concrete fullness should be fully clear' (*Ideas*, §69, p. 181). To be sure, their incompleteness is essentially different from the incompleteness of evidence peculiar to particulars – and most strikingly different from the evidence distinctive of perceptual things. But what Husserl wants to say, here, is that the essential difference between, say, persons and automata is given, as such, as an absolute difference in an *apodictic* evidence; it is *logically inconceivable* that, in some way or other, this difference not obtain in our world, *despite* the fact that the evidence of this difference does seem to be insufficiently detailed, precise, and fully intuitive. (We cannot now – if ever – specify all the criteria for personhood in such a way that every conceivable borderline case among the automata would be at once decisively excluded from personhood.)

(ii) possible, impossible, and essential *sorts of thetic positionality* (for example, it is certainly possible to hold various beliefs about a pumpkin and it is also possible for us to have wishes, hopes, and fears in regard to pumpkins, but it makes no sense to speak about acts of loving, admiring, or fearing directed upon a differential equation);[33]

and (iii) possible, impossible, and essential *styles, intensities, degrees and other qualities of intentional fulfillment* (for example, a perceptual object is necessarily, and is lived as being, 'an identity uniting modes of appearance through perspective continua',[34] so that the fulfillment of evidence for perceptual objects is necessarily neither an adequate nor an apodictic one; whereas what Husserl calls the 'immanent objects' of apperception are not evidenced in perspective variation[35]).

III: Self-evidence in a genetic phenomenology. In his later writings (the *Formal and Transcendental Logic*, *The Crisis of European Sciences and Transcendental Phenomenology*, and numerous other manuscripts as well), Husserl attempts to deepen his analyses of self-evidence. In these writings, the notion of *Sinnesgenesis* assumes a fundamental role, along with the notion of genetic constitution, which he uses to designate the phenomenological procedure of bringing *Sinne* to self-evidence in respect of their genesis, or formation.[36]

In the domain of the sciences, for example, it seemed especially important to Husserl that we recognize every *Sinn* as a *Sinngebilde* (a construction of *Sinn*, perhaps an element in a theoretical *model* of *Sinne*),[37] with its own peculiar conceptual origin and its own peculiar law-governed formation, or development. (Compare Wittgenstein, *Tractatus*: '2.1 We make for ourselves models of facts.') Accordingly, Husserl came to see his earlier work on self-evidence (and especially, the aspect of self-evidence that has to do with intuitive, or intentional fulfillment) as in need of supplementation and revision. His *Logical Investigations*, for example, explicate

---

[33] See *Ideas*, §141, p. 362 for Husserl's discussion of the '*Rechtscharaktere*' of different sorts of intentional act (e.g., perception vs recollection). Also see *FTL*, Part II, ch. 1, §59, p. 158 and ch. 7, §107, pp. 287–8.

[34] In regard to 'immanent objects', see *Ideas*, §44, pp. 125–6.

[35] On the distinctions of essence between immanent and transcendent objects, see *Ideas*, §§38 and 42–4; also *FTL*, Part II, ch. 7, §107, pp. 283–5.

[36] See Husserl's *Crisis*, p. 58.

[37] *Ibid.* pp. 113 and 130.

many domains of self-evidence; and they introduce fulfillment procedures for these domains. But they tend to ignore or suppress the fact that *Sinne* have an origin and a development within the context of the 'life-world' (*'Lebenswelt'*). To this extent, therefore, his investigations of fulfillment in self-evidence were profoundly incomplete. His later genetic phenomenology was designed to rectify this incompleteness.

I would like to conclude this paper, then, with a brief discussion of this supplementary methodology. My main concern is to defend this genetic methodology against the common view that it represents a return to his earlier psychologism and, in addition, transforms his phenomenology into a merely historical approach. In effect, what I want to show is that his later investigations are still genuinely phenomenological, and that they are designed to explicate the logic of the genesis of *Sinne*. Genetic phenomenology is a *genetic logic*.

First of all, the genetic investigations are, as such, neither psychological nor empirical. What keeps them within the framework of genuine phenomenology is the fact that they remain focused, like his earlier work, on the domain of *Sinne*. To be sure, their point of departure is the world we all live in. But this world serves only to provide them with certain 'clues', certain leading and provocative questions, and, too, with a certain subject-matter. But the subject-matter is *Sinne*, not psychic states and processes; and the method is one of transcendental description, not empirical explanation. And the 'connections' established are *logical*, not causal. Once under way, the investigations unfold solely in terms of the transcendental 'reduction'. Insofar as genetic phenomenology bears on empirical (or more especially, psychological) matters, it serves to elucidate them as *problems*, domains containing within themselves various *problems of meaning* (in the sciences, for example, these would include anomalies, difficulties attending abstraction and formalization, and counter-intuitive notions, for example, the notion of an elementary particle without mass).

Secondly, the genetic investigations of self-evidence make extensive use of historical knowledge, but they are not themselves, for all that, historical.[38] They are, on the contrary,

[38] *Ibid.* pp. 370–3.

investigations into the *logic* of certain *Sinne* (certain *noema*-complexes). History functions as a point of departure only in the sense that it shows us the *fact* that our meanings (and theoretical networks of meanings) have a history. If we take it as given that our meanings (perhaps most strikingly, scientific meanings) do indeed have a history, then we must proceed to explicate the logic of their histories.[39] For a phenomenology bent on radicality (returning to the roots, getting to the bottom of things), what this involves is a purely logical explication of various systems of meaning, showing how these systems (which we know to be *in fact* related in an historical, or temporal, continuum) are related to one another solely as systems of meaning. Ultimately, this shows, for Husserl, how even the most abstract and formalized systems of meaning are related in certain logical (and phenomenologically perspicuous) ways to the 'protological' systems of meaning operative in perception.[40] To accomplish this, however, is not at all to demonstrate the possibility of reducing the higher systems to the perceptual ones. A genetic *Geltungsfundierung* of the sciences simply re-establishes in living (present) self-evidence the logic of genesis that *connects* an idealization or formalized abstraction in the *objective order of science* to an analogous system of meaning functioning in the *subjective order of perception*.[41] Nor is it the intent of such a method to demonstrate the superiority of the perceptual field as a possessor of the truth of the world. What it does (or can) establish are their rightful places in our world.[42]

More specifically, Husserl's genetic phenomenology has three intertwined aims. (1) Negatively, to show that (and how) a perversion of objectivism and physicalism in scientific method has degraded the percipient subject's truths of perception – which are the subsoil from which, in fact, science constantly draws its vital nourishment – to the shadow-status of illusion (that which is 'merely subjective'); and positively, to restore to the percipient subject his proper domain of primacy and

---

[39] See *Ibid.* p. 124. In this regard, see also Ernst Mach, *Die Mechanik in ihrer Entwicklung historisch-Kritisch Dargestellt*, pp. 278–9; *The Science of Mechanics: A Critical and Historical Exposition of Its Principles*, trans. from the 2nd German edition by Thomas J. McCormack (Chicago: Open Court, 1960), p. 316.

[40] *Crisis*, pp. 124 and 141.

[41] *Ibid.* p. 140.

[42] *Ibid.* p. 125.

sovereignty. ('It is through a garb of ideas that we take for *true being* what is actually [the accomplishment of] a method.')[43] So if we ask the transcendental question, 'How is such an accomplishment of method possible?', and proceed to answer it in terms of a transcendental and genetic phenomenology, the 'subjective' truth of perception and the 'objective' truth of theoretical science will each have a *place*. And, what is more, they will be recognized to belong *together* in a unified continuum of worldly understanding. In this way, the process of *Sinnesäusserung*, or externalization of sense, that has tended to make the truths of science seem distant, obscure, threatening, and somehow severed from their humanistic roots, will be, finally, reversed.)[44] (2) To repossess the truth of science *as an accomplishment of* the percipient subject,[45] so that objective truth regains its human significance and can assume its life-sustaining responsibilities. (3) Finally, to advance the sciences themselves toward a new stage of auto-critique and enable them to reveal such untapped reservoirs of conceptual power as lie within them.[46]

Genetic phenomenology supplements the static, synchronic evidences acquired through the 'horizontal' method of explication that Husserl used in his *Logical Investigations*.[47] The genetic method of, for instance, Husserl's *Crisis* manuscript, 'The Origin of Geometry', is, by contrast, a 'vertical' method; as such, it yields meanings in a diachronic evidence that exhibits the peculiar logical *dynamics* of these meanings. For the sciences, genetic phenomenology prescribes a method of 'back-tracking', a procedure for retracing and (re)locating conceptual decisions, conceptual landmarks. In retracing the ancestry of theoretical concepts – which are nothing more than knots of *conceptual decision*, moments of insight into a web of theory-laden experience, genetic phenomenology hopes to make possible some fresh starts on new paths of research, since it shows us the ancestral concepts *as* decisions, *as* resolutions

---

[43] *Ibid.* p. 51; see further pp. 30 and 54.
[44] *Ibid.* pp. 231 and 343. See also *FTL*, Part II, ch. 7, §§101–3.
[45] *Crisis*, p. 121. See Sir Arthur Eddington, *Space, Time and Gravitation*, (Cambridge University Press, 1966), ch. XII, pp. 201–2.
[46] *Crisis*, p. 52.
[47] See the *Logical Investigations*, Vol. I, Prolegomena, ch. 9, §55, p. 207 and ch. II, §65, pp. 232–3. Also consider Vol. I, Second Study, ch. I, §6, p. 348.

(or attempts at the resolution) of webs of experience which *were* once, were previously, problematic: it enables, us, in fine, to 'reactivate' these webs of experience as *once more problematic*.[48] The genetic approach enables us, moreover, to understand the concepts of formalization as *formalizations*, hence as *exclusions* of numerous alternative 'readings' of experience. (Consider, for example, the logical primitives symbolized by '⊃' and '∈'. These notions are indeed theoretically useful and entirely legitimate. Nevertheless, it is important that we recognize them as formalizations which have excluded *and tend to conceal* alternative paths of formalization – paths which it just *might* some day prove fruitful or even imperative to explore.)

In the *Crisis*, Husserl has provided many illustrations of the genetic method at work. He has shown how this method helps us to understand, among other things, the discovery of a universal causality in nature, the mathematization of the qualities of sensible bodies, and Galileo's theoretical ascent from sensible thing-shapes to the concept of pure space-time. In a work as early as his *Logical Investigations*, of course, Husserl detailed and illustrated the phenomenological procedure of explication (bringing to evidence, fulfilling evidence). One of his illustrations involves the formula $(5^3)^4$. And he tells us, there, that its explication should proceed thus:

$$(5^3)^4 = 5^3 \cdot 5^3 \cdot 5^3 \cdot 5^3$$
$$5^3 = 5 \cdot 5 \cdot 5$$
$$5 = 4 + 1, \quad 4 = 3 + 1, \quad 3 = 2 + 1, \quad \text{and } 2 = 1 + 1$$
$$5 = 1 + 1 + 1 + 1 + 1$$

'This, finally, is the number $(5^3)^4$ "itself"!'[49]

But, in terms of the *Crisis* framework, this clarification would not suffice. Intuitively unfulfilled elements still shade the evidence. What *is* the number 1? What are the roots of this concept? Until we have answered these questions, we should

---

[48] See Husserl's *Crisis*, p. 363. Also, for a very fine survey-discussion of Husserl's genetic phenomenology and its affiliation with Heidegger's hermeneutic approach, see Theodore Kisiel, 'On the dimensions of a phenomenology of science in Husserl and the young Dr Heidegger', in *Journal of the British Society for Phenomenology*, Vol. 4, no. 3 (October 1973), pp. 217–34.

[49] See the *Logical Investigations*, Vol. II, Sixth Study, §18, p. 723.

not say, 'This, finally, is the number $(5^3)^4$ "itself".' The further fulfillment of evidence that his genetic method requires and makes feasible, here, involves grounding the number-concepts, especially the concept of the number 1, in concepts originally operative in our spontaneous perception of identities, unities, and multiplicities. Then, and only then, is $(5^3)^4$ rendered in fulfilling evidence.[50]

A glimpse beyond self-evidence

Phenomenology, for Husserl, is a guardian of philosophical humanism. And self-evidence is the touchstone of this humanism. How so? From one standpoint, it may seem that the aim of his project is simply to understand the nature and limits of human knowledge, and to extend thereby the scope, or purchase, of objective knowledge. For, as we have seen, it is within a framework of transcendental logic that the notion of self-evidence is cast and plays its first role. But there is also, in fact, another aim, beyond transcendental critique, or diagnosis, viz.: to offer a philosophical therapy. For, at the same time that we gain a deeper understanding of ontology and discover procedures for extending our acquaintance with the objects of our world, we shall also come to recognize, in the phenomenological *evidence* of these objects, the uniquely human contribution to the textures and trajectories of our world. Phenomenology thus facilitates a deeper and indeed more subjectively meaningful installment of man in the midst of this objective world. The notion of self-evidence dedicates phenomenology to this task: nothing less than the dream of reversing that decadence of meaning which Pinter's 'silences' so eloquently lament, and regaining for humanity its own *good* sense as its own. Through phenomenology, we are offered the chance to recognize what is reflected in and, in

---

[50] The genetic method of producing such self-evidence *neither opposes nor replaces* the enduringly great accomplishment of Gottlob Frege, whose strictly formal analysis and recursive definition of number, in *The Foundations of Arithmetic* and numerous subsequent writings (especially the *Grundgesetze der Arithmetik*), provide indisputably deep insight and powerfully systematic clarity. The bearing of Husserl's work on that of Frege cannot be discussed here. Suffice it to say, however, that, for Husserl, the formal definition of number yields a stage of self-evidence that must be supplemented, ultimately, with the fulfilling self-evidence of a phenomenological genesis of sense.

effect, released by, the evidence of our intended objects: our most primitive power to mean, our power to *bestow* meaning. We are offered the chance, finally, to re-cognize ourselves.[51]

[51] If I am right, then Husserl's phenomenology of self-evidence lends itself to an interpretation which somewhat bridges the abyss that separates Husserl's transcendental egology from Heidegger's hermeneutics of Being. For, as a therapy, the inward movement towards self-evidence breaks down the walls of spiritual solipsism and offers man, instead, an ecstatic deliverance from the suffering tyranny of the Self.

Self-evidence

A. J. AYER

Self-evident propositions are those that do not stand in need of proof. Not all analytic propositions are self-evident, though it is arguable that all self-evident propositions are analytic. In general, the fact that someone believes a proposition to be true does not entail that the proposition is true, however firm the belief. Even in the case of necessary propositions mistakes are always logically possible. On the other hand any process of proof must come to an end somewhere. A test serves no purpose unless we are disposed to accept what it appears to show. An empirical language needs to have meaning rules but these do not have to yield incorrigible propositions. These rules can not be expected to legislate with certainty for every possible case. There are areas in which their application will be doubtful, as is shown by the example of words referring to colours. There is, however, nothing to be done about our fallibility, beyond noting that it exists. Whatever system we adopt, we shall be taking a great deal for granted, which may go wrong. Any such system is liable to change, within the limitation of some principle of consistency.

Sir Alfred (Jules) Ayer is Wykeham Professor of Logic in the University of Oxford. His publications include: *Language, Truth and Logic* (1936), *The Foundations of Empirical Knowledge* (1940), *Philosophical Essays* (1954), *The Problem of Knowledge* (1956), *The Concept of a person* (1963), *The Origins of Pragmatism* (1968), *Metaphysics and Common Sense* (1972), *Russell and Moore* (1971), *Probability and Evidence* (1972), *Russell* (1972), *The Central Questions of Philosophy* (1974).

Experiences cannot be self-evident since they are neither true nor false. I shall follow the common practice of ascribing truth and falsehood to propositions. To say of a proposition that it is self-evident is to say not just that it is certainly true, but also that it does not stand in need of proof. One has only to understand the sentence which expresses it in order to be able to see that the proposition is true. Many philosophers have appealed to this notion of self-evidence, but there have been differences of opinion as to the range of propositions to which it can be applied. It has usually been taken to cover at least some of the true propositions of logic and mathematics, as well as propositions which are thought to be necessary in virtue of the non-logical concepts which they embody, such as the proposition that brothers are male siblings, or that whatever is red is coloured. Self-evidence has, however, also been ascribed to propositions which do not appear to fall into either of these categories, such as the proposition that every event has a cause, and some philosophers have claimed it for moral principles which they held to be true but saw no way of proving. An example might be that one ought not to take pleasure in another person's suffering.

The first point which emerges is that we cannot begin by taking the concept of self-evidence to coincide with that of being analytic. As we have just seen, self-evidence is claimed for propositions which at least do not appear to be incapable of being denied without contradiction; and conversely, many propositions which can plausibly be held to be analytic cannot with any plausibility be counted as self-evident. Logic and mathematics would be much easier subjects than they are if the conclusion of every theorem could be seen to be true, without the necessity of any proof.

A second point to note is that in saying of a proposition that it does not stand in need of proof, one should not be taken to imply that it is incapable of being proved. It might, indeed, be thought that when a proposition is capable of being proved, there would be nothing to gain, and perhaps something to lose, by holding it to be self-evident, but this would be to overlook the fact that deductive systems can have alternative bases. A proposition which appears as a premiss in one system may appear as the conclusion of a theorem in another. Consequently, if one is going to maintain that the premisses of a deductive system are self-evident, one may find oneself in the position of claiming self-evidence for propositions which one is also capable of proving.

A further distinction which we need to make at the outset is that between self-evident propositions, in the foregoing sense, and propositions for which certainty is claimed on the ground that in the circumstances in which they are advanced it makes no sense to doubt them. Propositions which are thought to be of this second sort are usually said to be incorrigible, the idea being that there is no possibility of a mistake which would call for their correction. In general, such incorrigibility has been claimed only for propositions which might be expressed by someone who was limiting himself to describing the nature of his present experience; propositions which would record his current thoughts or feelings or the quality of his sense-impressions; and it has been assumed that these propositions, being so limited in scope, would not carry any logical commitment to the occurrences of anything that was publicly observable: if they described the subject's current sense-impressions, their truth would not exclude the possibility of his being under some perceptual illusion. There are, however, philosophers, notably Wittgenstein,[1] who make substantially the same claim for propositions about the physical world which we unhesitatingly accept through the normal exercise of sense-perception or of memory, for those that record well-known historical facts, and even for propositions which express acknowledged scientific laws. They wish, in short, to confer a kind of immunity on all the propositions which it does not seriously occur to us to doubt; propositions which, for one reason or another, are so well established that to ask what is the evidence for them would seem out of place.

The difference between these so-called incorrigible propositions, in either extension of the term, and those that lay claim to self-evidence, in the sense that I first defined, is that self-evidence is supposed to be objective in a way that incorrigibility is not. The proposition that there is an expanse of green in the upper right-hand corner of my present visual field is arguably one of which the truth is known to me beyond any suspicion of doubt, but in that case it is only to me that it is so known. Others who observe my situation may confidently infer that this is so, but they do not speak with the same authority. Again, anyone

---

[1] See his book '*On Certainty*', trans. G. E. M. Anscombe and D. Paul (Blackwell, 1969).

with normal vision would be able to see the tree which overhangs the terrace where I am seated, but he would need to be in my present neighbourhood: merely to understand the sentence that there exists a tree at such and such a place would not make it evident that what it expressed was true. Similarly, such pieces of common knowledge as that the battle of Hastings was fought in 1066AD or that heating water causes it to boil rather than to freeze have had to be ascertained. There is nothing in these propositions, considered simply in themselves, that shows whether they are true or false. On the other hand, the truth of propositions which are said to be self-evident is supposed to be certifiable by anyone who understands the sentences which express them. It is sufficient to know what brothers are and what male siblings are in order to know for certain that brothers are male siblings. Anyone who has acquired the use of the mathematical concepts in question knows that $2 + 2 = 4$. Anyone who is morally enlightened knows that it is wrong to delight in another's pain.

The distinction is genuine, but there is a point at which it becomes tenuous. Does not one have to learn to reprehend cruelty, in very much the same way as one learns the facts of history or the rudiments of science? In so far as there is a difference, is it not due to the fact that moral principles are themselves of a different order from propositions of these other sorts? Whatever this difference may be, it is surely not the case that one has only to understand what is meant by taking pleasure in another's pain and also to possess the concept of something's being wrong in order to see that they go together. The proof that it is not is that many people, who do possess these concepts, have indulged in cruelty without thinking it wrong. We can say that this shows them to be morally unenlightened, but what does this come to beyond the fact that their moral attitudes are different from ours? Or to take another of our examples, surely it is just not true that anyone who understands what an event is and what a cause is will come to see that every event must have a cause. If one's view of the world is thoroughly scientific and if the science of one's time is deterministic, one may indeed be led to regard this proposition as unquestionably true; but one may just as easily reject it if, as can well be the case, one or other of these conditions fails to hold.

But now it may be objected that I am picking out just those examples in which the pretension to self-evidence is most dubious. What upholds it is no more than that the principles in question are principles for which those who hold them can give no further reason: it is not positively sustained by any necessary relation between the concepts which are combined in them.

I think that this objection is well-founded, but if we accept it the result will be that the candidature to self-evidence will be restricted to propositions for which the claim is also made that they are analytic. For if it is a necessary condition for a proposition to be self-evident that its truth can be determined simply through the consideration of the concepts which enter into it, then the only propositions which will qualify are those that are true in virtue of the meaning of the sentences which express them, and this is just the condition which is held to be sufficient for a proposition to be analytic. To say this is, indeed, to beg the question against those who hold that to apprehend the truth, say, of a proposition of elementary arithmetic, one has not only to command the relevant concepts but also to depend on *a priori* intuition. Since, however, the power to exercise this intuition is supposed to accrue to anyone who does command the concepts, the question is one that we can afford to beg in the present context. For even if it turned out that the claims to analyticity had been too generously accorded, the restrictions on the claims to self-evidence would remain the same.

The difficulty lies rather in the other direction. Since it is admitted that not all necessary propositions, whether or not we reckon them all as analytic, are self-evident, where is the line to be drawn? How is it decided whether such propositions stand in need of proof? Is it simply a question of the terms on which we are willing to accept them? In some cases we should demand that a proof be given, in others their truth would seem so obvious that to insist upon a proof would seem superfluous or even misguided. But clearly this is not a distinction about which there is likely to be any very general agreement. Not only do people differ in their perspicacity, but they differ in their standards of rigour. Most of us are content to take the truth of such a proposition as that $2 + 2 = 4$ on trust. A logician who is engaged in the enterprise of reducing mathematics to logic may take volumes to prove it. This may result even in his deriving propositions which seem to us self-evident from ones that do not. The single proposition to which Nicod reduced the primitive propositions of Russell's and Whitehead's *Principia Mathematica* is far too complicated for its truth to be obvious at a glance. Neither do we have to take it on trust. We can test it by the truth-tables and find that it comes out as a tautology.

The fact that there are differences of opinion as to what we are entitled to accept without proof does not itself entail that nothing qualifies for such acceptance. But the argument may be pressed further. The question may be raised whether someone's being certain that such and such is so is ever a sufficient reason for concluding that it is so. If we set aside propositions like '*A* exists' or '*A* is animated' which have to be true if it is to be true that *A* believes anything at all, does '*p*' ever follow logically from '*A* believes that *p*'? Except in the trivial sense in which a necessary proposition follows from any proposition whatsoever, it is not at all certain that it ever does. The doubtful cases are those of allegedly incorrigible propositions, in the narrower extension of the term. There is some plausibility in the idea of its not being logically possible, so long as merely linguistic errors are excluded, for anyone falsely to believe that he is in pain, or falsely to believe that there is an expanse of green in his present visual field, though even here I am inclined to think that one can devise counter-examples. There is no question but that one can misidentify the character of one's feelings or the qualities of one's sense-impressions, and the problem is only that of deciding when, if ever, such a mistake is to count as being factual and when as being merely verbal. Very often, I think, the distinction will be fairly arbitrary. However this may be, these are in any case not among the propositions which are thought to be generally self-evident. Even if, in appropriate conditions, they have their own way of being certain, they are not necessarily true. And when it comes to propositions which are taken to be necessary, then the answer to the question whether their truth is ever logically guaranteed by their being believed is surely that it never is. Whatever the example chosen, the fact that someone is convinced that some proposition of this sort is true will always be consistent with its not being true. In such a case, the only way in which the proposition that *A* is mistaken in believing that *p* can turn out to be contradictory is that if '*p*' is indeed necessarily true, then one will oneself be expressing a necessary falsehood in implicitly denying it.

This is not to say that people's convictions count for nothing. If *A* is known to be a competent mathematician, his acceptance of some proposition which he claims to have proved will be a good reason for our believing it to be true, even though we are not ourselves capable of following the proof. If he declares some step in the argument to be obvious, we shall allow that he is justified in making it, even though it is by no means obvious to us. The admission that he is not infallible, that there is indeed no point at which it is not logically possible that he should be mistaken, does not divest him of all authority. But the source of his authority is not the strength of his convictions but rather the fact that they have consistently or at any rate frequently turned out to be right. We take his word because we know that on previous occasions when he has given it his claims have been tested and certified.

But now the argument turns the other way. For how, we may ask, have his claims been certified? By the consensus of opinion among other mathematicians who have satisfied themselves that his proofs were in order; that their premisses were true and that the conclusions followed from them. No doubt the premisses would be propositions which had already been established, but for them to be established the same conditions would have to have been fulfilled. Again it is not necessary that the first links in the chain should simply be taken on trust. There may be procedures by which they can be checked. But then it has to be assumed that these requirements really are met, when they appear to be. It has also to be assumed that one step in the proof does really follow from another. Here too there may be methods of checking, but in the end there will be nothing for it but just to be able to see that things come out right. And what is this, it may be asked, but a final appeal to self-evidence?

Once more this is not to deny that mistakes are always possible. The point is rather that the process of proof must somewhere come to an end. If every step in a deductive argument had to be licensed by a special premiss, then, as Lewis Carroll showed in his Achilles paradox,[2] no conclusion could ever be drawn. The tortoise, in his fable, accepts '*p*' and

---

[2] See *Mind*, 1895, p. 278.

'if p then q' but requires to be shown that this is sufficient for the conclusion that q. He argues that there is need of the extra premiss: 'If, (if p, and if p then q), then q'. But then when Achilles adds this premiss to the others, the tortoise is still not satisfied. He requires the further premiss: 'If [if p, and if p then q, and if (if p, and if p then q) then q] then q' and so *ad infinitum*. The moral is that a rule of inference is something to be followed. If it is made explicit, and posited as a premiss, it loses its function. There will then be need for another rule. One wants to say that someone who accepts 'p' and accepts 'If p then q' is thereby committed to accepting 'q'. His recognition of this commitment is a mark of his understanding the expression 'If . . . then'. He has, indeed, to see that he is committed, but this need come to no more than his being able to apply the rule. It can be explained to him, but he has to grasp it.

Are we then to say that it is self-evident that if (if p, and if p then q), then q? What point should we be making? As a proposition, it can be proved, either by deduction from a set of logical axioms, such as the axioms of *Principia Mathematica*, or by consulting the truth-tables and finding that it comes out true under every assignment of truth-values to 'p' and 'q'. No doubt there are many people who can see at a glance that it is true, but that is of little interest, unless we are concerned with testing their intelligence. On the other hand, if it is taken as a rule, then the point is that it is straightforwardly applied. There could, indeed, be a rule which directed how it was to be applied; we might, for example, be instructed to detach the consequent if and only if the antecedent had been found to satisfy certain criteria of proof, and there could even be a directive for interpreting this rule; but the supply of directives has to give out somewhere. At some point, we have just to understand what we are expected to do, and act accordingly.

The analogy of a game may be helpful here. Suppose that I am playing a beginner at chess, and that I say 'Check-mate' and he says 'Prove it', I point out that the position of his king in relation to my bishop entails that it is in check, that, according to the rules and in view of the positions of the other pieces, there are just so many squares to which his king can move, that if it moves to this square it will be in check to the other bishop, if it moves to that square it will be in check to the knight, and so on until I have covered all the possibilities. His recognition that this is so goes together with his understanding how to play the game. It is of course logically possible that there is something which we have both overlooked, that there is, for example, a piece which he can interpose. It is logically possible that I have misremembered the rules of chess. It is logically possible that our vision is at fault, so that we are both mistaken in thinking that the king and the bishop really are aligned, with no other piece in between them. There is, however, not very much that we can do about these possibilities, beyond making the formal admission that they do exist. We can look up the rules, in which case we shall be assuming that they are correctly stated and that we are reading them correctly. Having made these assumptions, we are then just left to note how the rules apply to this particular case. If we think it necessary to check our eyesight, we can have it tested by an oculist, or we can call in a third person to inspect the board. But then we have to understand what these persons tell us. There is always the possibility of error, and there are always further tests that we can resort to. If I am doing a sum in arithmetic I can go over it again and again, I can call on any number of people to check it for me. I can have recourse to a computer, and then employ a second computer to check the first. In the end, however, it must always come down to my just being satisfied that I have got it right; and, unless I am very neurotic, this will happen quite early. If I am adding up a column of figures, it will probably be enough for me that I add it upwards and downwards and get the same result. The most timid householder does not usually make more than one inspection to make sure that he has safely locked the door.

The point is that a test serves no purpose unless we are disposed to accept what it appears to show. If its result is surprising, we may reasonably require that it be corroborated, but again this will be futile if the corroboration, when it comes, is not to be taken at its face-value. As I said earlier, the process of proof must come to an end somewhere; not indeed to an absolute end, since any question can be re-opened, but to a point where we are satisfied, where we see no use in carrying it any further. And just for this reason there are very many cases in which the need for proof does not arise. These are the cases in which we are satisfied straightaway, because the results of our calculations, or the interpretations that we put on what is presented to our senses, fit in with our existing stock of beliefs. We take it for granted that the outcome of any further experiments would be favourable, at least so long as they themselves were not suspect. Indeed, the only point of making them would be to add to the volume of evidence, since the conclusions at which we have arrived already have as strong a claim to credence as those that would result from any further test.

The attraction which philosophers have found in strictly incorrigible propositions has been that they seemed to provide an absolutely secure basis for knowledge. If their truth really did follow from their being believed, at least by the person to whose current experience they referred, there was not even the possibility of their being upset by any other evidence. Admittedly, their immunity lasted only so long as the fleeting experience which they monitored, but at least they brought the whole structure of our beliefs repeatedly into firm contact with the earth. They prevented it being left to hang in the air with its array of propositions defending only one another.

There is no doubt that this function needs to be performed, but it is dubious whether incorrigible propositions are needed to perform it. Is there really any profit in a security which so quickly vanishes? What we must have are rules of meaning which correlate the signs that we use with observable states of affairs. Even in the employment of a purely formal language, we need to be able to tell that such and such a mark or sound is an instance of such and such a numeral, or whatever it may be. It does not, however, seem to be necessary that our rules of meaning should be such as to apply without any possibility of error, or even that they should rest upon any such foundation. As I have suggested elsewhere,[3] we might very well manage with rules which licensed us to accept a sentence when there was no more than a high probability that the state of affairs with which it was correlated did in fact obtain. Indeed, it is with rules of this sort that we actually do manage. A child learns to use the names of physical objects under conditions where it is always at least logically possible that he is undergoing an illusion, so that the object in question is not really there. The occasions when this actually happens are, however, so infrequent, and the mistakes to which they give rise so easily

[3] See my article on 'Basic propositions'. Reprinted in my *Philosophical Essays*.

corrected, that the risk he is made to run is negligible. We could begin by teaching him to name his sense-impressions, but the gain in security would be outweighed by the lack of interest in what he would be learning to communicate. In the normal way our sense-impressions are of importance to us only as the springboard from which to jump to conclusions about what is physically present, and it is to the expression of these conclusions that our rules of meaning are adapted. If one is philosophically concerned with the analysis of perception, there may, indeed, be an advantage in introducing ways of speaking which make these inferences explicit, but no such terminology is required to give our language a sufficient anchorage in empirical fact.

In any event, no rules of meaning which operate at the level of observation can be expected to legislate with certainty for every possible case. There is likely always to be an area of imprecision within which it is not clear either that the term in question applies or that it does not. This is conspicuously so in the case of colours, where the fact that shades of colour spread over a continuous range entails that we repeatedly come upon border-line stretches where it is uncertain where one shade ends and another begins. This example may also serve to show how dangerous it can be to trust one's intuition. Thus, it might appear self-evident that if one object, *A*, displays some specific shade of red, and another object, *B*, is indistinguishable in colour from *A*, it also displays that shade. What else do we mean by their being indistinguishable? And then by the same principle, if *B* displays that shade and a third object, *C*, is indistinguishable in colour from *B*, *C* too will display it. But then, if the different shades of red are qualitatively continuous, it will follow that there are no different shades. For what is implied by their forming a continuum is that it is always possible to find a set of objects *A*, *B*, *C*, all falling within their extension, such that *A* is indistinguishable in colour from *B* and *B* from *C*, but *A* is distinguishable from *C*. In short, it is an empirical fact that the relation of being indistinguishable in colour is not transitive. It is for this reason that we are able to travel along a continuous line from one shade of colour to another. But now if we make what seems the obvious assumption that two objects which are indistinguishable in colour display the same shade, we render this relation transitive, and thereby abolish all the shades but one. Worse still, if, as appears to be the case, the colours in the spectrum form a continuous sequence we reach the absurd conclusion that everything is of exactly the same colour. To avoid it we have to allow, contrary to our intuition, that it is not a sufficient condition for *B* to display the same shade of colour as *A* that the two should be indistinguishable in colour. It is necessary also that there be no object from which either of them is distinguishable in colour and the other not.

This is a very strong condition, so strong indeed that there seems to be no way of making completely sure that any two objects satisfy it. We cannot examine all the objects that there are, and so long as even one remains unexamined, there is always the possibility that it would separate our pair. But surely we do continually judge with confidence what colour things look to us to be, and consequently whether or not the same colour term applies to them. Surely I can properly claim to know that the leaves on this branch above me are all now looking green. The answer is that I can apply terms like 'green' with confidence because of their comparative lack of precision. They apply to a range of objects which need not be indistinguishable in colour but are required to match one another roughly within limits that are not clear-cut. The sufficient condition for any two objects to satisfy such a term is again that they match just the same objects in the appropriate way. But in that case, since the matching need be only rough, we can be sure that this condition is fulfilled by objects, like these leaves, which come as it were in the middle of the range. There will, indeed, be objects with regard to which it is not clear whether they come within this range or another, but their existence does not threaten to separate the objects in the centre. To the extent that it is uncertain whether any such penumbral object matches any one of these leaves to a sufficient degree, it will be equally uncertain whether it matches the others. What follows is that the colour of the penumbral objects, for example, the objects which occupy the border-line between green and blue, cannot be certainly determined, but that is a tolerable consequence.

It does not matter to us that such concepts are vague, because the instances which fall upon their outskirts are relatively few, and they can anyhow be adequately characterized as belonging to the border zone of two neighbouring ranges. It is only if we wish to determine shades with such precision that any two objects which are discriminable in colour are held to display different shades that all attributions become uncertain. And the same applies to any other domain, such as that of sound, where the relation of being indistinguishable in such and such a respect is discovered not to be transitive. It is an empirical fact that there are these qualitative continuities, so that the vagueness in which we take refuge is not a logical necessity. There seems, however, to be no practical prospect of eliminating it.

If, as is normally the case, our rules of meaning relate to physical objects, their application will be rendered uncertain not only by vagueness but also by the fact, which we have already noted, that the existence of the things to which our signs refer will not be logically guaranteed by our having the experiences which justify their use. To continue with our example, it would, indeed, be absurd for me to entertain any serious doubt whether these really are green leaves. I have no reason to suppose that my senses are not functioning normally; my memory assures me that this tree has been here for years. I calculate that I must have seen it thousands of times. In summer its leaves are always green. Nevertheless, in making this perceptual judgement, I am going beyond the content of my present sense-experience. I am putting an interpretation upon my visual data which could conceivably be wrong. It is logically possible that I am undergoing an illusion. It is logically possible that my memory is playing me false. And this will remain the case, whatever further tests I carry out. The possibility that future experiences will lead me to revise my judgement can never be logically excluded.

But now we come back to the point that there is nothing to be done about these possibilities beyond just noting that they exist. They simply mark the fact that all our ordinary judgements draw drafts upon the future, and any draft upon the future can be dishonoured. So long, however, as we have no positive reason to believe that they will be dishonoured, the scepticism to which we are committed is purely formal. It becomes of interest only when it is brought to bear not on particular judgements, which are acknowledged to be fallible, but on the whole system of concepts which these judgements embody. But then we need arguments to show that these concepts are defective, and some grounds for thinking that a different system would serve us better.

Whatever system we adopt, there will be a great deal that we take for granted. Not only our common understanding of the meanings of the words we use, but also our ability to follow rules of inference; not only methodological principles and criteria of evidence, but a mass of historical and scientific information. We have moral and aesthetic principles for which it is arguable that no justification can be provided outside themselves. We have seen that various distinctions can be made with regard to the question how much of all this is to be regarded as self-evident, but this turns out also not to be a question of primary interest. The important points are that we learn in the end just to be able to see what a rule demands of us, and that any process of proof must come to a halt somewhere. It is, however, also true that any question can be re-opened and that the whole of our system, both the beliefs which enter into it and the processes by which they are formed, is liable to change. We cannot change it all at once, because we should then have no standpoint from which to change it, but no part of it is sacrosanct, not even its necessary propositions, including its laws of logic, since although they are dictated to us by the terms which figure in them, we might find it convenient to use different terms. We are limited only by a principle of consistency, which ensures that whatever move may be open to us, when we have made a given move, we have made that move and not a different one. For this is the minimal condition of our having any system at all.

To say that a proposition is self-evident is never an argument. At best it is an invitation to one's audience to look at things again, in cases where, if they are unable to see them as we do, we have no further argument to offer.

The Concept of
Prepredicative Experience

ROSS HARRISON

Husserl wishes to show in his newly translated work, *Experience and Judgement*, how the structure of predicative thought originates in the structure of prepredicative experience. Yet it is not possible to give the kind of description of prepredicative experience that Husserl desires. For even if we assume that prepredicative experience is independent of predicative thought, it is still possible for us to analyse experience only as it is thought about. This means that we cannot validly distinguish between those features of this composite structure which arise from the structure of prepredicative experience and those features which arise from the structure of predicative thought. Even if we do make the distinction this will not help Husserl since the resulting description of prepredicative experience presupposes description of predicative thought.

Ross Harrison is Lecturer in Philosophy at the University of Cambridge. He has published articles in *Analysis*, *The Philosophical Quarterly* and *Political Studies*. His book *On What There Must Be*, was published in 1974.

The recent translation of Edmund Husserl's *Erfahrung und Urteil* [1] into English has given English readers the chance to read an extended account of his analysis of prepredicative experience. In what follows I shall confine myself to consideration of this one work of Husserl's, and shall attempt to display what seems to me to be the essential problem involved in any such use of the concept of prepredicative experience. My interest is in this problem itself rather than in an exact exegesis of Husserl's account of prepredicative experience, or in an account of the role that the concept plays in the overall structure of his thought.

Husserl obviously regards his analysis of prepredicative experience as being extremely important. He says that 'The theory of prepredicative experience . . . is the proper first element of the phenomenological theory of judgement' (p. 27). This is because he thinks that it is only possible to give an adequate account of the logical categories and structures of judgement if it can be shown how these features of predicative judgements are founded on prepredicative experience. The structures discovered in predicative judgement have their origin in, and derive their validity from, the structure of experience prior to such predicative judgement or language. For example, Husserl takes the logician to start with simple, self-evidential, predicative judgements. He then criticises such a starting point because 'all predicative self-evidence must be ultimately grounded on the self-evidence of experience' (p. 41). A particular example of what he takes such grounding or origination to consist in can be given by his treatment of the subject–predicate form of judgement. The distinction between subjects and predicates obviously reflects a fundamental logical category, and Husserl starts his analysis of predicative judgements by remarking on the distinction between subject-form and predicate-form. However, he has before this carried on an extensive analysis of prepredicative experience, part of which is the distinction between the 'object-substrate' and its 'internal determinations' (see, for example, p. 113). This distinction in prepredicative experience is the foundation, or origin, of the distinction in predicative thought. Only when the distinction

---

[1] Edmund Husserl, *Experience and Judgement: Investigations in a Genealogy of Logic* (London: Routledge and Kegan Paul, 1973).

in prepredicative experience has been fully displayed in a phenomenological analysis can the nature and validity of the normal (predicative) logical distinction be understood. The essence of these predicative judgements is apprehended by means of an exploration into their origins, and such an exploration involves an extended account of the structure of prepredicative experience.[2]

Husserl is therefore committed not just to the claim that there is prepredicative experience but also to the claim that it is possible to give an extended analysis of the structure of such experience. Furthermore, since his analysis of the structure of prepredicative experience is meant to found, or clarify, his analysis of predicative thought, it seems to me that he is also committed to the claim that it is possible to discover and display the structure of prepredicative experience without relying on any awareness of the structure of predicative thought. It is these claims which provide the problem that I have with his use of the concept of prepredicative experience. This is because I find it difficult to see how any extended analysis of the structure of prepredicative experience could be completely independent of an analysis of the structure of predicative thought as expressed in language. In the first place I am doubtful whether the structure of one is totally independent of the structure of the other. In the second place, even if they are totally independent of one another, I do not think that this is something which we can ever find out; and it seems therefore that it is impossible for us to describe the structure of the one totally independently of describing the structure of the other. In the third place, even if this is also completely wrong and it is perfectly possible to describe the structure of prepredicative experience quite independently of the description of predicative thought, I think that this would only be possible if we can work from the structure of such thought to the structure of experience. So even if it is possible to give a description of prepredicative experience, it seems to me that this will only be because we can already give a description

---

[2] A more complete account of Husserl's dissatisfaction with the logical tradition emanating from Frege, and of what Husserl hoped to substitute for it, is given in the last paper of this collection, Dr Pivčević's 'Concepts, phenomenology and philosophical understanding'.

of predicative thought; and if description of prepredicative experience presupposes description of predicative thought, it cannot be used to clarify such description. This series of nested objections forms a rough statement of the problem that I have with Husserl's use of the concept of prepredicative experience. I shall now try to make the nature of the problem clearer, and to justify my belief that it is a genuine one. In doing so I shall often call predicative thought quite simply 'thought'.

If someone says that there is prepredicative experience as well as predicative thought, and that this experience has its own complex structure which is different from the structure of thought, a natural first reaction is that nothing could be more obviously true. We do not only live in a world of thought, it might be said, for thought is about something independent of thought. We have feelings and sensations whether or not we describe them or think about them. These feelings and sensations would have existed even if we had never thought or described. Animals clearly have sensations, yet it is normal not to attribute (predicative) thought to animals. So it would seem quite clear that experience and predicative thought were two quite independent things, and each capable therefore of having its own independent structure. In which case it would seem difficult to think that there could be a problem about the possibility of an extended description of the structure of prepredicative experience. It is true that language, and hence predicative thought, would be used in any such description, but the intention of this language would be to describe the structure of something which clearly existed independently of itself. Why then, it might be asked, should anyone feel that there was a problem about distinguishing between the structure of the predicative experience so described and the structure of the language used to describe it.

It still seems to me, however, that there is such a problem. The truth that lies behind the expostulation that experience is something quite separate from thought or language is that, as well as thought or language there is also experience. If all species of animals have experiences, and only one species of animal uses language or predicative thought, then it is quite clear that experiences can exist independently of thought. To talk of the possibility of prepredicative experience in this context is just to talk of the possibility of experience itself. Since, therefore, there is experience, and since such experience exists independently of predicative thought, it is clear that there is prepredicative experience. Sometimes when Husserl wishes to insist on the origination of forms of thought in the structures of experience, he does not want to do more than stress this truth that, as well as thought there is experience, and that the thought is about independent experience. He says for example that 'every activity of thought presupposes pregiven objects' (p. 19) or that 'all cognitive activity . . . presupposes this domain of passive pregivenness' (p. 30).

The problem, however, is not a problem of the possibility of the existence of prepredicative experience. It is, rather, the problem of whether the structure of this existing experience can be described independently of the structure of thought or language. The (admittedly independent) experience is judged or described whenever it is considered by us. This judged or described experience can be found on analysis to have certain structures. Since however these structures can only be displayed after the experience has been judged and described, it does not seem possible to distinguish between those parts of the structure which are the structure of independent experience and those parts of the structure which are the structure of thought or language. As we study experience, that is, for example for the purpose of phenomenological description and analysis, we are always dealing with an experience which is judged or described. The experience and the description always go together and can not be separated. In these circumstances it does not seem possible to distinguish between the structure of the experience and the structure of the description. What we have is the structure of the experience as described, and this structure might equally well be attached to the experience, to the description, to both, or arbitrarily divided between them. It does not seem possible, therefore, to arrive with any conviction at a description of the structure of experience totally independent of the structure of language. This, then, is the main problem that I have with Husserl's account. We may easily agree that there is experience independent of thought and language, and that this thought or language is about something totally separate from itself. It does not follow from this that it is possible to describe the structure of the one totally independently of description of the structure of the other. On the contrary, since we can only deal with experience which is already thought about or described, it seems totally impossible to decide which parts of the resulting structure reflect the structure of experience and which parts reflect the structure of language.

This problem is the problem which any extended description of the structure of prepredicative experience faces. It has been called, for example by Lothar Eley in an afterword to this edition, the problem of 'the circle of language'. The problem is how, operating within the circle of language, it is possible to say what it is like outside the circle of language. It is possible to say that there is an outside, that as well as language there is something independent of language which language describes. This is why I agreed that there was experience, and prepredicative experience, in reply to the expostulation above. However, once we try to describe the nature or the structure of this outside, we are forced to do so in terms of thought or language. This means that we are not really outside, and so are relying on the structure of thought or language.

It might be thought that it was possible to escape from the circle of language by saying that dependence upon language, and upon the structure of thought, while describing prepredicative experience was a merely methodological requirement. That is, it might be argued that we had to use language in describing prepredicative experience just because we have to use language in the description of anything. This, however, it might be said, was purely accidental and should no more be thought to influence the nature of the experience described than description is usually thought to influence the nature of what is described. We may have to use language to describe experience in the way that we have to use eyes to see the world, but this does not mean that we cannot distinguish between the structure of language and the structure of experience any more than our having to use our eyes means that we cannot distinguish between the changes in the appearances of things which arise from changes in the objects themselves (such as their being painted a new colour) and changes in the appearances of things which arise from changes in our eyes (such as seeing them double or having jaundice). We can make such distinctions in the case of our eyes, so it would seem that we should also be able to do so in the case of our predicative thought.

There are, however, two important respects in which the case of the eyes is different from the case of thought, and which are sufficient to ensure that the suggested analogy is not a good one. The first, and more important, difference is that we do not have to use our eyes in order to perceive the nature of the world, while we do have to use predicative thought in judging the nature of the world. That we do not have to use our eyes is shown by the fact that blind people are able to perceive the nature of the world, and by the fact that it is always in principle possible to construct a machine which provides the information which we normally receive visually (such as colour) in a form acceptable to another sense. Because we do not have to use our eyes, it is possible to consider our dependence on our eyes for such information as the colour of objects as being merely methodological. We could, for example, construct a machine which emitted a different tone of sound for each different wavelength of light fed into it. Let us suppose that this machine would make the same distinctions between objects as we at present do in our visual colour discriminations. If it did, this would show that being different in colour was (or represented) a difference in the objects themselves, and was not just an effect produced by the eyes. In such a case, that is, it is possible to make the required distinction between those parts of the experience which are produced by the eyes, and those parts of the experience which are produced by the independent object. This is, however, because in this case we can have independent access to the object. Our reliance on our eyes is in this case genuinely methodological, and this is shown by the fact that it is possible for us to do without it. The case of predicative thought or language, which is the present problem, is quite different. Here it is impossible to do without predicative thought, and it is impossible to have independent access to the objects thought about. This means that the dependence on predicative thought or language is not merely methodological, and so means that it is impossible to distinguish between those features of the resulting structure which arise from the nature of thought and those features of the resulting structure which arise from the nature of the experience itself.

The second important respect in which the case of the eyes is different from the case which provides the problem is that in it merely accidental and changing features are picked out as arising from the nature of the eyes or the nature of the independent object. Yet what Husserl wishes to display for prepredicative experience is its essential, that is unchanging, nature. Now when we have a changing situation it is often possible to tell by the manner in which the changes occur whether the change is a change in the medium or a change in the independent object. For example, if spots occur in one corner of the film whatever the scene is, we think that the spots are a result of the film and not of the scene. However, in Husserl's case, we are concerned with the essential and unchanging structure of prepredicative experience and the essential and unchanging structure of thought. Since we must consider these two structures together, and since we are interested in the unchanging features of each, it is impossible to distinguish between the two structures by seeing how the one changes with respect to the other. Again it is the case that the two elements whose features we wish to distinguish always appear together; and so again it is the case that there seems no means of deciding which features of the composite structure originate with each element.

I have tried to show by criticism of this suggested analogy with the case of the eyes why our dependence on thought and language in the study of experience is not merely a methodological requirement, and why therefore we cannot justifiably describe the structure of prepredicative experience. Of course, the whole topic of perception is philosophically problematical, and someone who has a different view of perception will no doubt fail to be convinced by criticism of the analogy. It is nevertheless worth realising that the perceptual analogy depended upon realist assumptions in which it was assumed that the object of perception is independent of the perception itself. The aim was to show that even if we make a similar realist assumption about the independence of predicative thought and prepredicative experience, there is still nothing analogous in this case to the possibility there is in the perceptual case of distinguishing between those features of our experience which are due to the perceptual mechanism, and those features of our experience which are due to the independent object. Now if we started with idealist assumptions about the nature of perception, in which it was assumed that there was not an independent object, then the question of such a distinction would not arise, and so there would be no pressure for thinking that there ought to be a similar distinction in the case of predicative thought and prepredicative experience. My object was to show that even in the most favourable interpretation of the perceptual analogy it still gave no reason for thinking that our dependence on language was merely methodological, or that we were not locked in a 'circle of language'.

In any case, whatever is thought of the analogy, the heart of the problem remains. This arises, it will be remembered, because it is necessary for us to study experience as that experience is predicatively judged or linguistically described. For even if it was not so judged when it was experienced (as, for example, in the case of animals), it is necessary for us so to judge it when we are engaged in any study of it, or in any attempt to display its essential structure. Since we can only study experience as judged and described, and since this coincidence between thought and experience is universal and not merely methodological, it is impossible to distinguish between those features of the composite whole which arise from the structure of experience and those features which arise from the structure of thought. So even if we make the realist assumption that thought is quite independent of experience, it still is not the case that extended description of the essential structure of prepredicative experience is possible. Husserl in spite of himself must work inside language. It does not seem therefore that he can ever be sure that the structure of experience that he describes is the structure of experience quite independent of the structure of language. In the end, his insistence on the necessity of a study of prepredicative experience seems to come to no more than an insistence on the necessity of the study of experience (of any experience); and his emphasis that the object whose structure he studies is *prepredicative* experience seems to come to no more than the emphasis that *there is* experience independent of thought, that it is not just the structure of thought that is being studied.

At this stage I think that it is useful to look at the way in which a similar problem arose for a group of philosophers opposed to Husserl, the Logical Positivists. Fairly shortly after the publication of the manifesto of the Vienna Circle, the Logical Positivists divided into two groups over the nature of fundamental, basic, or (as Husserl would say) self-evident statements. On the one hand were philosophers such as Schlick and Ayer who believed that direct statements of immediate experience could function as verifiers while themselves never being in need of verification, because there was no possibility of such statements being altered or mistaken. On the other hand was Neurath, and after him Carnap and Hempel, who took a more conventionalist view and held that no statement was immune from the need for verification or from the possibility of revision. On the contrary, all statements, including immediate statements of experience, were to be accepted or rejected according to how well they fitted into the totality of statements accepted by the 'culture circle' in which we happen to live. This claim of Neurath and his followers produced at times a tone of baffled outrage in the replies of Schlick and his followers. For it seemed to them to amount to, or to involve, the claim that what we experience depends upon the language we use. If the nature of our direct immediate experiences are to be taken as different according to the culture circle to which we belong, then it seems that we can never break out of the circle of language and can never have direct experience of the world.

Such bafflement can be found, for example, in Schlick's paper 'Facts and Propositions'.[3] He starts by describing how he wrote an earlier controversial paper while 'overlooking the blue bay of Salerno'. The implication is that, whatever his culture circle might say, this is the experience that he has. He goes on to describe how he compares statements in Baedeker with 'reality' by looking at such things as cathedrals. 'A cathedral', he says, 'is not a proposition or a set of propositions'. It needs no more than a few such simple examples, Schlick obviously thinks, in order to shock Neurath and his followers into realising that they are attempting to live in a universe inhabited only by words, and have forgotten experience altogether.

The problem here seems to be the same as the problem posed by Husserl's description of prepredicative experience. On the one side we have a group of philosophers who emphasise that

---

[3] Moritz Schlick, 'Facts and propositions', *Analysis*, Vol. 2, no. 5 (1935). This paper is a reply to Hempel's paper in *Analysis*, Vol. 2, no. 4 (1935), which was an attack on the earlier paper of Schlick's mentioned here, 'Ueber das Fundament der Erkenntnis', *Erkenntnis*, Vol. 4.

we cannot get outside the circle of language and who emphasise that the nature of the experience we have will therefore depend upon the nature of language. On the other side we have a group of philosophers who hold that this is wholly absurd, and that the only result of such claims would be the abolition of all experience and a type of linguistic idealism. A philosopher who supported the latter group although himself outside the ranks of the Vienna Circle was Russell. Here is one of his attempts to show that the Neurath–Carnap–Hempel position is absurd:

We may illustrate Hempel's position by a fable: At a certain period when his finances were not flourishing (so the fable avers), he entered a cheap restaurant in Paris. He asked for the menu. He read it, and he ordered beef. All this since entering the restaurant was language. The food came and he took a mouthful. This was confrontation with facts. He summoned the restaurateur and said, 'this is horse-flesh, not beef'. The restaurateur replied, 'Pardon me, but the scientists of my culture circle include the sentence 'this is beef' among those that they accept'. Hempel on his own showing would be obliged to accept this with equanimity. This is absurd, as Carnap in due course came to realise.[4]

Russell here resembles Schlick in that he obviously feels that he only has to point out the consequences of this doctrine for anyone to realise that it is absurd. Yet this appearance of absurdity only arises from the fact that Neurath and his followers look as if they are trying to abolish experience. If instead they are only taken to be claiming that statements or judgements about experience depend upon the structure of our predicative thought as well as the structure of prepredicative experience, then they look less absurd.

The truth which lies behind Russell's and Schlick's objections is the same as the truth which I said above lay behind Husserl's claims. This is that there is experience, and that experience is something different from predicative thought. I experience the sea at Salerno whatever I may be thinking, I experience the meat in Paris whatever the nature of my conversation with the restaurateur. It does not follow from this, however, that when I describe the nature of these experiences my description is totally independent of the way in which my

[4] Bertrand Russell, *My Philosophical Development* (London: Allen and Urwin, 1959), p. 218.

thought and language happen to operate. Nothing could seem to be more totally independent of the nature of thought or language than that my experience is experience of a blue sea. Yet once we remember that different linguistic communities, or culture circles, divide the colour spectrum differently, so that a member of one culture circle will describe this experience as being similar to an experience which a member of another culture circle would not think that it was similar to, then it seems that my description of the nature of this experience is not totally independent of the nature of my predicative thought. The same point can be made about Russell's fable. Russell obviously thinks that it is absurd that Hempel should give way with equanimity. Yet if it really is the case that the scientists of the restaurateur's culture circle (which is a circle which must be taken to include Hempel as well) would all describe the meat as 'beef', then there seems no reason why Hempel should not give way. He has the experience all right, and no one would suggest that he does not have the experience that he has. However, it is perfectly possible for him to be mistaken about its nature. In the end, if he continues to disagree with everyone else he must be taken to have no insight into the nature of his experience, into what it is *like*, into what experiences are similar to it. Russell's fable, of course, looks as if it has the opposite conclusion, but this is because it is designed to make Hempel look in the right and the restaurateur look a crook. But in that case we may take the restaurateur to be simply lying about the scientists of his culture circle, in which case there is no reason for Hempel to give way at all.

If this is the case for the simple judgements of immediate experience with which these positivists deal, how much more must it be true of the total structure, or essence, of experience with which Husserl deals. However much we stress that language is of something independent of itself, the fact remains that we can only describe or represent this independent thing in the way that our language allows. As Wittgenstein says in the *Tractatus*, 'the limits of my language mean the limits of my world'.[5] We cannot build more structure into the exper-

[5] *Tractatus*, 5.6, Pears and McGuinness translation (London: Routledge and Kegan Paul, 1961).

ience than exists in the language with which we have to describe the experience. Husserl refers to Kant in *Experience and Judgement* and uses Kantian arguments in order to demonstrate that our experience takes place in time and in one single time (see, for example, p. 164). Now Kant distinguishes between the conditions which apply to experience (empirical knowledge) which arise from the essential form of intuitions and which arise from the essential form of concepts. However in a famous phrase he declares that 'thoughts without content are empty, intuitions without concepts are blind'.[6] Anyone who takes this sentence seriously must realise that in the end a distinction between the structure of prepredicative experience and the structure of predicative, or conceptual, judgement of this experience is artificial. If analysis is to be possible we must deal with a composite structure, otherwise we are blind. All of which means that we are restricted to the limits of the language.

It is of course perfectly possible to work back from this composite structure and to say that it reflects the structure of one of its elements, experience, even though it is impossible to examine this element in isolation. The simplest way to do this is just to assume that the structure of the composite which is analysed reflects the structure of experience. Any distinction which appears in the analysis, for example that between subject and predicate, can then be taken to arise from a distinction in experience. The trouble with this is that it is impossible both to do this and then go on to clarify the structure of the composite by saying that it arises from the structure of prepredicative experience. Clarification cannot work in both directions. If we discover the structure of prepredicative experience by examining the structure of experience as described and reading back this structure into one of its elements, we cannot then go on to clarify our description of the composite structure by saying that it arises from the structure of this element. If, because it sends people to sleep, we read back into opium that it contains the *virtus dormitiva*, we cannot then turn round and, by way of explanation or clarification, say that opium sends people to sleep because it contains the *virtus dormitiva*.

[6] *Critique of Pure Reason*, B75, Kemp Smith translation (London: Macmillan, 1929).

Even if it is possible, therefore, to give a description of prepredicative experience by the simple device of asserting or assuming, that the structure of judged experience is the same as the structure of unjudged experience, this will not help Husserl in his general project.[7] For if he is to clarify description of judged experience (or judgement) by displaying the origin of its structure in the structure of unjudged experience, then he must be able to give a completely independent description of the structure of unjudged, or prepredicative, experience. Yet I do not see how he could do this; it certainly will not be achieved by any method which involves working back from the description of (predicatively) judged experience.

It is natural to think of the relation between predicative thought and experience in terms of an Aristotelian distinction which Husserl also employs, that between matter and form. Experience is the matter, thought is the form, and we only have to deal with the composite structure, this matter in this form. Now Husserl wants to say that experience also has a structure, and so it is natural to assume that it has the structure which allows it to result in this form. As Husserl says 'We can also say that before every movement of cognition the object of cognition is already present as a *dynamis* which is to turn into an *entelecheia* (p. 29)'. The trouble is that once we start reading back into the matter properties which arise from its ability to be given a certain form, we end up with a situation in which matter can only take the form it does take. This both spoils the form–matter distinction and is also totally non–explanatory if we are trying to explain why it has the form it does have. The alternative is just to say that there is matter, and to study it as it assumes various forms. This is analogous to the statement that I have several times made that all that we can say is that there *is* experience. Judgement is the judgement of something, the form is the form of something. However, when we wish to study it, we can only study it as fully formed, study it as moulded by predicative thought.

It seems to me, therefore, that however we argue back from the structure of predicatively judged experience to the struc-

---

[7] Here and in what follows, I use 'judgement' in what Husserl would call its 'narrow' sense. Husserl wishes to claim that judgement in 'the broadest sense' is something which is already present in prepredicative experience (p. 61).

ture of prepredicative experience (and there are more sophisticated ways of doing this than the simple assumption that the two structures are identical), we are still left with the situation that the only structure which we can analyse, produce, understand or describe is the structure which we analyse in language (or predicative thought), and which is therefore the structure which this language (or thought) allows. We can never in the end distinguish between the essential features of this structure which arise from our thought and language and the essential features which arise from something independent of it. For if we could do so, this would be to suppose an independent or external position, outside of all thought or language, which is impossible. If we realise that thought or language is deficient in some way, this is something we think or describe, and so is not to go outside thought or language. It is, rather, to substitute a more adequate thought or language for a less adequate one. There have, of course, been many famous attempts to assert that the really important things in life lie outside the boundary of language and attempts made to show, suggest, or indicate, their nature; for example Bradley on experience or Wittgenstein on the mystical. However Wittgenstein's magnificent tautology on this subject, that 'whereof we cannot speak, thereof we must be silent',[8] is as true for Wittgenstein himself as it is for anyone else. As F. P. Ramsey remarked 'if you can't say it, you can't say it, and you can't whistle it either'. The world we describe, including our experience, is the world our language allows us to describe, and one therefore which lies inside the boundary of language. We can of course assert that its structures are given pre-linguistically, or prepredicatively; that is, that they are in the experience before it is described. In the end, however, this means no more than that there is an independent experience; that, as well as language, there is something described in it. If, therefore, there is going to be discovery of the structure of our experience by reflection on its inner, or essential, nature, then this will be discovery of the structure of our experience as that experience is described in language. That is, if there is going to be phenomenology at all, then it must be linguistic phenomenology.

---

[8] *Tractatus*, 7, Ogden translation (London: Kegan Paul, 1922).

Austin's 'Linguistic Phenomenology'

ANTHONY MANSER

The paper first explores some likeness between the methods of Husserl and Austin which are apparently not due to the influence of the former on the latter. It then considers the philosophic core of Austin's method, his 'linguistic phenomenology' or consideration of 'what we should say when'. It then examines how far Austin remained true to this ideal in his later work.

Anthony Manser is Professor of Philosophy at the University of Southampton. Besides a book on *Sartre* (1966), he has published articles on a variety of topics in various journals. At present he is working on some likenesses between Hegel and Wittgenstein.

Austin clearly had an enormous influence on contemporary British philosophy and produced a number of papers which deserved to be described as classical contributions. By his fellows he was considered to be a thinker in tune with the Oxford philosophy of his period, mainly thought of as 'linguistic analysis, ordinary language philosophy' and so on. Hence it is surprising that he himself talked of his own method as 'linguistic phenomenology'; this characterization found no echo in the writings of his followers, even though they adopted many of his techniques. In this paper I want to explore the meaning of the phrase 'linguistic phenomenology' and to see in what way Austin's use is related to the continental use of the word.[1] At the same time it will be necessary to make an assessment of Austin's philosophical status. In spite of his domination of Oxford or at least of the Oxford philosophers of his own and the succeeding generation, I do not think he is a great philosopher, not to be counted among the central figures of this century, Russell, Moore, Wittgenstein and Ryle. This is perhaps shown by the contrast between his critical and his constructive work, perhaps best exemplified by that between *Sense and Sensibilia* and *How to Do Things with Words*. Both were reconstructed from his lecture notes, but the former has a strength and directness which is missing in the latter. This strength seems to come from the critical line of *Sense and Sensibilia*, from its destructive analysis of the views of three of his contemporaries. Austin treats them as an Oxford tutor deals with a student's essay; he shows how they have failed to examine their assumptions, to think for themselves, to take an unprejudiced look at their subject-matter. He is the archetypal Oxford don and his dominance was due to the way in which he treated the work of his fellow philosophers to the same kind of criticism as they were accustomed to mete out to their pupils; it is hardly surprising they were scared of him, particularly when he could do this better than they could.

As I have said his use of the term 'phenomenology' to characterise his work is surprising for that philosophy seems

---

[1] References to the works of Austin are included in the text, and are given as follows:
PP   *Philosophical Papers*, 2nd ed. (Oxford, 1970).
HTD   *How to Do Things with Words*, ed. J. O. Urmson (Cambridge, Mass., 1962).
SS   *Sense and Sensibilia*, reconstructed by G. J. Warnock (Oxford, 1962).
SA   *Symposium on J. L. Austin*, ed. K. T. Fann (London, 1969).

to have had no influence in Oxford; Husserl and other post-Fregean Europeans were largely unread in the forties and fifties. As a young don, Gilbert Ryle had lectured on some of those philosophers, and had even written a long and comparatively sympathetic review of Heidegger's *Being and Time*. However, his own philosophical development does not seem to have depended on their writings. His later considered view, which I think was shared by most of those doing philosophy in Oxford, was: 'In short, Phenomenology was, from its birth, a bore. Its over-solemnity of manner more than its equivocal lineage will secure that its lofty claims are ignored.'[2] This could never be a description of Austin's work, which was seldom solemn and never boring; he did not leave a mountain of manuscript material nor did he engage in the continual rewriting of a programme for a philosophy which was never written. Further, there is no evidence that Austin ever seriously read a page of Husserl. Whatever he may have meant by 'linguistic phenomenology' there is no reason to see it as a reference to any influence of Husserl.

Nevertheless there are certain similarities between the two. Both wanted to get rid of the prejudices which philosophers have inherited and start philosophy afresh, as is shown by Husserl's slogan 'Back to the things themselves' which I think Austin would have been willing to re-echo. Both thought of philosophy as an enterprise which had been solitary but which should become co-operative, a team effort (cf. *PP*, p. 175). In each case this seems to have been due to the belief that a method had been discovered, one which was comparatively easy to learn but which required the examination of too many examples for any single individual to undertake. In Austin's case this involved working through the dictionary (cf. *PP*, pp. 186–7). Finally, in both cases the result of the new turn was the discovery of a multitude of 'acts' whose existence had previously been unsuspected or ignored. Husserl found a whole series of 'mental acts': 'we must distinguish "*straightforwardly*" *executed* grasping, perceiving, remembering, predicating, valuing, purposing, etc., from the *reflections* by means of which alone, as grasping acts belonging to a new level, the straightforward

---

[2] G. Ryle, review of Marvin Farber, *The Foundations of Phenomenology*, *Philosophy* (1946), p. 268.

acts become accessible to us.'[3] Austin's 'acts' were linguistic
or 'speech' acts; it is regrettable that a stylist like Austin should
perpetrate such a form of words, and still more regrettable that
it should have become part of the current philosophic terminology (or mythology). Husserl's talk of 'mental acts' at least
follows a philosophic tradition and groups together a set of
things which have no common name and which at least seem
to go together. It is hard, however, to distinguish the uttering
(or making, doing) of 'speech-acts' from speaking. In its origin
in the work of Austin the distinction is clear; it marks off uses of
words which are 'doings', such a promising, from other uses,
such as stating. The importance of the notion of 'performative
utterances' need not be pointed out here. But as Austin worked
on the distinction it became more woolly until eventually
everything became an 'illocutionary act' of one kind or another.

Part of the trouble may arise from Austin's original distinction; there is reason to suggest that he drew the line wrongly
from the start. Mats Furberg (*SA*, p. 452) has pointed out that
there are special forms of words the uttering of which constitutes the doing of a certain action. Promising is one example, but
there are many other similar and more ceremonial formulae
which need not even be in the language of the speaker or hearer,
e.g. '*Le roy le veult*'. These are often not addressed to a particular
person but to 'whom it may concern'; when the foreman of the
jury says 'Guilty' then the prisoner is guilty. Furberg says of
such 'performatives': 'Their speaker as it were presses a button
in a social machine, and after that the machine works without
his interference – or if it fails, it is not necessarily his business to
put it right' (*SA*, p. 453). The characteristic of such devices is
the invocation of some social mechanism which may be that of
the law, as in the case of the foreman of the jury or may be less
formal, as in the case of ordinary promises. In both cases it is
in accordance with our ordinary way of talking to say that an
action has been performed; in Austin's words: 'This is one way
in which we might justify the "performative – constative"
distinction – the distinction between doing and saying' (*HTD*,
p. 47).

There could be grounds for talking of performatives as
'speech-actions', i.e. doings which necessarily involve the

---

[3] *Cartesian Meditations*, trans. Dorion Cairns (The Hague, 1969), p. 33.

utterance of words, and in contrast we might then introduce another term, 'speech act', to apply to utterances which were not examples of 'doings' in the strong first sense. This latter would merely serve the purpose of a general term for any utterance not included in the first class, though it is not clear that it would really be necessary to employ it. However for one so attentive to the details of English usage, Austin's apparent carelessness with the words 'action' and 'act' is remarkable. The same things are sometimes described as the one, sometimes as the other (cf. *PP*, p. 235 & p. 238). There are too many such examples to enumerate here, but it is a revealing exercise to go through the text of *How to Do Things with Words* underlining the occurrence of these words. Of course there are problems in this area, namely those that led Austin to become dissatisfied with his original 'performative–constative' distinction. Sometimes we want to say 'He didn't do anything; he just talked', whereas at other times his talking might be what he did in the sense that it could be praised or blamed, e.g. 'He gave away the secret'. Professor Cerf has discussed this problem at length (*SA*, pp. 359–68); what I am saying is largely complementary to his discussion.

I feel inclined to say that once the firm ground of the ritual formula for a speech-action has been left behind there is little basis for a clear distinction, which is why the term 'illocutionary', introduced to replace 'performative', eventually comes to embrace all utterances. The editors note a marginal remark which concludes: 'won't all utterances be performative?' (*HTD*, p. 103n). Austin himself says: 'Surely to state is every bit as much to perform an illocutionary act as, say, to warn or to pronounce . . . 'Stating' seems to meet all the criteria we had for distinguishing the illocutionary act' (*HTD*, p. 133). As 'illocutionary' is introduced by Austin, it is hard to quarrel with its usage, but it does lead him into oddities. For example, he puts the following on the same level:

I state that he did not do it.
I argue that he did not do it.
I suggest that he did not do it.
I bet that he did not do it. (*HTD*, p. 133)

Only the last is a clear 'performative', and it is hard to imagine the first two as complete utterances. We would normally expect their completion by some additional phrase, e.g. 'I state that he did not do it on p. 111' or 'I argue in Chapter xi that he did not do it.' But these would be reports or descriptions of what I did elsewhere, not the doing of them and hence not 'illocutionary acts'. Here the attempt to classify has clearly led Austin into trouble. This could be put in the form that he has deserted his phenomenological method and this is the source of the difficulty, a point I discuss further below.

For if there is to be classification of 'speech-acts' then it seems to be necessary that there should be always something in the form of words used which specifies, or at least enables us to discover, what was being done by the speaker. And this seems to me doubtful. Kierkegaard uses a parable of the escaped lunatic who tried to convince others that he was sane by only uttering true statements; he constantly asserted that the earth was round. To his surprise, this was not accepted as evidence of his sanity.[4] He had forgotten the further fact that even true statements have to be relevant, to have a role in the situation in which they are made. But this role is not necessarily something which can be seen from the utterance itself. Austin goes some way towards incorporating this point by his third category of linguistic acts, the 'perlocutionary' (*HTD*, p. 101). But this only applies if the effect on the hearers is one which the speaker intends. Austin did not seem very interested in this third class of acts, but I think it is clear that the same form of words can be used to achieve many different kinds of effect, and it is only the total context which will enable us to pick out what was intended, and even here there is the possibility that both speaker and hearer may be in doubt even after looking closely at the situation. It is true that normally we expect any remark made to have some reason for its utterance beyond the fact that it is true. To see what the reason is may well always be to see 'what I was doing' in uttering those words. But 'what I was doing' may sometimes naturally be thought of as an 'act', at other times as an 'action'. The kind of difference I have in mind here can be indicated by the pair 'telling a story intended to interest those listening' and 'making a brave attempt to keep the conversation going'. There is a sense in which non-performative utterances may be actions, i.e. things for which praise and blame are

[4] *Concluding Unscientific Postscript* (Princeton, 1968), p. 174.

appropriate, or only acts, i.e. utterances which can be attributed to a person but from which nothing particular follows. I am not happy with this distinction, but it does seem to be the case that in philosophy the word 'act' is a general term referring to anything which can be described by an active verb. Whether a particular utterance is an act or an action can only be decided by reference to the whole context, not by looking at the words themselves.

Austin was, I think, aware of this point; at least I take this to be the sense of his remark: 'The total speech act in the total situation is the *only actual* phenomenon which, in the last resort, we are engaged in elucidating' (*HTD*, p. 147).[5]

The repetition of 'total' gives an air of inclusiveness, but it is not clear what either the 'total speech-act' or the 'total speech situation' are meant to be, nor how the latter is supposed to be distinguished from the total situation, which would include not only the relations of the people involved but also the social structure as a whole. It seems improbable that such a totality could be meaningfully spelt out. What Austin really needs here is something more like the Wittgenstinian 'form of life', which is not meant to be spelt out in detail but which implies the connection between language and the social structure, that which makes it possible for men to converse, to commiserate, to tell stories, to write verse, to give and to obey orders and so on. It is not that Austin neglects altogether the social dimension as Husserl tended to, but rather that his view of speaking tends to be abstract and formal; there is often a suggestion in his writings that the language of the Oxford Common room is somehow the pinnacle of its development. Here again the reason for the problem is the desertion of the phenomenological aspect, the very search for generality which Austin himself so often castigated as the bane of previous philosophising.

The exploration of the curious likenesses between Husserl and Austin is not meant to suggest any influence of one on the other. They arise partly because of a faith in method, the same in each case, that of looking, without blinkers, in detail, at particular examples in order to dispose of certain philosophical

---

[5] There are two minor points which can be made about this quotation. First, the use of 'phenomenon' is perhaps part of the reason for Austin's use of 'linguistic phenomenology' as a description of his method. Second, the use of 'actual' may have connections with Austin's fondness for 'act'.

problems. Austin's *Philosophical Papers* is a record of his success in this area. His failure springs first from his forgetting the degree to which the search for *the* method has itself been the source of so much of philosophy from Descartes on and secondly from a tendency to misdescribe his own activity. Perhaps it should be added that the attempt to look at the world 'without blinkers' frequently succeeds in getting rid of one set whilst failing to notice another. Certainly he wanted to distinguish what he was doing from what had come to be called 'linguistic philosophy' or 'ordinary language philosophy' or 'analytic philosophy', as he states when tentatively introducing the 'mouthful' of 'linguistic phenomenology' (*PP*, p. 182) as a description of what he was doing. This was partly to distinguish his work from that of old-style grammarians – 'old-style' because he was well aware of the changes which were taking place in the grammatical study of language. He even speculated: 'Is it not possible that the next century may see the birth, through the joint labours of philosophers, grammarians, and numerous other students of language, of a true and comprehensive *science of language?*' (*PP*, p. 232). This would get rid of 'one more part of philosophy' though there would still be plenty of it left.

A 'science of language' would not be equivalent to philosophy. Many people had felt that 'linguistic philosophy' involved a trivialisation of the subject, an abandonment of concern for what used to be considered the important and substantive questions the subject dealt with. Austin obviously had some sympathy with this view; he did not feel that what he had said in, e.g. 'A plea for excuses' was *merely* about the uses of words in the way that a linguist might be said to be concerned with them. It was not a matter just of 'what we say' but of 'what we say when', and this, I think is the main reason for his adoption of the title 'linguistic phenomenology'. Austin expressed it in this way:

When we examine what we should say when, what words we should use in what situations, we are looking again not *merely* at words (or 'meanings', whatever they may be) but also at the realities we use words to talk about: we are using a sharpened awareness of words to sharpen our perception of, though not as the final arbiter of, the phenomena (*PP*, p. 182).

There seems to be a tension between the two parts of this remark, the first part of which (down to the colon) seems admirably to characterize Austin's method, whereas the second gives away too much and implies a remarkably old-fashioned view of the relation between words and the world.[6] That this is not an accident of expression is shown by a slightly earlier passage: 'words are not (except in their own little corner) facts or things: we need therefore to prise them off the world, to hold them apart from and against it, so that we can realize their inadequacies and arbitrariness, and can relook at the world without blinkers,' (*PP*, p. 182).

The 'what we should say when' formula certainly does not involve such a separation between words and the world. Furthermore, he does not employ such a separation when actually working on problems. For example his conclusion against Strawson that 'the condition of the cat is something-in-the-world' (*PP*, p. 156) is something which commands agreement, but certainly does not involve one in looking at the world to reach that agreement. Again I cite the long discussion of anger and its signs and symptoms in the paper 'Other Minds' (*PP*, pp. 105–16), which clearly teaches us a lot about anger (and not just about 'anger'), and yet does this by telling us how we normally *talk* about anger. There is no mention of anything psychological or physiological, no suggestion that we need to look at angry men. As a result of reading what Austin has to say, we become clearer about what anger is, and so are no longer liable to be taken in by what Wisdom and other philosophers have said it must be. Of course *examples* are employed, but not samples. Partly as the result of Austin's work, we are now all aware of the importance of examples in philosophy, but, as he often points out, these need not be actual things that have happened in the world. At the beginning of 'Three ways of spilling ink' he says:

First, let us consider some cases. Actual cases would of course be excellent: we might observe what words have actually been used by commentators on real incidents, or by narrators of fictitious incidents. However, we do not have the time or space to do that here. We must instead imagine some cases (imagine them carefully and in detail and comprehensively) and try to reach agreement upon what we should in fact say concerning them (*PP*, p. 274).

It should be noted that 'actual cases' do not here only comprise

---

[6] I owe the substance of this point, as well as many others, to a discussion with Mr David Pugmire on an earlier draft of this paper.

things that have happened, they also include what novelists have written. 'Imagined cases' are those thought up by the philosopher. The disadvantage of these latter is that we may not think up a wide enough range, suffer from a one-sided diet. That they do not refer to the 'real' world is of no significance in investigating 'what we should say when'.

The situation is quite different in the case of an empirical study of objects clearly 'in the world'. Budding gemmologists are advised to take every opportunity of handling precious stones, because: 'Descriptions of stones, however detailed and lucid, and illustrations, however good, cannot wholly replace visual experience, and readers are advised to study the cut stones exhibited in museums . . .'[7] In the field of excuses the law courts are obviously going to offer good examples, because there men are so often concerned with excusing their conduct. But an imaginary example will reveal as well the distinction between 'by mistake' and 'by accident' (*PP*, p. 185n). In the case of gemmology, samples are what the learner requires. In philosophy at an early stage a genuine case may be helpful in convincing the learner that what is going on is not mere playing with words (cf. Regina v. Finney, cited by Austin, *PP*, pp. 195–7), but it is still playing an exemplary role, as is shown by the way in which the philosopher handles it. This will be different from the lawyer's discussion; for him the case is a sample of how the law actually operates.

Thus the way Austin's 'linguistic phenomenology' operates in practice does not demand a look at the world as distinct from the words used in describing it. What he is doing could be characterized in words taken from a philosopher in what is often regarded as a different tradition from Austin's:

Reality is not what gives language sense. What is real and what is unreal shows itself *in* the sense that language has. Further, both the distinction between the real and the unreal and the concept of agreement with reality themselves belong to our language. I will not say that they are concepts of the language like any other, since it is clear that they occupy a commanding, and in a sense a limiting, position there. We can imagine a language with no concept of, say, wetness, but hardly one in which there is no way of distinguishing the real from the unreal. Nevertheless we could not in fact distinguish the real from the unreal without understanding the way this

[7] G. F. Herbert Smith, *Gemstones*, revised F. C. Phillips (London, 1972), p. 4.

distinction operates in the language. If then we wish to understand the significance of these concepts, we must examine the use they actually do have – *in* the language.[8]

If we look at his procedure in dealing with 'real' (*SS*, pp. 62–7, *PP*, pp. 86–9) and the related discussion of 'fact' (*PP*, pp. 154–74), we find that this is what he is doing; it is the use of the concept *in* language which is at issue – the 'nature (grammar, logic)' (*PP*, p. 105) of 'real', not the 'nature of reality' in the way an old-fashioned metaphysician might be thought to have envisaged it. It is because they are both working in this kind of way that Austin can be seen to be like Wittgenstein, as has often been claimed by writers on contemporary philosophy. However to liken the two is to miss all that is distinctive about Austin, both his strong and weak points. If a name is required for the 'what we should say when' method of procedure, then 'linguistic phenomenology' will do as well as any other.

What also needs then to be emphasised is that it is not *a* method of philosophy, but *the* method; there is no other available. This is what those who have criticised philosophers for being concerned with mere words have failed to grasp. They feel that there is reality 'out there' which can be pointed to or otherwise indicated without the use of words and which can be employed to check on our vocabulary. Though there are cases where one language does not have a concept which exists in another, e.g. we have no English word equivalent to 'chic' or 'tabu', it is only because we have come across these *concepts* in another language that we have felt the need to introduce them into our own. There are also the trivial cases where a new entity is discovered and hence a new name is required, but these are discoveries made within a particular science which has its methods of giving new names when needed. Philosophy, it has long been clear, is not that kind of a discipline, does not 'discover' new types of entity and hence, as was pointed out at least 150 years ago, 'stands in no need of a special terminology';[9] By the same token, philosophy is bound to leave everything as it is; there are no gaps in our language which could be pointed to by the philosopher.

I have only sketched briefly this view of philosophy because I

---

[8] Peter Winch, *Ethics & Action* (London, 1972), pp. 12–13.
[9] Hegel, *Science of Logic*, trans. A. V. Miller (London, 1969), p. 32.

assume that it is well known and understood at the present by those engaged in philosophy. My argument is that Austin exemplified this when at work but failed to grasp the full nature of what he was doing when he came to talk about his method. He appears to have accepted too easily the remarks of hostile critics and hence to have given away too much in such passages as those I have already quoted from 'A plea for excuses'. It might be possible to give an innocuous interpretation of 'prising words off the world', taking it to mean that we are examining them and not using them to make substantive statements, but such phrases as 'relook at the world without blinkers' cannot be explained away so easily. The charge of triviality is an infuriating one, particularly when one knows that one is doing something important, is genuinely making progress in an area where philosophers have been bogged down for a long time. If all that were at issue were isolated remarks which were inserted to convince opponents that they were mistaken, then it would be possible to ignore them and concentrate on the real meat of linguistic phenomenology. Unfortunately this is not the case. There is a kind of general view of language, particularly in the later writings, which is both at odds with his earlier practice and disastrously wrong, a denial of the method of linguistic phenomenology. It is this which leads him to produce *How to Do Things with Words*. In the remainder of this paper I want to try and show how Austin goes astray.

There are two main reasons that I have been able to discern; first, the urge to generality which I have already mentioned, and second, certain aspects of Austin's view of language, in particular his functional and evolutionary notions. He can give a very good reply to those who object to the study of the use of words by saying that usage varies:

When we come down to cases, it transpires in the very great majority that what we had thought was our wanting to say different things of and in *the same* situation was really not so – we had simply imagined the situation *slightly* differently: which is all too easy to do, because of course no situation . . . is ever 'completely' described (*PP*, pp. 183–4).

Shortly after, however, he implies a rather different view:

Certainly, then, ordinary language is *not* the last word: in principle it can everywhere be supplemented and improved upon and superseded. Only remember, it is the *first* word (*PP*, p. 185).

The implication seems to be that the work of the philosopher can lead to improvements in ordinary language. The examples that Austin actually cites are Psychology and the Law. As I have already said, there is no problem in language being changed as a result of empirical discoveries, and it is possible to see how the need for new distinctions can arise in the law and later get incorporated into ordinary language. Austin never suggests any alterations that need to be made in our normal way of talking as a result of his investigation of excuses or whatever; the only forms that come under attack are from the language of philosophers and these are almost by definition not ordinary language. Only if the philosopher could look at the 'world' without the aid of words would he be able to see their 'inadequacies and arbitrariness' and so suggest improvements.

Part of the reason lies in his belief that 'Words are our tools' (*PP*, p. 181), coupled with the idea that it is possible to talk of the 'fittest' or 'most efficient' forms of speech: 'Let us also assume, what is in a sense a tautology, that *in the very long run*, the forms of speech which survive will be the *fittest* (most efficient) forms of speech' (*PP*, p. 281). Incidentally he only uses this notion to account for one rather minor, and to my mind dubious, feature of English, 'the survival of words in groups where similar-sounding words mean similar things'. He does not attempt to justify the claim that the notion of efficiency will account for the 'whole general evolution of morphology, syntax and grammar (*ibid.*)'. It is not clear how he could even begin to do so. We can talk of the evolution or development of a tool or some similar artefact on the basis of efficiency, but this is because it has a function which can be stated independently of its use. The user knows what he wants to achieve by means of the tool, and so can consider how to improve it. He may not be able to do so; many hopeful inventors find that their ideas cannot be translated into reality because there is no substance in the world with the appropriate properties. An invented word may fail for lack of euphony, as is said to have happened with the original name for 'lawn tennis', but the invention of names for new things is a rare event in language, not part of its normal growth. Connected perhaps with this is Austin's surprisingly Augustinian account of the origin of language: 'Briefly, let us assume, for the sake of argument and because we actually have no right to assume anything else, that 'in origin' speech consisted in any person making any noise in any situation to signify anything (*PP*, p. 281). This view of naming, the notion of words as tools and the related notion of efficiency all seem to point to a separation of language and the world which is not implicit in the 'what we would say when' formula, though it is explicit in the second half of the quotation on p. 116.

It is possible to compare words and tools in a way which does not give rise to problems, as Wittgenstein does: 'Think of the tools in a tool-box: there is a hammer, pliers, a saw, a screw-driver, a rule, a glue-pot, glue, nails and screws. – The functions of words are as diverse as the functions of these objects. (And in both cases there are similarities).'[10] The latter is concerned to break the hold of certain ways of thinking, to make us realise that not all words function in the same way. The talk of efficiency almost seems to push in the opposite direction. Certainly the idea of words as tools is deeply embedded in Austin's thinking – he tells us how to *do* things with words. At times language (or at least 'speech acts') seems to take on a manipulative aspect, as in the definition of 'perlocutionary': 'Saying something will often, or even normally, produce certain consequential effects upon the feelings, thoughts or actions of the audience, or of the speaker, or of other persons: and it may be done with the design, intention, or purpose of producing them...' (*HTD*, p. 101). It may seem that this charge is unfair to Austin, but unless there is some such notion implicit in what he says, it is hard to see how the notion of 'efficiency' or 'fitness' can begin to get a hold. I am not sure how we could come to see that: 'The explicit performative formula, moreover, is only the last and "most successful" of numerous speech-devices which have always been used with greater or less success to perform the same function (just as measurement or standardization was the most successful device ever invented for developing *precision* of speech)' (*HTD*, p. 73).

It is not clear why we can be confident that the 'more primitive' or 'vaguer' performative was intended to perform the *same* function as ours. Only if we could know the overall purpose of language could we begin to assess the fitness of particular devices in it. There are, of course, many problems with the use of the term 'fitness' in connection with biological evolution. It is because we can attribute the goal of survival to organisms that we can count as succesful those that do, can say that they

---

[10] *Philosophical Investigations*, §11.

are 'fit'. Unless we can similarly attribute some such goal to language, or to speaking, we are debarred from applying the word to it. Certainly we do not talk, or talk in the ways we do, because we have found that it *pays* to do so.

Part of the trouble is that Austin does not seem to take seriously the relation between language and society; he makes a few perfunctory references to the way 'in which language develops in tune with the society of which it is the language' (*PP*, p. 245), but these seem either gestures in the direction of accepted views or else to involve the same disastrous separation of words and the world, to imply that there is a recognised problem for which a linguistic solution is introduced:

If I say something like 'I shall be there', it may not be certain whether it is a promise, or an expression of intention, or perhaps even a forecast of my future behaviour, of what is going to happen to me; and it may matter a good deal, at least in developed societies, precisely which of these things it is. And that is why the explicit performative verb is evolved – to make clear exactly which it is, how far it commits me and in what way, and so forth (*PP*, pp. 244–5).

It seems that, as with certain other dubious features in his later philosophy, the notion of evolution was originally introduced by Austin as a negative one, to counter certain common views:

our common stock of words embodies all the distinctions men have found worth drawing, and the connexions they have found worth marking, in the lifetimes of many generations: these surely are likely to be more numerous, more sound, since they have stood up to the long test of the survival of the fittest, and more subtle, at least in all ordinary and reasonably practical matters, than any you or I are likely to think up in our arm-chairs of an afternoon – the most favoured alternative method (*PP*, p. 182).

If we read this passage as a defence of a method under attack there is much to be said for it. Only when it becomes a positive doctrine, something which explains the functioning of our language, do the flaws become apparent. Of course I am not denying that languages do change over time, nor that there is a 'fit' between the language and the society of which it is a language – how could it be otherwise? My objection is that Austin switches from a phenomenological view of language, one which looks at it from the inside as it were, to an external view which holds it apart from the world.

Austin appears to have invoked the notion of evolution in order to explain language in some sense, and the same is true of the classification which bulks so large in *How to Do Things with Words*. It is possible to see why he gets into this position given his original starting point, his concern with performative utterances. It seems to make sense to explain the existence of, say, the institution of promising in terms of the role it plays in our form of life, because we can indicate the disadvantages we would feel if deprived of that institution. Naturally such an explanation will refer to our desires and interests. If we can classify all forms of 'illocutions', it seems to follow that we can similarly explain them in terms of desires and interests and that thus a general explanation of a large part of language will have been obtained. What is incoherent here is the idea that it is possible to talk of 'desires and interests' independently of a language and form of life, as if they could exist prior to their embodiment. Austin is forced into this position by what might be called his 'linguistic *epoché*', his prising words off the world.[11] It might be claimed that the error is implicit in the title *How to Do Things with Words*, for this can be seen to embody the suggestion that words are things which we can use to obtain effects that might be obtained in other ways.

Thus it is the abandonment of his own 'linguistic phenomenology' which leads Austin astray. Ironically enough the motive for this abandonment seems to have been that very desire for generality which he had so often castigated in other thinkers. Austin's permanent contribution to philosophy lies in the detailed application of his method to particular cases. What he does in 'A plea for Excuses' and other such writings can legitimately be called 'linguistic phenomenology', though with the proviso that it is not a new method of philosophising but simply what philosophy itself is in this day and age.

[11] Austin's reliance on 'divinest Etymology' should also be considered in relation to this point. All I can say here is that it seems that one can refer to etymology to confirm a point already established phenomenologically, not use it to make a substantive one on its own.

On the Sense of
Method in Phenomenology

RICHARD M. ZANER

The difficulties and risks involved in *talking about* phenomenological methodology are like those involved in *talking about* philosophy itself. Phenomenology is conceived essentially as a principle of philosophical criticism, and its chief method is that of *reduction* and *epoché*. Phenomenological reduction is explained in terms of the 'shifts of focal attention', and consequent 'reflective orientations', which permit philosophical criticism of any given context (art, science, etc.), any belief, value, idea; and, most importantly, the explication of that 'natural attitude' which involves the belief in the existence of a world 'out there'.

Richard M. Zaner is Easterwood Professor of Philosophy at Southern Methodist University, Dallas. His publications include: *The Problem of Embodiment* (The Hague: Martinus Nijhoff, 1964); *The Way of Phenomenology* (New York: Pegasus Press, 1970). He has co-edited *Existentialism and Phenomenology* (New York, 1973), as well as three volumes in the series *Selected Studies in Phenomenology and Existential Phenomenology* published by M. Nijhoff.

1. The problem of method in phenomenology centres on the concept of *phenomenological reduction*. Admittedly it was not until after 1913 – the year in which Husserl published Book One of his *Ideas* – that the term 'phenomenological reduction' began to feature prominently in Husserl's writings. Nevertheless he had made use of something like reduction long before this (especially in connection with the practice of ideation, in his *Logical Investigations* (1900–1), and in his lectures on inner-time consciousness (1905–6) later published under that title), but the actual formulation of the method came only with the *Ideas*. Subsequent reflection throughout his career led to many variations, modifications, and revisions, although it does seem apparent that the central methodological point remains.

Unlike what has come to be known as 'reductivism' (e.g., in philosophy of science), the phenomenological notion has nothing whatever to do with any attempt to simplify or economize, much less to try and explain one region by showing it to be reducible to another. Rather, the basic thrust is found in the literal meaning of the term 'reduction': a leading back to origins, beginnings, which have become obscure, hidden, or covered over by other things. What Husserl, in *Ideas*, calls the 'fundamental meditation' of phenomenology throws light on a rudimentary and unquestioned 'natural' commitment to, there being 'the world'. Not unlike what Santayana calls 'animal faith', or Hume 'belief', Husserl speaks of the 'natural attitude' and its 'general thesis', which is not so much a judgment as it is a rudimentary attitude towards 'what is': viz., *that* there is a 'world' over and above whatever may be cancelled out of it under the name of 'hallucination' or 'illusion'.

This fundamental attitude at the root of our every experience of things (as things *in the world*) is an 'attitude': i.e., an orientation towards things (in the world), a way of regarding which is not so much an explicit action as it is an implicit *informing* of our lives. It is, moreover, 'natural': i.e., expressive of the fundamental tendency of consciousness to 'posit' or 'take a stand toward' whatever it encounters or experiences. The 'phenomenological epoché and reduction' is the systematic effort to bring that natural attitude itself into focus. Thus, Husserl's mathematical metaphor of 'bracketing' (*einklammern*) in no way denies what is naturally believed in or posited by natural consciousness; it rather is a deliberate effort to 'suspend' or 'put in abeyance' that attitude in order to examine it in depth.

Several more preliminary remarks might be useful. To the extent that it is the inherent tendency of consciousness to 'posit' or 'take a stand towards' whatever is encountered, any particular process or act of awareness is a specific 'orientation' with respect to such 'objects', and thus the latter always have a specific 'sense' or 'meaning' as a function of the specific type of orientation at hand in any particular case. Thus, while driving my injured son to the hospital, and coming upon a red traffic light, the light has the sense not only of 'stop' (thanks to the context of traffic rules and regulations) but of 'critical interruption', possibly 'disastrous', in terms of 'what I am doing' – i.e. my 'stance' toward such objects of awareness. It is the same for every possible awareness and object of awareness. In this sense, Husserl insists (1) that every awareness, even the simplest, is not merely an awareness *of* something, but includes some modality of 'positing' (*Positionalität*): the awareness has its doxic ('belief'), emotive, valuative, volitional components. And, (2) Husserl contends that every *awareness-of*, and *that-of-which* there is the awareness, are *essentially correlated* (he terms this the 'correlational apriori'). Hence, to analyze any objectivity whatsoever commits one to the analysis of its correlated mode of awareness, through which that objectivity is presented or otherwise encountered; and, to analyze any awareness (perception, memory, anticipation, judgment, symbolization, etc.) necessarily commits one to the analysis of its correlated objectivity. The awareness (*noesis*) has its objective correlate (*noema*): this complex is expressed by the central Husserlian concept of intentionality (*Intentionalität*).

To be sure, most of the time we are not explicitly aware of things *as they are presented through specific acts of consciousness*, any more than we are explicitly aware of our own acts of awarenesses *as consciousnesses of specific objective correlates*. That is, our focal attention is for the most part directed simply to objects, and rarely to *objects-as-meant* or *intended*. The methodological step expressed by the 'reduction and epoché', as will be argued shortly, is designed expressly to enable the reflecting philosopher to bring that correlational apriori to *explicit attention*.

The reduction is therefore a strictly methodological step to enable the philosopher to make explicit what is all along implicit and taken for granted by each of us. In the following I try to make this important step clearer, and to show how it is connected with the act of philosophical reflection more generally.

The latter, as Bergson put it, 'does violence' to our 'natural' ways of thinking, in that the philosopher attempts to explicate (make explicit) what is taken for granted, the hidden, and obscure, in every dimension. Phenomenological reflection, then, turns out to be the fundamental philosophical act of criticism, carried out 'to the end'.

However, when reading phenomenological literature the impression that one often gets is that the method of phenomenological reduction is not only impossibly difficult and complex, but that it is a veritable embarrassment, an effrontery, to cognition. Phenomenologists who write about *epoché* and reduction seem plainly insulting, or self-indulgent. One example, perhaps the most notable, will suffice to illustrate the situation.

Noting that 'speaking *about* phenomenology presupposes having actually passed along its way',[1] Eugen Fink then goes on to say that

Every discussion of the phenomenological reduction, no matter how incomplete, finds itself faced with the unavoidable difficulty of being compelled to speak about it as if it were an activity of knowledge which it is always possible to perform, and which from the very start lies within the horizon of our human possibilities. In truth, however, it does not at all present a possibility for our *human* existence. The unfamiliarity of the reduction is therefore not only an unfamiliarity with it as a fact, but is also an unfamiliarity with its possibility. Although we also say that all talk about a particularly difficult kind of knowledge quite remote from our everyday knowing (for example, the knowledge of physics) presupposes *actually having been involved with it* . . . a discussion of the reduction not only signifies an appeal to its actual performance, but also imperatively requires the performance of an act which places us beyond the horizon of our own possibilities, which 'transcends' our *human* possibilities . . .[2]

The reduction purports to be a focusing on and suspension of the deeply-rooted 'natural attitude' which ultimately defines our existence as human beings. Because of this, Fink continues, nothing within the context of 'natural living' can either explain or motivate the suspension of that 'attitude'. Hence, its radical unfamiliarity:

---

[1] Eugen Fink, 'The phenomenological philosophy of Edmund Husserl and contemporary criticism', in R. O. Elveton (ed. and trans.), *The Phenomenology of Edmund Husserl: Selected Critical Readings* (Chicago: Quadrangle Books, 1970), p. 103.

[2] *Ibid.* p. 105; subsequent quotations from this article are from the same place.

The reduction becomes knowable in its '*transcendental* motivation' only with the transcending of the world. This means that the reduction is its own presupposition insofar as it alone opens up that dimension of problems with reference to which it establishes the possibility of theoretical knowledge. This strange paradox of the beginning of philosophical reflection finds expression within the fundamental perplexity into which all attempts to explicate the phenomenological reduction fall. Unmotivated and unfamiliar with respect to its possibility, every exposition of the phenomenological reduction is in a unique way *false*.

The reason for this is, perhaps just as strangely, readily at hand: philosophical reflection – to use Bergson's words again – requires us 'to do violence' to our usual ways of thinking; the mind 'has to reverse the direction of the operation by which it habitually thinks, has perpetually to revise, or rather to recast, all its categories'[3]. In other words, not only the specific philosophical act of *epoché* and reduction, but philosophy itself, are essentially *alien* to 'the everyday'. Thus, Fink concludes:

Being shut off from the dimension of the 'transcendental' belongs to the essence of the imprisonment within the world which defines the natural attitude. Phenomenology's problem is not one which can be explained within the compass of the natural attitude. The introduction to philosophy presents itself as the *exemplum crucis* of the *leading out* of the natural attitude which begins with the natural attitude.

The dilemma is not an unfamiliar one, of course. One need recall only the deeply perplexing question neatly rooted in Plato's myth of the cave. Once the questioner is freed from his bonds, he is somehow able to prod and pry others loose from theirs. But how is this possible? And, even more, who frees the first from his bonds? Husserl, the founder of and still principal figure in phenomenological philosophy, was plagued with this strange issue all his philosophical life. Near the apex of his career, he could write only that the philosopher of necessity needs

a resolution of his own through which alone, only and originarily, he created himself (as) a philosopher, a primal investiture, so to speak, which is originary autocreation. No one can get into philosophy accidentally.[4]

---

[3] Cf. Henri Bergson, *Introduction to Metaphysics*, trans. T. E. Hulme (Indianapolis and New York: Bobbs-Merrill, 2nd ed., 1955), p. 51.

[4] Edmund Husserl, *Erste Philosophie* (1923–4), Part II. Husserliana VIII (The Hague: Martinus Nijhoff, 1959), p. 19.

The 'embarrassment' which so many phenomenological writings seem intractably to trade on, thus, turns out to be inherent to philosophy itself. This, at least, is Husserl's view – one which he and others have seen as the central theme of philosophy since Descartes. For Husserl, Ludwig Landgrebe correctly stresses,

The task of philosophy is thus no longer merely the grounding of the knowledge of the world by means of the sciences; it is rather the justification of striving for knowledge ... (which) need not be taken as a self-warranting and unquestionable possibility for man, so that its justification need only be the adequate foundation of the methodological steps by which cognition is obtained.[5]

The point in all this is two-fold: first, the problem of 'talking about' phenomenology is, ultimately, the same as 'talking about' philosophy itself; and, the method of 'epoché and reduction' must be understood as essential to the 'task of philosophy' itself – the justification of the very striving for knowledge itself. But there is a further point to be made: the question concerning the justification of philosophical reflection – the 'seeking-to-know' anything, hence of *methodology* – is no mere idle pastime. Throughout his career, Husserl's writings have a marked urgency: the future of reason, hence philosophy and all other epistemic endeavours, is now at stake, thanks to 'a sort of collapse of all naive cognitive and scientific values',[6] the presence of which can be witnessed in many facets of modern culture. The act of philosophical reflection, therefore, has necessarily an *ethical* import.[7] When the guiding values and norms of life and thought come under radical suspicion, then what is called for is a radical criticism of life and thought.[8] The method of *epoché* and reduction is accordingly no mere intellectual game. It turns out to be an imperative *task* which necessarily reaches to, indeed through, the very roots of our existence as human beings.

As such, there can simply be no question of understanding

---

[5] Ludwig Landgrebe, 'The problem of the beginning of philosophy in Husserl's phenomenology', in Lester E. Embree (ed.), *Life-World and Consciousness: Essays for Aron Gurwitsch* (Evanston: Northwestern University Press, 1972), p. 44.

[6] Husserl, *Erste Philosophie*, p. 196 (reference in note 4 above).

[7] Landgrebe, *op. cit.* pp. 44–9 and 51–3 (reference in note 5 above).

[8] Cf. Husserl's essay, 'Philosophy as rigorous science', included in *Phenomenology and the Crisis of Philosophy*, trans., notes and introduction Quentin Lauer (New York: Harper Torchbooks, Harper & Row, 1965), where this theme is articulated in detail. It was published in 1910.

this 'method', much less what is purportedly disclosed through its use, except on condition that one *actually undergoes* it. In Ortega's terms, one cannot acquire knowledge unless in his own life one finds that he *has to know*.[9] Which is just what Socrates claimed: to know is an actual happening occasioned by encountering directly a fundamental *aporia* – the actual experience of not-knowing and knowing that one has to know in order to continue to be oneself.

2. With that as background, it is hopefully possible to say something 'about' this method. First, without suggesting that this is the whole of the matter, it nevertheless seems clear to me that a good deal of the mystification about the method has its source in that 'crisis of reason'. I mean: whatever may be the inherent difficulties of the reduction, if Husserl is correct in his sense of the radical crisis of contemporary human life and reason, then it is hardly surprising that the effort to come to terms intellectually with that crisis appears cognitively and linguistically tortuous. If philosophy cannot be regarded as automatically 'self-justifying', then neither can language, much less other modes of epistemic endeavour. Within the fundamentally historical setting of phenomenology, indeed of philosophy, what is of the utmost importance is finding a *way into and through* (*meta-hodas*) the issues at hand. The problem of the 'crisis of reason' is inseparable from the problem of method, as is the problem of the sense and justification of reason. In different terms, 'method' and 'knowing' are but two facets of the same. If the crisis makes a radical criticism necessary, the 'way' of conducting that criticism is equally necessary. Phenomenology, as Husserl constantly emphasized, is the discipline of philosophical criticism; its 'way' is, moreover, that delineated by the terms, '*epoché* and reduction'. These can now be given some sense.

3. I provide two examples, as clues to the method. First, assume that a serious problem crops up in a person's life – where 'serious' indicates only that the matter is serious for him. What happens? Among other things,[10] the occurrence of the problem

---

[9] See his *What is Philosophy?* (New York: W. W. Norton, 1960), especially chs. 5, 10 and 11.
[10] See Richard M. Zaner, 'The radical reality of the human body', *Humanitas*, Vol. II, no. 1 (1966), pp. 73–87; and *The Way of Phenomenology* (New York: Pegasus Press, Bobbs-Merrill, 1970).

signifies that it has become important for him to know what and
how matters actually stand, what things really are.[11] His usual
ways of acting and thinking have proved to be inadequate, or
wrong, and precisely in view of the 'seriousness-to-him' of the
situation it becomes imperative that he find out 'what is really
the case'. If his values, beliefs, habits, etc., are inadequate or
lead to wrong conclusions, he can no longer presume their
efficacy. Instead, he must 'stop and think', as Dewey said; i.e.
he is obliged to probe and question in the effort to find out, to
know what is correct. The 'problem' calls for 'resolution', and
if his ways of handling these do not work he is forced to seek
other ways. He may well continue, or want to continue,
holding to those values and beliefs; but to the extent that they
prove inadequate or wrong in the face of this concrete problem,
he must set them aside and seek for others. And, to the extent
that finding, knowing, is important to him, he has little choice
but to 'think things through for himself'. He 'stops' – i.e. calls
into question and seeks for possible other ways of dealing with
the situation. If he is serious and deliberate, his course of action
and thought will be to assess the things themselves *for himself*.

He knows already from his own experience the difference
between accepting something to be true on the basis of actually
encountering it himself (in the way appropriate to it); accepting
it on the basis of his past experience; on the basis of someone
else's judgment (who may or may not have himself actually
encountered it); and so on. He knows, too, that these bases
for acceptance are not equally good: accepting on the basis of
one's own experience is in general by far the best. He therefore
tries to obtain the best possible evidence to enable him correctly to assess the situation, and to settle the issue.

From this it is a small step to the fundamental principle of
phenomenological methodology – necessary to understanding
epoché and reduction. As stated by Dorion Cairns, it is:

*No opinion is to be accepted as philosophical knowledge unless it is seen to
be adequately established by observation of what is seen as itself given 'in
person'. Any belief seen to be incompatible with what is seen to be itself
given is to be rejected. Towards opinions that fall in neither class –*

[11] Husserl makes this point emphatically; see his *Formal and Transcendental Logic*,
trans. Dorion Cairns (The Hague: Martinus Nijhoff, 1969), pp. 277–8.

whether they be one's own or another's – one is to adopt an 'official' philo-
sophical attitude of neutrality.[12]

Our knowledge is lodged in judgments, and judgments are
not only assertions about certain states of affairs; they point to a
mode of encounter appropriate to those states of affairs – the
mode of evidence that justifies the judgments concerned. We
know from everyday life that not every judgment is based on
that actual mode of encounter called 'sense perception', or
even an encounter with individual things. We believe in, and
incorporate our beliefs into judgments about, an incredibly
rich range of affairs other than those directly open to sense
perception: past affairs, mental affairs, political and social
goals, laws and social 'recipes of action', institutions (family,
marriage, church, etc.), symbols, signs, ethical, aesthetic and
religious values, and on and on. Hence, where the principle
asserts the necessity of 'adequate observation', this must be
taken both literally and contextually: one must 'get at' the
affairs themselves, observe them in the way most appropriate to
them, and what kind of observation is called for will necessarily
vary according to the nature of what we judge about, believe in,
or seek to know.

The principle asserts, then, that no belief is philosophically
acceptable unless it is established on the basis of adequate
evidence. This is a condition of legitimacy of epistemic claims.
However, such claims not only have this epistemic function,
but also what Cairns calls a 'communicative function'. One
may say that all epistemic claims are essentially dual in
character: *they assert something to be the case, and they serve as communicative guides.*

Statements that are strictly phenomenological in the Husserlian
sense are to be used as guides for observation, much as one might
use a previous observer's description of a landscape as an aid in
distinguishing its features while all the time it lies before one's
eye's . . . (Such) assistance is useful not only because some observations
are intrinsically difficult but also because prejudices are likely to

---

[12] Dorion Cairns, 'An approach to Husserlian Phenomenology', in F. Kersten & R.
Zaner (eds.), *Phenomenology: Continuation and Criticism, Essays in Memory of Dorion
Cairns*, Phaenomenologica (The Hague: Martinus Nijhoff, 1973), p. 224. Husserl
incorporates this into what he calls the 'normative principle of evidence', *Cartesian
Meditations*, trans. Dorion Cairns (The Hague: Martinus Nijhoff, 1960), p. 14.

induce one to overlook or explain away what is actually there to be seen. The Husserlian phenomenologist's appeal to 'immediate' inspection is not made on the assumption that a Husserlian phenomenological proposition need only be understood for its truth to become evident forthwith. The truth of an opinion is seen 'immediately' only when its coincidence with a given fact, as judged on the basis of the very matters entering into it, is seen. And often it is a long and hard road to a position from which one can see the truth of an opinion – 'immediately'.[13]

The first clue to understanding *epoché* and reduction is, then, this fundamental principle of method – one which is plainly present in our daily lives, and which demonstrates the dual character of every result obtained.

4. A second clue can now be advanced. The situation faced by the person in the above example (oversimplified though it was) can be described in slightly different terms. Any 'problem' (or: disturbance, crisis, dilemma, in life) stands out from a background of what is unproblematic; in fact it is only by reference to the latter that anything can stand out as 'problematic', 'unfamiliar', 'unexpected', and the like. Moreover not only does the unexpected, unfamiliar or unusual call attention to itself, but what has hitherto been accepted as familiar, expected and usual is brought into question. At the least, some elements of what has been taken for granted come into question – which elements, how many, and the degree to which they are at issue, depends on the person's concrete situation, his prevailing tasks and interests, and the seriousness it has for him. To the extent the person takes his situation – ultimately, his life – seriously, the problematic situation is critical for him; and to the extent that he seriously *seeks to know* 'what and how things actually are', he is himself called on to be critical: to question, seek, find out, assess, justify. That is, he must cease taking for granted what has been up to now accepted as unquestioned. This move is, of course, strictly contextual: in actual situations it is exercised only to the point where the issue is resolved, the unfamiliar made familiar, the unexpected accounted for, and the person has for his prevailing purposes no need to push matters any further. Even though it is a mode of critical thinking, it is restricted to the matters at hand, and lapses when resolution is achieved. Still, the *kind* of thing he does is

[13] *Ibid.* p. 227.

not nothing, and provides a basic clue to understanding phenomenology and philosophical reflection generally.

The phenomenologist engages in criticism, and the kind of thing he does is thus a *descriptive explication* of what is taken for granted; he seeks to make explicit what is implicit. He makes these affairs 'present themselves' for his reflective inspection, in the way appropriate to them, and on that basis makes judgments about them which are epistemic, communicative and critical in character. He seeks lasting cognitive possessions – knowledge – which are necessarily continually subject to further reflective criticism.

The crucial point here concerns the *kinds of affairs* which occupy his attention. The *epoché* and reduction have their place here: they and they alone can make accessible to the reflecting philosopher those affairs which concern him. We are witness to a radical collapse of guiding norms and values – one which sets up the imperative task of giving a radical criticism of life and reason. It would, however, be a serious error to think that any particular historical situation totally defines the prime tasks of philosophy. However urgent that crisis is, what is important is the astonishing insight it makes possible: that whatever may come into question in our practical and even our theoretical lives, our every thought and action as human beings living within the world, is undergirded by a rudimentary, wholly implicit *belief in the world*. More particularly, we discover that whatever is, and in whatever way it is, is experienced by us thanks to the continuous functioning of determinable processes of consciousness – and is, thus, strictly correlative to these. Underlying these processes and acts through which 'what is' is experienced or otherwise comes into our awareness, is that belief in the world itself. Santayana had glimpsed this primordial commitment to the world, naming it 'animal faith'. Hume, too, saw it rather clearly in what he called 'custom and habit', our inadvertent belief which alone saves him from total scepticism.[14] This elemental 'existing-within-the-belief-in-the-world', as Fink calls it, is the critical disclosure, the prime matter to be focused on:

---

[14] See Hume, *A Treatise of Human Nature*, Selby-Bigge edition (Oxford University Press, 1888). 'We have', he says, 'no choice left but betwixt a false reason and none at all', a judgment he comes to after determining that all connections lie 'merely in ourselves'. See pp. 266, 268.

What is of decisive importance is the awakening of an immeasurable astonishment over the mysteriousness of this state of affairs. To accept it as a self-evident fact is to remain blind to the greatest mystery of all, the mystery of the being of the world itself, the world which first receives meaning and the acceptance of its being from the flowing world-apperceptions, and this in terms of every content with which the world could conceivably be given to us at any moment.[15]

Hume came to the verge of this, seeing that whatever is, is strictly correlative to, or a function of, our subjective beliefs. But, instead of grasping what he had discovered as the prime philosophical issue, Hume took it as a motive for despair and scepticism.[16] Where he faltered, Husserl picks up and seeks to secure the insight, by insisting on the need for a radical criticism precisely of that marvellous 'inattention', the mysterious workings of that 'inadvertence': 'belief'.[17]

5. Such a criticism, in other words, signifies a radical and liberating reflection which 'stops at nothing'. Landgrebe puts squarely:

Only the universal resolve to stop at nothing that appears self-evident, and with this the preparedness for a constant control of our language, can lead further, step by step, in such an enlightening liberation. This resolve to perform the reduction – and that means a resolve to be prepared not to put up with, and simply not to let remain, anything of the pre-given and of the accepted – constitutes thus the only presupposition for the 'critique of life'.[18]

The *epoché* and reduction, then, fundamentally mean this resolve and preparedness to take nothing for granted. This makes clear as well, however, that there can be no straightforward exposition of this 'method', the 'talk about' it is in the strictest

---

[15] Fink, *op. cit.* pp. 109–10 (reference in note 1 above).

[16] Hume, *op. cit.* pp. 102ff., 215, 266ff., *passim* (reference in note 14 above).

[17] Husserl, deeply appreciative of Hume, discerns behind his scepticism the fundamental problem of transcendental philosophy, noting however that Hume did not push his inquiry into that critical region. See Husserl, *Formal and Transcendental Logic*, *op. cit.* pp. 256–7; and Husserl, *The Crisis of European Science and Transcendental Phenomenology*, trans. David Carr (Evanston: Northwestern University Press, 1970), pp. 96–7.

[18] Landgrebe, *op. cit.* p. 47 (reference in note 5 above).

sense *an appeal for its actual performance*.[19] All talk about it, thus, is 'false' to the precise extent that it is not done; the 'doing of it', however, is nothing else than the 'first authentic *discovery of the belief in the world*'.[20] To grasp subjectively the way human life is rooted in the world, is to have made the decisive discovery: that you are a human agent in the world continually living within that elemental commitment to, that animal faith in, the world. To have discovered that belief, that natural attitude, is at the same time to have discovered oneself as the human performer of the belief. And, with that, one recognizes that the multiple 'objects' within the world are all given or otherwise presented, with some modality or other, through or by means of certain processes and acts of consciousness; the two, awareness (consciousness, experience) and object, are strictly correlates, and cannot be studied except within that context.

This double disclosure is but the first step, one which Hume and others came close to. What is then required, if one would pose it as a philosophical problem, is *to shift one's focal attention to it for its own sake, to probe and explicate it with the resolve to stop at nothing*. This deliberate, explicitly adopted philosophical shift of attention, we can now say, is what is to be understood as the '*epoché*'; the resultant 'orientation' or 'attitude' – that self-consciously maintained resolve to reflect radically on whatever presents itself – is the 'reduction'. If one has grasped this, it then becomes clear that a number of other shifts of attention and their consequent reflective orientations are possible. When one begins to grasp and on that basis to describe 'objects' strictly as they are experienced, one sees also all the other 'facts' which have been present all along prior to the initial discovery and its *epoché* and reduction. The *epoché* and reduction signify only that one's focal attention has been shifted in order to view this complex itself, for its own sake. The difference – one secured by the deliberate shift of attention and its maintained orientation – is that now one's focus is on the *world-as-believed-in* (and its various 'objects') and, correlatively, *oneself-as-believing-in-the-world*. Apprehending this correlation – the 'correlational Apriori', as Husserl called it – permits one to begin to appreciate that, however significant this step in

---

[19] Cf. Fink, *op. cit.* p. 106 (reference in note 1 above).
[20] *Ibid.* p. 110.

truth is, it is still *critically incomplete*, is not itself yet free from all presuppositions. Most importantly, one must go on to recognize that even at the level of this reflective orientation one is still accepting one's own mental life and its particular processes and acts of awareness (perceiving, remembering, loving, wishing, judging, inferring, and the like) as going on within the world, as *mundane*. That is, he must needs go on to recognize, disengage and subsequently explicate that very sense of mundanity itself, i.e. the experiencing of oneself as a being-within-the-world along with other beings-within-the-world. This is the discovery of the fundamental *status* of one's own mental life, one which is presented to reflection as more fundamental than one's experienced status as 'mundane'.

To put it differently, the reflecting philosopher must at some point push his inquiry still further; his own discovery of himself as believing-in-the-world (and its correlate: the world-as-believed-in) and this reflective examination of this fact reveals that his consciousness is experienced and believed in as worldly, among other worldly affairs. Because of that, the act of discovery cannot itself be a mundane act; it cannot be at the same level as the other mundane acts one has disclosed. As Landgrebe puts it, 'This possibility of . . . self-knowing, which is the presupposition for man's ability to turn himself critically toward all valuing and everything that is valued and everything that exists, is not derivable from anything else . . . It is a *transcendental experience* in the following sense: it is the ground on the basis of which there is experience. . .'[21]

In still different terms, the reflective act of apprehending oneself as a worldly human creature believing in (in very much the sense which Hume gave to this), acting in and on, the world, and the world as the strict correlate of these (a point which Hume failed to grasp) – this reflective act is itself something to be focused on. The attentive focus on it, and on any other act of reflection whatsoever, shows that it cannot be derived from anything else; rather, it makes possible all other acts of reflection or 'self-knowing'. It is something authentic in its own right, and *needs to be accounted for*. Doing so reveals that one is confronted with a different, and more fundamental, status of

---

[21] Landgrebe, *op. cit.* p. 52 (reference in note 5 above).

oneself and one's mental life, than its status as worldly: one's transcendental status.

One final way of putting the point may be helpful. I find myself as a being who is an *object in the world*, and also I find myself as a *subject for whom* all objects are objects. But, included in the latter is myself: I find, that is, that *dual status itself*. I am reflexively aware of my being both an object and a subject in and for the world. *That reflexivity itself* reveals a more fundamental status of my being: my being as *transcendental ego*. The focus on this status is the transcendental *epoché*, and the appropriate orientation towards it is the transcendental reduction. So far as it is legitimate to say that my reflection on these affairs is a mode of experience (reflective experience, on the basis of which judgments are made), it is legitimate and necessary to call it transcendental experience.

6. *Epoché* and reduction, therefore, are terms designating these various shifts of attention and the reflective attitude or orientation maintained in order systematically to study whatever is thereby found. Such terms as 'bracketing', 'suspension', and the like, used to characterize these methodical steps designate no more and no less than that. To focus on the natural attitude is effectively no longer to take it for granted. But this reflective focusing assuredly does not signify the disappearance of the belief in the world 'out there'. This belief is there all along, and is not even grasped as such except by means of the *epoché* and reduction.

If a radical critique of life is called for, this can only mean that one must resolve to stop at nothing – which expresses the fundamental sense of phenomenology. In this sense, phenomenology is in no way merely one more metaphysical stance alongside others; it is rather understandable solely as the central discipline of philosophy itself: that of fundamental criticism, whose prime 'ways into and through to' its themes and problems are a series of epochés and reductions, only some of which have been indicated here. The point of this essay is merely that phenomenology has its place within the nature and tasks of philosophy, and is not one more 'point of view' on the nature of things alongside other 'points of view'. However interesting and valuable such points of view may be they all presuppose the kind of fundamental criticism herein described.

7. A final comment seems desirable. It is well known that Husserl frequently characterized his work, especially what he came to call 'transcendental phenomenology', as a 'transcendental idealism'. At the same time, he just as often spoke of phenomenology as a genuine 'empiricism'. While it is doubtlessly true that one ought not to place much stock in such labels, for they can too easily become mere catchwords conveying little substantive meaning, what I have been concerned to show in this essay is that, conceived as philosophical criticism, and established on systematic and methodologically firm foundations, phenomenology is quite properly conceived not only as transcendental idealism but as a *new empiricism* – so long as such terms are understood with the sense Husserl gave to them.

Phenomenological philosophy is 'transcendental', one can say, because it is *foundational*, seeking to uncover and explicatively to analyze the necessary presuppositions of every actual and possible object and process of consciousness, leading ultimately to the grounds for philosophical reflection itself. It is therefore also 'idealism' because, as criticism, it is obliged to turn to consciousness itself as a complex of acts and processes by and through which alone are objects of any and all types whatever presented, experienced, or otherwise made known. This, however, in no way entails the claim that all objects are either 'mental' or reduced to consciousness; to the contrary, objects are for the most part transcendent to (empirical) consciousness, and a great many of them are strictly 'non-mental'.

The 'empiricist' feature of Husserl's philosophy consists in this: that this philosophy insists that positing anything beyond all possible experience of any kind is sheer nonsense, and that it is to the 'things themselves' of experience, and precisely *as* experienced (in whatever way), that one must ultimately appeal for all evidence and knowledge. But it is a 'new' empiricism, because 'experience' has been critically disclosed as manifestly richer and enormously more stratified and differentiated than any tradition empiricism understood it to be. Husserl expressed this complex sense of his work even more succinctly:

This idealism is not a product of sportive argumentation, a prize to be won in the dialectical contest with 'realisms'. It is sense-explication achieved by *actual work*, and explication carried out as regards every type of existent ever conceivable by me, the ego, and specifically as regards the transcendency actually given to me beforehand through experience: Nature, culture, the world as a whole. But that signifies: systematic uncovering of the constituting intentionality itself. *The proof of this idealism is therefore phenomenology itself.*[22]

It is to the 'uncovering of the constituting intentionality itself' that the battery of epoches and reductions – focal shifts of reflective attention – are directed, and it is from the phenomenon of intentionality itself that these methods receive their fundamental sense and justification: 'sense-explication achieved by actual work'.

---

[22] Husserl, *Cartesian Meditations*, trans. Dorion Cairns (The Hague: Martinus Nijhoff, 1960), p. 86.

Phenomenology and the Meaning of Realism

J. N. FINDLAY

Husserl's philosophy is phenomenological, i.e. it studies things solely *qua* appearing to consciousness or 'constituted' by and for consciousness, and suspends all transcendent affirmations. This theory was first developed in the abstract fields of number and logical form, and later extended to the givenness of objects in space and time, to intersubjective life and to primitive, 'pre-predicative' experience. Husserl at one point in his development affirmed, on epistemological and ontological grounds, the dependence of all objectivity on constitutive subjectivity; but this affirmation involved a departure from the phenomenological suspense which he had inculcated and of which he had made such valuable use.

J. N. Findlay is Professor of Philosophy at Boston University. He has held professorial chairs in Philosophy at several British and American universities. His principal works are: *Meinong's Theory of Objects and Values* (1933, 1963); *Hegel: A Re-Examination* (1958); *Values and Intentions* (1961); *Language, Mind and Value* (1963); *The Discipline of the Cave* (1966); *The Transcendence of the Cave* (1967); Translation of Husserl's *Logical Investigations* (1970); *Axiological Ethics* (1970); *Ascent to the Absolute* (1970); *Plato: The Written and Unwritten Doctrines* (1974).

The character of the illumination shed by Husserl on philosophy is at once brought out by the title he gave to his system: it is a phenomenological philosophy, a systematic study of 'the appearances'. It is a study of everything whatsoever in so far as it appears or is given to consciousness, even of such things as are given as transcending consciousness, or as always partially eluding it, and it is also a study of the *manners* in which such appearance is achieved, the manifold 'acts', noeses or conscious stances which can themselves, with some initial reluctance, be made to appear before consciousness, thus revealing such second-order character as they may have over and above whatever content appears *in* them. And even the appearances of such higher-order stances and manners can themselves be made to appear in a yet higher-order stance or act – the phenomenology of philosophical phenomenology. But while this systematic study of 'the appearances' attaches great weight to the distinction between rationally justified, reality-revealing 'appearances', and those which lack such prerogatives, it does not cast the latter into the outer darkness. It recognizes, with the wiser Greeks, that 'that which is not', even that which is inherently absurd, is something that can be 'meant', intended, brought before consciousness, even in an incomplete manner 'perceived', and that it must in a sense be part of 'the phenomena' if only to be excluded from its more rationally ordered segments. The phenomenology of fiction, wild or tame, is as definite and important as the phenomenology of fact and science, and the phenomenology of illogic and even of fragmented senselessness as of the well-formed, well-attested, inwardly and outwardly consistent matter of fact and truth. And its conception of what can 'appear' before consciousness is not restricted to what enjoys the palpability of sense. It includes whatever can be 'read' (as we like to put it) into the things given to our senses; their deficiencies, their background, their likely continuations, their membership of certain kinds, their conformity to these or those standards and so on indefinitely. And 'the appearances' further include all those detached meanings which language above all renders it easy for us to grasp, though their ability to make an appearance prior to and independent of linguistic aid is also something that cannot be doubted: the vague menaces and presences and atmospheres which haunt us, the more precisely clipped contents associated with regularly used adjectives and common names, or with well-constructed sentences, or even with detached connectives, expletives and other disject parts of syntax. Even if no 'realities' can be adjudged fit to correspond to such subjectively experienced 'senses', something plainly *appears* before us whenever we have experience of them, and their own occurrence as appearances likewise constitutes itself as a phenomenon. And even if, in certain special ways of considering the matter, it may be thought reasonable to 'base' the conscious appearances and whatever appears in them, whether wholly or in part, on peculiar arrangements which do not form part of their intrinsic structure or content – as when we drag in processes held to occur in nerve-cells or make use of other forms of extrinsic basing – this does not bring the content of such basing a jot closer to that of 'the appearances' in question, and it further obliges us, no matter what rationality there may be in such 'basing', to see how the things it uses to base conscious appearances, are themselves set before us as objects in certain other conscious appearances. Nothing whatever can climb by a back stair into the charmed circle of consciousness: it can only enter by the front door, by being consciously introduced or acknowledged. Either it must be something that is in some way 'there' or 'constituted' for and by consciousness, or it must consist in something's being thus 'there' and 'constituted', i.e. it must either be something apparent or it must be the appearing of what is thus apparent, which appearing can itself also be made apparent. For surd 'causes', environmental 'conditions', underlying 'mechanisms' etc. there can only be a derivative, complexly constituted place in a pure study of 'the appearances'.

In what follows I shall try to show that while Husserl's inquiry into the structure of appearances yields many invaluable philosophical insights, Husserl misapplied his own method by proceeding to adopt what was, in effect, an idealistic stance, indicating that the being of the natural world consisted, in the final analysis, in this world being constituted by a transcendental consciousness. I shall, however, argue that this capitulation to idealism makes little difference to the merit of Husserl's intentionalist analyses or to his contributions to logical theory.

Husserl continued and developed Brentano's conception of

the mental or psychic as the sphere of self-transcending intentionality, incapable of being understood except as directed upon what may in some cases wholly lie outside of its being, and which can as readily be located nowhere at all as in any preserve or segment of the real. The self-evident absurdity of trying to describe a state of mind, without importing into one's description matters which are certainly not among the real constituents of the state in question, is one of those basic insights which it takes the highest genius simply to acknowledge, and not to distort by some inappropriate analysis in terms of whole and part. No one, we may say, can understand Husserl's phenomenology who has not grasped its transcendently realistic roots in the intentionalism of Brentano, roots which Husserl may have ingeniously 'bracketed' in various higher-order conceptions, but which in a sense remained intact and unharmed within such brackets. Those who, like most of Husserl's French interpreters, have approached him from an exclusively subjectivistic, neo-Kantian standpoint, basing themselves on his writings since 1913, and who largely bypass or ignore Brentano, never will rise to a full understanding of his phenomenology.

The beginnings of Husserl's interesting object-constituting phenomenology are to be found in the remarkable *Philosophy of Arithmetic* of 1891. There Husserl tries to show how, starting from given items that need have nothing in common beyond the fact that we pay heed to them all – a vastly better foundation for a philosophy of number than Frege's connection of numbers with common 'concepts' – we can, by collecting such items together in a single reference, set up for ourselves a new, higher-order object called an aggregate (*Inbegriff*) or a plurality (*Vielheit*), from which we can progress, by carefully abstracting from the *character* of the items thus collected, and considering them each and all merely as indeterminate 'somethings' abstractly brought before consciousness, to a generalized aggregate or plurality consisting only of such indeterminate somethings, in which however (though Husserl fails to make specific mention of the point) we must be careful to preserve the diversity or distinctness of the indeterminate items thus collected. Something and something (else) is one such generalized aggregate, something and something (else) and yet again something (else) is another, and so on indefinitely. Obviously we are fabricating for ourselves pure cases of the natural numbers, and we can then, by abstracting from any residual individuality still clinging to the notion of 'something', and concentrating only on the structural type present in all of them, progress to the new notion or generic object Natural Number, as well as to its various specific forms, the natural numbers. For any plurality to consist of something and something (else) and something (else) is for it to be a case of the Natural Number Three, and the Number Three is nothing but being a member of this species, a mode of approach which is not importantly different from that of *Principia Mathematica*. The background of such number-constitution is, however, psychologistic, since it involves *acts* of collection and abstraction, and at the period represented by the *Philosophy of Arithmetic*, such acts are even included in the significant content of the number-concepts or objects thus constituted, an aggregate being a complex explicitly held together by a psychic act of collection, while its constituent 'somethings' are items abstractly considered as mere objects of consciousness.

In the *Logical Investigations* of 1899–1901 this taint of psychologism is removed from the analysis of numerical and other formal notions. What we have before us when we consider a group or an aggregate may have been assembled before us by a mental act of collection, but we need not *reflect* on that act of collection for the group to appear before us: the aggregation together of *A* and *B* and *C* is not *given* as an aggregation imposed on *A*, *B* and *C* by our psychic activity. In the same way the abstraction of consisting of something and something and something may have been set before us by a mental act of abstractive ideation, but the ideation in question seems to play no part in the abstracted pattern itself. The *Logical Investigations* extends this notion of psychologically constituted, but not psychologistically analysable, objectivity to all the entities of reason which occur in logical theory: to the infinitely various senses or meanings, misguidedly called 'concepts', which occur in thought or speech, and which remain phenomenologically *objective* even if set before us by various subjective acts of abstractive ideation – such meanings as those of the phrases or words 'the victor of Jena', 'the Schloss at Berlin', 'culture', 'religion', 'above', 'below', 'white', 'alike' etc., to the ideal Species, e.g. Triangle as Such, Act of Will as Such, given us through abstractive ideation, but as thought-themes wholly objective, to the meanings expressed by formal connectives such as the copula, the signs of negation, disjunction, identity, conditionality etc., which though set before us through various non-independent mental syntheses or modalizations, introduce us to various factual forms which have nothing subjective about them – that either *A* or *B* will happen, that the victor of Jena *was* the defeated at Waterloo etc. – to the meanings conveyed even by incomplete, synsemantic fragments such as the 's' of plurality or of third-person action, which are to Husserl phenomenologically objective – to the meanings lastly which may involve inner contradiction, e.g. wooden iron, but which are none the less objective contents genuinely present to our thought, and wrongly rejected as meanings because we cannot concretely *envisage* anything that might correspond to them or fulfil them.

Husserl also ranges among the ideal objectivities set before us by various synthetic acts of predication etc., the states of affairs, the completed propositional meanings, true or false, that assume such a central place in Logic: that squares have equal diagonals, that Halle is on the (river) Saale etc., concatenations which include no reference to what people conceive, believe, or ought to conceive or believe, but only to what obtains or is the case no matter what people may choose to think. Logic then assumes the role of an objective discipline, telling us how various objective meanings can be fitted together into complex cases of meaning, e.g. *the passing postman* or *that the postman is passing*, and how diverse cases of meaning can be predicatively or conditionally or otherwise combined into propositional unities which then either may be or cannot be or must be the case, or whose being the case has as a consequence that other similar unities must be or may be or cannot be the case. Only secondarily is Logic a science which teaches us how to think and reason; primarily it sets forth the ordering structures of various manifolds of entities and of the possible connections that may obtain among them. This depsychologized view of Logic is more elaborately set forth in the *Formal and Transcendental Logic* of 1929, where Husserl sketches a Formal Ontology dealing with entity-types such as Individuals, Predicates, Relations, Aggregates etc. among which States of Affairs are merely included as a particular type, and also a Formal Apophantics which deals primarily with propositional

unities and their laws of formation and transformation, and
only secondarily with the other formalized entities which occur
in such unities. But behind all this formalized Apophantics and
formalized Ontology are the pure acts of thought, involving
various syntheses, predications, identifications, connections
etc., through which all these entities are set up as objects for
thought, and without which they could not be there for us at all.
Husserl is, however, so far from conceiving these acts as *arbitrarily* subjective or constructive, that he is inclined to speak of a
'categorial intuition' in their case. Negation, identity, alternat-
ivity, conditionality etc. may be given to us by subjective
modifications and combinations, but they are as void of
subjective *content* as being a detergent or being an oyster, and
we confront plain cases of the former as we may of the latter.
Phenomenologically Husserl is plainly right: the logical forms
and connectives in questions enter into all that we perceive or
into all that we refer to reality.

Husserl's constitutive phenomenology therefore begins its
career in the somewhat queer sector of the entitites of reason: its
presuppositions and its methods are, however, even in the
Logical Investigations, soon carried over into the world of natural
things and into the sphere of the acts in which we perceive and
think of such things. And here Husserl employs the same device,
little understood in this new connection, that he has already
employed in dealing with the entities of reason. He conceives
that there may be appropriate modifications of subjective
experience whose nature or function it is to *enable* us to perceive
various qualities in the external, natural things before us,
without being either the *same* as, or even remotely *like* the latter.
This strange, but on examination illuminating doctrine he took
over from the Polish philosopher Twardowski, from whom his
contemporary Meinong also borrowed a corresponding concept
of psychic *content* (*Inhalt*). On this view there are sensory affec-
tions of the conscious person which *correspond* to such perceived
features of natural things as their various colours, shapes,
sizes, resonances etc. – colours, shapes, sizes, resonances etc.
cannot be immediately 'lived through' – but which, without
being themselves noted or considered, or at all like what we
note and consider, are such as to lend themselves to a peculiar
use by an act of interpretative reference (*Auffassung*) which sets
before us a correlated object. It is, e.g., by being sensuously

affected in the unique, chequered, outspread way in which we have experience of light that we are able, by an interpretative use of this experience, which none the less we do not notice, to have objects visually set before us in varied colours and positions. Husserl makes use of the term *Sinnesdaten*, which *seems* to mean the same as the English 'sense-data', and he also talks of the material (*Materie*) of perceptual and other experiences, but such terms, together with the word *Auffassung*, which we have translated as 'interpretation', have wholly misleading associations for the English philosopher, since the data and materials he speaks of have no separateness from our lived subjectivity, and are not normally brought before consciousness, and since the 'interpretation' which animates (*beseelt*) them objectively certainly does not interpret them, in that it has no consciousness of them at all. It is, however, the presence in experience of Husserl's hyletic sense-data which gives perceptual awareness the 'seeing' character which distinguishes it from unfulfilled, unseeing thought, the character of seeming to set the 'thing itself' before us in perception. There are, however, 'materials' of a phenomenologically different kind which set a thing before us in imagination, and also in unfulfilled thought, when we 'know what we mean' but neither see it nor picture it.

The *Logical Investigations* also starts to explore a trail that the *Ideas I* of 1913 and Husserl's later work were to explore very much further: the notion of the perceptual encounter with natural things as involving a perpetually extended and extensible 'synthesis of identification' in and through ever varying cases of 'fulfilment'. An object appears and reappears before us as the *same* thing in ever new confrontations, in which ever new sides of it achieve intuitive fulfilment, while others lapse into nonfulfilment, but in what counts throughout as the direct presence of the 'object itself'. What is thus intuitively given through an appropriate use of sense-material, both fluctuates and also maintains its identity through time, and is always surrounded by a halo or 'horizon' of other aspects that future experience will bring to light, but which are no longer or not yet given in sensory fulfilment. And no matter how much we vary and enrich our perceptual acquaintance with the physical thing, it must remain incomplete, synthetic, never totally presentative: the complete confrontation with a natural thing in all aspects is rather in the nature of a transcendental idea than a possible achievement, it is something we move towards, but cannot ever wholly attain. Husserl is later in the *Ideas* to say that even a God could never perceive all sides of a physical thing, though here he seems to be excluding the possibility of a non-successive synthesis of which even *we* in *our* experience have limited acquaintance. Husserl has, however, provided us with a satisfactory elaboration of much that is obscure and vague in the Kantian conception of synthesis, and his views also are quite in harmony with the less deep-going opinions of phenomenalists, verificationists and pragmatists and other Anglo-American contemporaries.

The analyses of the *Logical Investigations* are carried much further in Husserl's various lectures and papers on the *Phenomenology of the Inner Time-consciousness* (1905–11), perhaps the finest of his works, and an unsurpassably great philosophical achievement. Here Husserl gives Time the central place in the life of consciousness and its objects which Kant also accorded to it, and he points out how, in endless self-reiteration, it combines permanence with flux, the immediate past being retained and its order preserved in a fixed gradation of modes, and the immediate future similarly prefigured in a parallel schema of phases, both schemata remaining formally invariant while ever new content rushes through them. What Kant wrote of with half-intelligible profundity, and what William James embalmed in memorable poetry, here achieves portentous clarity. Husserl also tells us how contents that have 'flowed' in orderly fashion through this invariant schema, are themselves 'constituted' as having their own invariant identity which they maintain as they retreat indefinitely into the ever further past, and how natural objects having other dimensions than the temporal come to be given a definite historical spread and position in the indefinite medium of cosmic time. But the analysis terminates in the further remarkable insight that, while all immanent and transcendent objectivities have thus to be constituted as temporal through various immediate acts of retention or protention, or various more widely ranging forms of memory or indirect inference, the flux of our own awareness cannot be thus 'constituted'. We are not the flowing set of conscious phases that we are, unified yet changing, because we hold ourselves together reflectively or tack our past on to our present and our future: such a doctrine would obviously involve an unintelligible infinite regress. Obviously we do not constitute ourselves the unified persistent persons that we are as we constitute the unified persistent objects that are there for us: in constituting such objects, consciousness without more ado may be said to constitute itself (*Zeitbewusstsein*, §39). The subsequent reflection which recapitulates what we thought and experienced, depends on the non-reflective living-through of the flowing continuity which is consciousness itself. Husserl has here given form and substance to the perceptions which Kant tried to formulate in his Transcendental Deduction, his Analogies of Experience and his Refutation of Idealism: that, while things can only come to be there for us in so far as we successively unify them, we ourselves can only come to be there for ourselves in so far as we have successively unified *things*. There is, however, much in Husserl that shows him to be not fully in possession of these subjective–objective insights, and to be at times dominated by a subjectivism that can only be called 'one-sided'.

Part I of the *Ideas towards a Pure Phenomenology and Phenomenological Philosophy* was published in 1913, and here the most arresting, novel part is to be found in the Second Section. This part, however, contains many of the illegitimate, surreptitious slides in position on which we shall later comment, while the remaining parts contain much of the infinitely patient, detailed analyses on which Husserl's reputation must ultimately rest. The theme of the Second Section is that of a methodological route towards phenomenological insight characterized by a suspension, an *Epoché* or holding back, of what Husserl calls the natural attitude, meaning by this our unquestioning belief in the independent reality of a world of spatio-temporal, mind-transcendent things. This natural attitude is not to be scotched nor even superseded by systematic doubt – this would be a Cartesian stance which Husserl at first resists, and into which he only later falls – it is merely to be anaesthetized, temporarily 'put out of action', or, what is the same, its deliverances are to be temporarily put 'into brackets'. The brackets in question are those of intentionality: we are to see the natural world, not as in unreflective stances it gives itself out to be, but as something throughout acknowledged, posited and recognized as having this or that structure by consciousness. The suspension of conviction consists in the fact that, from this new standpoint, metaphysical or ordinary questions about 'reality' cease to have relevance. An unreality systematically posited would, *qua* posited, not differ from a corresponding reality: both would be 'bracketed' in precisely the same way. The suspension of natural conviction is therefore only possible because nature becomes bracketed for us in the various conscious acts and procedures which put nature before us, because we treat it as an object of second intention, as something believed in or given and not in its independent right. The suspension of natural conviction therefore leads at once, and not by an accident, to the bringing into view of the conscious acts and procedures through which contents were posited: in putting the positing of some natural object or feature out of action, we by a change of regard bring its positing, the thought of it, into the picture. We are made aware that there undoubtedly was such a positing, and that we are now reenacting both a remembrance of it and a neutralized version of its content. To suspend one's natural conviction in physical things, other people, the past, the future, the hidden laws behind things, the idealities of morals and mathematics and the numinous objects of religion, is to find, not only the complex awareness of these objects crowding in upon us as a new hierarchy of objects, but also all the objects of those same awarenesses. These return upon us, however, only in the *modus* of matters believed, entertained, sensuously envisaged or confidently posited as things independent of our thought and being. The whole natural world, the world of embodied mind and the world of detached ideality, therefore return upon us in all their well regulated pattern, together with all the fragmented unreality and absurdity that they exclude.

What are now envisaged are, however, only the matters apparent to consciousness, and the conscious appearances in which they are thus apparent, and this means that even the natural being and place of the individual who thus suspends conviction is itself suspended: he becomes in his suspended state mere consciousness in general or consciousness as such, or the transcendental Ego who transcends the conscious person, because the latter has itself to be constituted by the former's thought. The technique of suspense means that we are prevented from importing into our analysis of the appearances things which are neither appearances nor matters apparent, things which come from another extrinsic causal order, and which can break into the appearances only by nonapparent violence, and not as matters duly acknowledged, constituted and consciously given. The new suspense-technique means, further, that we cease to regard objects as truly independent of the acts that constitute them for consciousness, and they are accordingly only there to the extent and in the light in which consciousness constitutes them: it is possible for Napoleon to be given only as the conqueror of Jena, and the defeated at Waterloo not to be part of what is thus put before consciousness. A new, abstractly attenuated object, the *noema* or object-*qua*-thought-of, now takes the place of the real object of the natural attitude: the concretely real Napoleon is now only the imperfectly given *X* to which a growing series of *noemata* is synthetically related (*Ideas I*, §131). The new conception of the *noema* takes the place of the old 'material' of mental orientations which in the *Logical Investigations* was supposed to mediate the reference to mind-transcendent things.

Limitations of space and time render it impossible to comment in detail on Husserl's remarkable constitution of other conscious persons in the Fifth of his *Cartesian Meditations* of 1931: he correctly discerns that other conscious subjects are primitively part of 'the phenomena', and that all objectivity is given as objectivity to the whole community of subjects, and not to the single subject alone. And while foreign subjects are constituted not quite directly, but by an *appresentation* attaching to the behavior of their living, natural bodies, there is not therefore anything derivative or questionable in our *acceptance* of their supporting presence. Husserl in fact assumes that the world of monads or subjects has a much more firmly constituted place in the phenomenological order than the natural objects which are merely there *for* them all.

Limitations of time and space also render it impossible for me to comment on Husserl's later teaching regarding the 'life-world' and 'prepredicative' experience. (See *Erfahrung und Urteil* and *The Crisis of the European Sciences*.) Husserl believes that our original, passively lived experience involves in an undistinguished total mass many of the highly articulated relational, modal, generic, social, valuational and introspective features that are afterwards teased out of it by 'predicative' thought. Husserl's doctrine on this point is the antithesis of Wittgenstein's. If Wittgenstein denies the reality of pre-linguistic 'meanings', Husserl makes them infinitely rich and numerous, and prior to predication as well as to language. We, e.g., perceive snakes as snakes and flee from them, long before we can pronounce the predication 'This is a snake'. As is usual in such clashes, Husserl is right, and Wittgenstein obviously wrong: the former builds on the actual appearances, the latter on an abstract semantic theory. Husserl further thinks that some of the higher exercises of predicative assertion represent rather an impoverishment of the rich wealth of pre-predicative life than an extension or clarification of the latter. The mathematico-scientific view of the world may have become part of the phenomena for suitably educated men, but the phenomena contain more things than have ever been distilled from them in such education.

It now remains to complete our brief discussion of Husserl's phenomenological analysis by adverting to the great confusion which to some extent mars it all. This is the transformation of the suspense of natural conviction, the 'bracketing' of nature necessary to achieving the phenomenological standpoint, into a refusal to return to an unbracketed nature, into the metaphysical assertion that it can only live and be within intentional brackets. The phenomenologist slips, by what Kant would have called a 'transcendental subreption', into treating the being of the natural world as consisting simply in its constitution by consciousness, a step not in itself reprehensible if taken boldly and metaphysically, but wholly reprehensible if treated as a mere extension of the phenomenological suspense. The reasons that Husserl gives for his immense change of front are mainly to be found in *Ideas I*, §49 and §55: their most dogmatic proclamation is to be found in *Formal and Transcendental Logic*, §99.

Husserl's arguments for his new-found subjectivism are to a large extent Cartesian: despite his original denial that the suspense of the natural attitude involves *doubt* as to the existence of the natural world, it is plain that Husserl in some sense thinks that the existence of the natural world is not wholly indubitable, and that he attaches importance to the fact that, however prolonged and uniform our acquaintance with some natural object, such acquaintance is always a matter of incomplete, one-sided, sensible slants, and that whatever we extrapolate from such slants could always be refuted (*Ideas*, §§43, 44). It is, in fact, possible, Husserl believes, that nothing like a persistent, law-governed natural reality exists at all, and that only a chance show of order which will not be sustained induces us to think otherwise. The existence of our *awareness* of an apparent natural reality is, however, beyond doubt, and so offers us an apodictic foundation for philosophy. Such a line of argument has, however, long been exposed as being almost totally without merit. For the self-constitution of consciousness, if at all significant, involves a going beyond the flashlight awareness of the instant, if indeed there can be such a thing as an undeveloping, momentary consciousness, and the constitution of the consciousness of other persons is, if anything, far more open to question than the constitution of physical things. The phenomenological analyses of consciousness proposed by Husserl are, moreover, all open to question. Husserl himself changed his position regarding the pure Ego, and differed on many points from his contemporary Natorp. And it is quite arguable, even if ultimately unacceptable, that talk about conscious acts is all a reflection and interiorization of language, and that there are no inwardly discriminable processes of positing, synthesis, ideation and what not, though without analysis there may well appear to be such. The experimental researches of Titchener at Cornell (see his great but forgotten *Experimental Psychology of the Thought-processes*) and the less disciplined researches of Wittgenstein, certainly deserve consideration, even if they have finally to be rejected. Doubt regarding the apparent particularities of natural being seems further, as many have argued, and Husserl himself in a 'bracketed' sense often admits, inseparable from faith in natural reality as a whole. Husserl has provided no good or even meaningful reason for doubting that the natural world exists, however much that existence may also have to be 'constituted' or rather reconstituted for our minds, and that its processes *have* an important causal relation to the acts of constitution just mentioned, being in fact responsible for the 'fulfilment' of those acts through appropriate data, and that natural objects are increasingly given as they are in and for themselves, in an unbracketed and not merely bracketed sense, both through the normal perceptions of men and the theories of the less methodologically prejudiced scientists.

Husserl's second set of reasons for his idealistic change of front lies in the ontological conviction that the being of anything not consciously constitutive of other things and of itself, is necessarily parasitic upon, relative to the being of what is thus consciously constitutive, and what so enjoys an absolute existence. As Husserl puts it in *Ideas*, §49: 'The immanent being (of consciousness) is doubtless an absolute being in the sense that it in principle *nulla re indiget ad existendum*. The world of the transcendent *res* is on the other hand throughout dependent on an actual, and not merely logically conceived, consciousness.' Or again: 'The whole spatio-temporal world, in which human being and the human ego have their subordinate individual reality, has by its very sense merely an intentional being, one that enjoys the merely secondary, relative sense of a being *for* a consciousness.' This ontological conviction of course makes nonsense of the Cartesian doubt which Husserl has elsewhere been practising, and certainly violates the phenomenological suspense that he has elsewhere recommended. And as a metaphysical dogma, it is without cogency for many who, taking their lead from Kant's Refutation of Idealism, can make no sense of a conscious life without permanent, independent objects in space with which consciousness can be busied, which objects must be actual and not merely logically conceived, and which must actually control, and be actually felt to control, the constitution of natural objects by consciousness. Husserl's great metaphysical step can, moreover, only be fully defended provided a philosopher is willing to make a large number of affirmations going far beyond what Husserl, as a phenomenologist, shows any willingness to make, e.g. the Kantian or Fichtean willingness to affirm the half-conscious activity of a productive imagination which in some manner prearranges the same set of natural appearances for all, or the thought of a God who imposes the same order of fulfilling appearances on all subjects. It is interesting to note that though God is seldom mentioned by Husserl, he acquires something like a necessary place in such references as *Ideas I*, §51 and §58 and that he even received something like religious worship at the time of Husserl's death. One would, however, have welcomed a more explicit, better worked out Husserlian theology. But once we concede that how things are in and for themselves is a different question from how things are given as being, necessary as is the interlacing overlap and coincidence of the phenomenological with the ontological orders, the ontological gates are at once thrown wide open: phenomenology can pursue its pure description of the appearances while admitting that some of them reveal an independent, causal, natural setting. It can also bed down with nominalism and sensationalism, and become a mere account of what we find it natural to say. It can readily be harmonized with the almost infinitely elaborated Platonism represented by Meinong, who believes in an indefinite array of real and unreal, psychic and non-psychic objects, or with the older Platonism which deduces variety from a few ultimate paradigms. This is not to condemn Husserl's later 'transcendentalism' out of hand – though whether it should be called 'transcendental' may well be disputed – but it was a sad mistake to mix up so old and so questionable a subjectivism with the fine new claims and methods of Husserl's science of 'the appearances'.[1]

---

[1] I have derived great stimulus for the writing of this paper from Robert Sokolowski's excellent book, *The Foundations of Husserl's Concept of Constitution* and also from Iso Kern's *Husserl und Kant*.

The Idea of a Phenomenological Ethics

If phenomenology is a science, its function is to yield factual knowledge of some kind, rather than to issue norms or imperatives. Hence it cannot expect to generate an ethics. Scheler's 'non-formal ethics of value' may look like a counter-example. But the objective 'value-facts' he professes to find in emotional acts of love, preference, etc. are open to many objections, and even if they were not, could provide no reason why anyone should do anything to realise them. Phenomenology may thus be useful in studying moral experience, but can do nothing to recommend or vindicate any particular form of morality.

Peter Heath is Professor of Philosophy at the University of Virginia. He published (in 1954) the first English translation of a work by Scheler, *The Nature of Sympathy*, and has since produced a number of translations from German, an edition of De Morgan's logical papers, and a commentary on Lewis Carroll entitled *The Philosopher's Alice* (1974).

One does not have to be very far gone in phenomenology in order to realise that – at least as its founder conceived it – it is very intent on being a science. Husserl never wearied of insisting that what he had discovered, invented or mapped out under that name was indeed a rigorous and professional discipline, whose truth-claims were equal if not superior to those of the most exact empirical sciences, and this, after all, has been one of the main reasons for contending that phenomenology is not just a new kind of philosophy, or an old kind in a new guise and terminology. If phenomenology is *not* a science, and does not yield knowledge, then its claims to novelty and independence are largely fraudulent, and most of the rationale of its procedures would immediately disappear.

It would be an error, of course, to infer from this that phenomenology is itself an *empirical* science, or anything like one; its subject-matter does not consist of things or phenomena in the usual sense, but rather of essences or subsistent meanings, detached from their embodiment in anything actually existing, and the method of their discovery is likewise a peculiar one, requiring a special sort of armchair scrutiny that needs training and practice if it is to yield any reliable results. For all that, it is, or can claim to be, a science, in the sense that anyone who does undergo the necessary training will – or at least ought to – arrive at exactly the same insights as his fellow-phenomenologists. Their conclusions are thus in principle verifiable, and can legitimately be regarded as reports of something public, independent of the observer, and uncontaminated by the subjective biasses which disqualify the ordinary methods of introspection, and which the phenomenologist, needless to say, has been at special pains to discard.

Husserl himself, as the founder-discoverer of the new discipline, was not unnaturally more concerned to explain and justify his method, and to map its territory in outline, than to spend much time on phenomenological 'field-work' for its own sake. Hence the fact that – like other eminent philosophers – he notoriously made little or no contribution to ethics is not in itself evidence that he could not have done so had he wished, or that his procedure is inherently unsuitable or irrelevant to the problems of ethical inquiry. Nevertheless it is significant. It suggests, if nothing else, a recognition on Husserl's part that what he had claimed to find was a way of obtaining *knowledge,* independently of sense-experience, concerning various kinds of *a priori* fact. And from this it seems to follow, not only – as Husserl himself said – that phenomenology is itself in intention a neutral and 'value-free' form of investigation, but also that its findings will be neutral too, in the sense that they cannot and should not be expected to exert any direct influence upon the desires, wishes, feelings, etc, of the phenomenologist himself, or of those whom he seeks to instruct. His role is merely that of an observer, reporter, analyst, taxonomist and so on, and his sole business is to provide information. Even if, as is at least conceivable, his investigation should reveal 'norms' or 'values' among the essences, they would strictly be 'value-facts' in this context, and his account of them would likewise be purely descriptive and not normative in character. If confined in this way to the mere making of descriptive statements *about* values, it is evident that the phenomenologist can no more set up as a moralist than a jurist can as a judge, and will be essentially an onlooker in the field of ethics proper, insofar as the latter is taken – as it generally is nowadays – to be the subject-matter of normative rather than factual discourse.

This is not to say, of course, that phenomenology is in any way cut off from inspecting and classifying the facts of 'moral experience' 'moral feeling' or the 'moral life' – assuming any such facts can be found. Husserl himself may have envisaged such a task, but was hardly the ideal person to perform it, since the 'transcendental idealism' of his later years seems to have made it correspondingly difficult – his critics would say impossible – for him to emerge from the egocentric predicament and to 'constitute' other selves on any footing that would make for intelligible moral relationships between them. Nevertheless, if his method can be detached from his metaphysics, there seems no reason why it should not be used, either to throw light on the peculiarities of moral reasoning and feeling, or – more ambitiously – to refound a science or theory of the moral sentiments, of a kind but little developed since the days of Adam Smith.[1] What that method seemingly cannot do, however, is to enter the moral arena as such, without for-

[1] There is a capable treatment of this subject in T. D. Campbell, *Adam Smith's Science of Morals* (London, 1971).

feiting its claim to be a science. It is the old story of 'ought' and 'is'. If morality is essentially concerned with 'oughts', and if these are intrinsically incapable of derivation from the existence or subsistence of any kind of fact, then no amount of inquiry, however rarefied, among eidetic essences, values and the like, can expect to terminate in a genuinely normative ethics, or to furnish reasons for acting in one way rather than another. The jurist can say what the law is, but it is not his business either to make or apply it, or to air his opinions about what it ought to be. The phenomenologist, on his own showing, is in very much the same boat. *Mere* knowledge – even of the difference between right and wrong – is notoriously impotent to determine conduct or decision; and yet anything more than mere knowledge must necessarily lie beyond the province of a strictly conceived science of *a priori* fact.

At this point the argument confronts a formidable obstacle in the writings of a well-known if somewhat unruly figurehead of the phenomenological movement, Max Scheler. Second only to Husserl himself in the subtlety and variety of his discriminations, and considerably broader than his master in range of interest and insight, Scheler is reputedly a moralist of no mean order – the greatest of this century, in the opinion of his admirers, who do not scruple to compare him with Aristotle and Kant. Now that *Der Formalismus in der Ethik und die materiale Wertethik*, his chief work on the subject, has at long last been translated,[2] there will be more chance of assessing these claims, and less excuse for the neglect he has hitherto encountered in the English-speaking world. If anyone can make a case for phenomenological ethics, it assuredly has to be Scheler. With the doubtful exception of von Hartmann, a hesitant recruit to the phenomenological cause, no other member of the school has attempted anything on so large a scale, or can be reckoned so eminent an authority. It will obviously be necessary to take his views into account.

For this purpose it will fortunately be needless to rehearse those views in detail – a lengthy and complex undertaking, which has in any case been well performed already by persons

---

[2] M. Scheler, *Formalism in Ethics and Non-formal Ethics of Values*, trans. Manfred S. Frings and Roger L. Funk (Evanston, Ill., 1973).

qualified for the task.[3] All that is required in the present context is to set forth in brief and general terms the *type* of theory
that Scheler is committed to, together with its more obvious
drawbacks, and then to ask whether, so far as it remains
phenomenology, it can properly be called an ethics, or *vice
versa*. If the 'non-formal ethics of value' turns out to be defective at the very point one would expect, namely in making
the transition from a quasi-factual knowledge of value to the
problem of justifying norms of obligation, that will confirm
the impression already gained, that the role of phenomenology
is on the periphery rather than at the centre of ethical inquiry,
and that it cannot in fact generate a distinctively ethical view
of its own. This is to classify the discipline, not to condemn it.
For, historically speaking, there has certainly been room for
the type of inquiry to which phenomenology *can* legitimately
aspire, and there is no good reason for thinking such studies
to be useless or outmoded. The natural history of 'moral experience', whose aim is to establish how and why people judge
and act as they do, but not to vindicate those judgements or
enjoin those acts as obligatory (or the reverse), is clearly a
helpful, and perhaps a necessary, *approach* to ethics,[4] and
whether or not it deserves to be *called* ethics is largely a matter
of words. The main reason for withholding the title is in fact
to prevent confusion between the factual and normative types
of inquiry – a distinction which Scheler, in particular, seems
to have been habitually prone to neglect. The fact that he is
really rather good at the first, and really rather bad at the
second, is responsible for much of the unevenness and disorder
which even his more devoted admirers confess to finding in
his work.

Scheler's declared ambition was to go beyond Kant, and a
large part of *Der Formalismus* is accordingly given over to a

---

[3] See, for example, among shorter accounts, A. Schutz, *Collected Papers* (The Hague,
1966), Vol. III, pp. 133–78; H. Spiegelberg, *The Phenomenological Movement*, 2nd
ed. (The Hague, 1965), Vol. I, ch. v; J. N. Findlay, *Axiological Ethics* (London, 1970),
ch. IV; and W. Stegmüller, *Main Currents in Contemporary German, British and American
Philosophy*, trans. Albert E. Blumberg (Bloomington, Ind., 1970), ch. III. The best
book on Scheler in English (of a sort) is Manfred S. Frings, *Max Scheler* (Pittsburgh
and Louvain, 1965).

[4] For a good instance of how to do it, see M. Mandelbaum, *The Phenomenology of Moral
Experience* (Baltimore and London, 1955).

running criticism of Kant's ethics. The attack is not altogether *à outrance*, however, since the assailant professes a high regard for his opponent, and largely agrees with him in his hostility to eudaemonist and utilitarian ethics. For all that, Scheler advances as comprehensive a set of objections as could well be found to the whole tenor of Kant's conception of the moral life, finding it empty, narrow, mean and almost wholly indifferent to the wealth and diversity of human temperaments, to which a formal and universalistic preoccupation with the pure notion of duty can naturally do no justice at all. Whether such objections are well-founded, or directed at anything much more than a caricature of Kant, there is again no need to discuss. The only real purpose of the criticism is to define the tasks and display the merits of the opposing view, and this it may succeed in, whether it is fair criticism or not.

Scheler is no less anxious than Kant himself to insist upon the objectivity of moral principles, their independence of the empirical desires and wishes of the agent. What he objects to is the rationalistic method of securing this by narrowing the scope of the ethical to a purely formal adherence to the principle of universalisability. The moral law, as Kant conceives it, is wholly devoid of content, and its *a priori* authority as the imperative of duty has its source only in the autonomous practical reason of the agent himself. It is the same law for all, only because every individual, as a possessor of practical reason, is exactly the same as every other. Here as elsewhere in the critical philosophy, objectivity is founded on a postulate of *a priori* uniformity, and has indeed no other source. Scheler sought objectivity of a kind that would do more justice to the uniqueness and individuality of persons, and found it, rather crudely, perhaps, in the postulate of an independent realm of values, existing outside the agent and disclosed to him by way of his emotions. The checks and pressures, aspirations and aversions, which constitute the moral life consist essentially of responses to the perception of these values, and more particularly in acts of choice and preference between them. Although emotions disclose values, and presumably actuate responses to them, they do not in any way create or constitute the realm of value, nor is it arrived at by reflecting on or abstracting from emotions. What happens, rather, is that values are presented intentionally *in* the emotion itself, and precede –

so Scheler says – any detailed acquaintance with the facts. You take to a person on sight, say, as someone to trust, and though bitter experience may prove him unworthy of your confidence, that does not mean that you were wrong in discerning, through your feeling, the value of trustworthiness. You simply detected it in the wrong place.

It will be seen that Scheler's phenomenology differs from Husserl's in being – at one level, anyway – an amateur pursuit. Anybody can do it, and indeed everybody does, without training and without trying and without even knowing that they are doing it. Nothing is heard here of the painful processes whereby 'essences' are supposedly to be wrung from the phenomena. Schelerian values are simply intuited 'eidetically' in a more or less instinctive fashion, by a process analogous to sense-perception, and one in which reason plays no part. The description and analysis of values or emotions – Scheler's own particular *forte* – is no doubt a more intellectual undertaking, though even here the appeal is mainly to an inspection of the 'facts', with argument at a premium and little in the way of precautions or constraints. The *logique du coeur* is sufficient, it seems, even for the uninstructed, to yield not only the presence of values, but also the relations of order and hierarchy among them, so that we can tell directly, if we will, not only that something has a value-property, but also that it is higher or lower in the scale than other values. An elaborate guide to the hierarchy is of course provided by Scheler himself, but since no-one is exactly a stranger to this realm, there seems no reason why such guidance should be heeded, or needed, by anyone prepared to rely on his own insight. Our everyday decisions and preferences reflect this insight in any case, and a right ordering of values will recognise and give priority (if Scheler is correct about it) to those which are more lasting, more readily shareable, more satisfying, less dependent on other values, and less subservient to natural appetite.

These are bold claims, unclouded, apparently, by any suspicion that there may in fact be rather less in the situation than meets the phenomenological eye. One ought, at any rate, to look carefully at such a bill of goods before accepting delivery. It is true, of course, that we do often size up a person or state of affairs evaluatively, before knowing anything much about him or it, and that many of our decisions rely on impulse or 'seat of the pants' intuitions, rather than on rules or reasoning. Such facts are worth remembering, as a corrective to some of the fables of other moralists, and as a reminder that (whatever the explanation), emotions, inclinations and feelings are by no means so blindly uninformative as certain theories would suggest. But that hardly warrants assigning them the superior cognitive powers that Scheler is anxious to accord to them. The reasons of the heart are often enough persuasive; they are not so often right.

The *a priori* – or non-natural – character claimed for these deliverances is also a somewhat reckless and inflated way of explaining what has since come to be regarded as a truth of logic, or even of language: that statements of value are not formally deducible from statements of fact, or, more flatly still, that some words ending in -able or -ible are not exhaustively definable in terms of the corresponding words ending in -ed. Because a thing is admirable, that does not mean that anyone actually has admired it; and the fact that they have admired it is not a conclusive reason for saying that it ought, or deserves, to be admired.

That admirability, and other such properties, are objective features of things, or essences subsisting on their own account, is another conclusion drawn, not only from such logical considerations as the above, but also from the psychological observation that our liking, approval and admiration (or the reverse) seem very often to be *elicited* from us by the thought or perception of an object, and are not simply conferred or projected upon objects at our own arbitrary pleasure. But mere impressions of this kind are a slender foundation on which to build an ontology, nor does it in the least follow from these facts that the act of approval has to be construed as a sort of perception (or response to perception) of a non-natural property lurking in or behind the object approved of. Quite apart from the unsoundness of the analogy with sense-perception, there is no *economy* in such a theory. It creates unnecessary difficulties almost as fast as it manufactures superfluous and questionable entities, and one does not have to look much further into Scheler before finding him obliged to wrestle with them.

First on the list comes the obvious objection, that if there really were such a world of subsistent values, as accessible to naked eye observation as the stars in the sky, there ought to be little (if any) more disagreement about evaluative questions than there is about matters of fact. This has to be countered by hypotheses concerning deception, falsification and impoverishment of the capacity to perceive values – in short, by an invocation of the principle of phenomenological *defect* to explain why not only individuals but whole cultures may be rendered impervious to the presence of this value or that. The factual arguments for the view that values are *themselves* relative are thereby converted into evidence for the relativity of our perception of value, while preserving the integrity of the objective value system as such. The system is still 'there' for all to see, but not everybody is equally good at seeing it. One would like to know in that case, however, why *anybody's* account of such a system – including Scheler's – should have the right to be thought final and authoritative, and why it should still be the case, even when these values are clearly pointed out by experts, that half the world should pay no attention to them, and the other half continue to bicker incessantly about each other's choices and preferences and priorities, even among such values as they are collectively willing to accept. One of Kant's main reasons for rejecting the attempt to base ethics on the emotions was precisely that the latter yield no agreement, provide no proof of anything, and so have no claim on the acceptance of anyone but the individual who feels them. Scheler may think he has a way round the difficulty, but it is hard to see what it can be. For there is really no future in maintaining that emotional insight into values is somehow direct and self-authenticating for everybody, while at the same time insisting that both individual percipients and the cultures they belong to are inherently subject to 'perspectival' and other distortions, which blind or blur their vision of what is there to see. He cannot have it both ways, and if – as seems all too likely – the defects in question are universal, so that no single witness can be relied on, we may as well give up hope of ever getting dependable information about the world of values by way of our emotional responses to them. The god-like immunities of the professional phenomenologist are of little or no avail in this connection, for Scheler has not only made it too easy for everyone to *be* his own phenomenologist, but also too difficult for anyone – phenomenologists included – to escape the toils of the 'sociology of knowledge', and the scepticism and relativism which inevitably go with the admission that all such knowledge is conditioned by factors it is historically impossible to escape.

Scheler appears at times to concede that authentic and complete insight into the entire value-system is an unattainable ideal, though one to which succeeding cultures and superior individuals may hope progressively to approximate. This begs the question, of course, if there is no *other* means of telling who these superior persons are. For the ordinary individual, situated in the culture that history happens to have deposited him in, there seems, therefore, in the end, to be no better recourse than to follow his own lights, do his own thing, as it were, and respond as best he may to such values as he can find to respect. It may, indeed, be good for his morale in doing so, to be persuaded that these values actually are absolute and universal. But what reassurance can Scheler have to offer that they really are the *same* values as those available to everyone else? As a matter of fact, he says the very opposite, alleging on occasion that the values disclosed to a given person, though as objective as ever, are essentially private and peculiar to himself. This is not quite the same as the discovery by a particular individual (e.g. a moral teacher) of values that have hitherto eluded detection by others. Such discoveries, once made, can be shared, whereas the private value is the sole concern of its perceiver, and presumably remains so. Its appearance is not common, which is just as well, for if it were the general rule, the 'non-formal ethics of value' would have little apart from a vacuous claim to objectivity that could serve to distinguish it from the most extravagant kind of subjective antinomianism, and the battle to base ethics on a common foundation of phenomenological insight would have been lost before it had begun. Even as it is, the possibility of intrinsically private values is as disconcerting as would be the appearance in the ordinary world of intrinsically private physical objects. Just as there is nothing to differentiate the latter from hallucinations, so there would be nothing by which to tell of the former that they are not value-delusions, errors of conscience and the like, and it would clearly be far more dangerous to believe in their reality than in that of more orthodox values, which, however commonplace or dubiously authentic, at least have the virtue of commanding the adherence of other people as well as oneself.

The dogmatic objectivism of Scheler's value-theory, the difficulties that beset it, and his own attempts to escape from these difficulties, are sadly reminiscent of the problems of naive realism in the theory of perception, and the traditional endeavours to come to its aid. The main differences are that his energetic defence of an unhopeful cause is hampered additionally by the absence of any commonsense belief in what he is defending, and by considerable doubts as to whether there is anything there to theorise about at all. Perhaps the saddest thing of all, however, is that even if none of these problems existed, and everything that Scheler has to say about the reality of his world of values were unreservedly granted to be true, it would still be not the slightest use to him as a foundation for a genuinely normative ethics. It might be a well understood fact that such a realm of values existed, that unimpeded access to it was accorded uniformly to every member of the human race, and that the relevant emotions of mankind were constantly directed to mapping and surveying it. That would still provide no reason at all why anyone should ever act on this knowledge; we could all be in perfect agreement concerning the facts of the value world, and yet remain no more moved to action by them than we are tempted to physical appropriation by contemplating the aesthetic glories of a picture-gallery or museum. In attempting to base ethics on a knowledge of the good, Scheler has forgotten the will; in more modern terms, he has overlooked the now well-established principle that an imperative cannot be logically derived from premises that contain only statements of fact.[5] That in Scheler's case the facts in question are non-natural value-facts has no effect on the logic of the situation. All that can follow from statements about such facts is another factual statement – *about* values, maybe, but not itself a value-statement. In his own terms, the most that can be generated from an emotional cognition of a value is a declaration that that value 'ought to be'; but this – as he well knows – is simply a consequence of the principle that the existence or realisation of a value itself

---

[5] Cf. W. Stegmüller, *op. cit.* p. 131 (reference in note 3 above).

has value, and is a far cry from the 'ought to do' which lays upon somebody the obligation of actually realising it. The attempt – predictably made – to extract the one from the other – *ex pumice aquam* – is no less predictably a failure. Given a static firmament of values, it is, after all, extremely peculiar that a certain number of them should insistently *demand* to be realised, often at the expense of their betters, and not just in a general way, but by particular persons at particular times and places; there is really no accounting for it on a scheme of Scheler's sort, and it is no wonder that it embarrassed him, and that he disliked the notion of duty. Kant may have erred in putting too much stress on the notion, and neglecting those aspects of the ethical structure which carry no such weight; but at least his arch has a keystone, whereas Scheler's, for all its greater richness of ornamentation, does not.

Brief and sketchy as they obviously are, the foregoing remarks make no pretence of being a demolitionary critique of Scheler's entire system, still less a root-and-branch dismissal of all forms of phenomenological or axiological ethics. Their purpose, rather, has been to show up, in a necessarily simplified way, a few of the more evident drawbacks of a system which, if not necessarily typical, is at all events an undeniably distinguished specimen of its kind. Husserl called Scheler's phenomenology 'fool's gold', and in the end would have none of it; one sees why, but the observation scarcely does justice to *Der Formalismus*, which for all its failings is in many ways a most interesting and arresting book. Granted that its method may have been unsatisfactory, it did nevertheless throw up a large number of worthwile *aperçus* on many aspects of ethics, which deserve a more sober setting. A chastened form of the doctrine might well be able to preserve a fair proportion of these, while improving their chances of general acceptance, and although no such reconstruction can be so much as contemplated in the present context, it is at least possible to point to three main features which the Schelerian theory might be better off without. Their removal, to be sure, would clip its wings severely, but the operation would also help to reanchor it more securely within the phenomenological fold.

In the first place, there is the 'ontologism' which forms so incongruous and vulnerable a feature of the theory, and which turns out in any case to afford it but little protection against the scepticism it seeks to repel. The phenomenological programme, after all, was expressly designed by Husserl to avoid any such hazardous commitments, and though the price of doing so may be to confine exploration solely within the bounds of 'consciousness', there can be little doubt that it is there only that the phenomenologist is properly at home. Schelerian perceptions of value, such as the feelings of liking, approval, respect, awe and so on, are admitted data of consciousness, and can be studied for what they are worth without necessarily going on to ask awkward and possibly misleading questions about the what and whereabouts of their intentional objects (though the propriety of this model could certainly bear some further inquiry on its own account). The variation and seeming relativity of the value judgement can then itself become a mere datum, to be studied calmly for its own sake, without having to be seen as a menace to be neutralised, or an objection to be explained away. Such a programme, though it could not aspire to establish the existence of any extra-mental ethical facts, could still hope to broaden the scope of traditional ethics, and might even furnish the contemporary metaethicist with patterns of analysis a trifle more rewarding than 'Jones is a good man', 'Shut the door, please', and 'This is a good cup of tea'.

The second point on which reform might be desirable follows naturally from the first. It is to reinstate the distinction between those who make value judgements and those who make a scientific study of their occasion and content. On Scheler's theory, this distinction, though always apparent in practice, is blurred by his insistence that values are self-evidently given in the emotional value-experience, and that the only obstacle to their clear perception by everyone is to be found in personal obtuseness, self-deception, cultural conditioning and the like. By concentrating on value judgements as phenomena, and refusing to dispense guidance about values, the phenomenologist is not only absolved – as he should be – from entering the axiological fray, but can also claim to be doing something which the ordinary evaluator is not well qualified to do for himself. His subjects may delude themselves as usual into believing their judgements 'true', but he will no longer feel obliged to correct either the judgements or the belief, or to claim in doing so an immunity to delusion which he does not and cannot possess.

A third and final point, also a corollary of the first, is that the drawing up of *a priori* schemes of order and dependence among values, though an interesting game to play, is not the province of phenomenological inquiry. The ordinary man, and the moralist, may in concrete cases debate the competing claims of patriotism, friendship or religion, and have every reason for doing so, since it is their practical decisions, or the value of their advice, which depend upon the outcome. The phenomenologist has no such concern, and need have no interest, therefore, in whether these estimates are 'correct' (whatever that may mean). The very last thing that is required of him is an abstract decision to the effect that one of these values takes official precedence over the other. His business is merely to examine the way in which debates of this sort are conducted, and from this to determine, if he can, how the customary priorities are arrived at. It is no affair of his to moralise about the result, and still less to engage on the strength of it in gratuitous excursions into metaphysics, whose effect can be only to confuse the aims of his discipline, and to bring it into disrepute.

Phenomenology of Freedom

PAUL RICOEUR

The phenomenology of freedom is, first, an implicit phenomenology involved in various contexts – philosophical, ethical, epistemological, political, theological, etc. An 'explicit phenomenology' of freedom which lays bare the descriptive core of the phenomenon of freedom common to all such contexts is possible only in connection with a linguistic analysis of ordinary language. The principal topics with which I concern myself in this paper are: intention, motives, reasons, act and agent.

Paul Ricoeur is Professor of Philosophy at the University of Paris and at the University of Chicago. His main publications (in English translation) include: *History and Truth* (1965), *Freedom and Nature: The Voluntary and the Involuntary* (1966), *Husserl: An Analysis of his Phenomenology* (1967), *Freud and Philosophy* (1970), *The Conflict of Interpretations* (1974).

Implicit phenomenology

Phenomenology of freedom is not an invention of the moderns;
nor is it an invention of the so-called 'phenomenological school',
if the latter term is understood to refer exclusively to Husserl
and the philosophical movement which he inspired. There
exists an *implicit* phenomenology of freedom which is embodied
in philosophical descriptions and analyses of the phenomenon
of freedom within particular contexts. What I shall call the
'explicit phenomenology' of freedom, on the other hand,
involves an attempt to 'bracket out' or 'neutralize' these contexts, with a view to isolating the descriptive core of the phenomenon of freedom which remains the same in all cases. In what
follows, I shall give a few examples of such contexts. Only by
'neutralizing' these contexts can phenomenology give substance to its claim that it proceeds 'without presuppositions'.

The 'ethical' context: Aristotle.   It is within an ethical
framework that Aristotle first gave an analysis of the voluntary
and the involuntary action – an analysis which, though not
formally separated from the rest of his discussions, has clearly
distinguishable features of its own. This analysis, included in
Book III of the *Nicomachean Ethics*, in conjunction with the
developments carried out by the medieval thinkers and by the
seventeenth-century Cartesian psychology, contains valuable
hints as to the possible link between phenomenological and
linguistic analysis – a point which we shall take up again later.
Aristotle based his analysis on the descriptive terms relating
to human action occurring in the Greek language as it had been
forged by poets and orators. He began by drawing a distinction
between the actions performed 'voluntarily' and the actions
performed 'involuntarily'. Involuntary actions result from
external constraint of some kind and are characterized by the
insufficient awareness, on the part of the agent, of the circumstances; voluntary actions, on the other hand, are initiated by the person who acts; they are performed 'knowingly'.
Following Aristotle, philosophers have traditionally defined
voluntary actions in terms of the interiority of the cause and
the awareness, on the part of the agent, of the circumstances
of the action.

Within the class of voluntary actions Aristotle distinguishes the smaller class of actions performed 'by preference'. The delimitation of this concept is Aristotle's own contribution; coming to us through Latin translations, this concept has dominated our concept of decision or choice. Aristotle applies to it his method of analysis by proximate genus and specific difference. The proximate genus of decision is 'wish', that is, the optative mood (which in Greek is expressed by a word which has the same root as the verb *to will*; a similar link is retained in the French expression *'je voudrais bien'*). 'Wish' is indeed of the same family as 'will' but it can relate to things that are not dependent upon us (e.g. the wish that a particular athlete win, that fortune be favourable to me etc.), to impossible things (wish not to die) or to distant aims (e.g. that the sick are restored to health). Moreover, wish is rooted in the life forces which relate it to 'the desirable in general', – the desirable including that which is pleasing to the body as well as that which is pleasing to the spirit. The sphere of preference coincides with the sphere of our immediate efficacy, where we are in command of the means. At the same time, the specific difference which characterizes this sphere is easily discernible: decision presupposes the possibility of alternative courses of action and an act of 'deliberation'. Thus, the voluntary could be defined as 'deliberated desire', bearing in mind that this deliberation relates to the means rather than to the ends.

This analysis contains abundant possibilities for elaboration, as the definition in terms of 'deliberated desire' suggests. The will, on the one hand, is rooted in the life-force which powers all human activity; on the other hand, the will partakes of reason which, by joining itself to desire, becomes *practical* reason. This can be seen in the 'practical syllogism', which is reasoning about, and weighing up what is desirable. Thus, we can see in Aristotle's philosophy of freedom the forerunner of both the 'voluntarism' which stresses the force of acting and the initiative of choice and the 'intellectualism' for which a will enlightened by rational motives alone is properly human.

However in the *Nicomachean Ethics* it is in purely ethical terms that the problem of the will is posed; the inquiry into the problem forming the central part of an investigation into the principal forms of what the Greeks called the 'living will' and which could be translated into modern terms as 'judicious action'.

The 'theological' context: Augustine. All the possibilities of Aristotle's implicit phenomenology of freedom could not have been fully explored if his approach had not been supplemented in the Christian West by a theological reflection, which, in diverse ways, guided and inspired philosophical anthropology until Kant.

The psychology of will was refined and deepened by a meditation on *evil*, or sin. Christianity brought the concept of the infinite into the focus of attention; Hegel saw in this the turning point between the Greek world and the modern world. To this 'new form of the world' belonged the conception of the will as 'infinite'. The Aristotelian metaphysics of finite action was now enriched by a metaphysics of the desire for God and by an analysis of evil. This can best be seen in Saint Augustine. Here, *voluntas* is revealed in its terrible splendour in the experience of evil and sin; the will has the power to deny being, to say 'no', to 'turn away *from*' God and to 'turn *towards*' his creatures. This awesome power to 'fall away from' – this *posse peccare* – is the very mark of the infinite in the will. Perhaps there was no true concept of freedom in Western philosophy until Western thought had been confronted with the problem of what Saint Augustine called the *modus defectivus* of the will.

In this respect, Augustine's two great quarrels – first with the Manichaeans and later with the Pelagians – constituted an extraordinary conceptual laboratory. Against the Manichaeans, he had to disprove the idea that evil was something substantial; evil is not a thing, it has to do with the will; it is not already there, we ourselves make it. The possibility of turning towards the 'nothingness' of evil is an essential characterizing feature of the will itself. Against the Pelagians, on the other hand, it was necessary to show that having this defect is a 'manner of enduring', a quasi-nature of sorts; that we are, in a sense, the captives of the nothingness of evil. In trying to conceptualize 'original sin' on the basis of the symbols of the fall and of captivity, Christian theology has thrown light on a hidden dimension of the human will, where the power to act finds its limit in a feeling of impotence which is also constitutive of our nature.

Theological speculation contributed in yet another way to a deeper understanding of the human will: if there is something

like a divine will how can the human will, of itself, begin anything that has not been foreseen and, in one way or another,
willed by God? This problem raises not only the problem of
'predestination' – or, more precisely, the problem of the
predetermination of human beings, by God, to eternal sal-
vation or eternal damnation – but also the problem of the
divine grace which predetermines the movements of goodness
and charity in the human will. How can man be the author and
master of his own actions if they are thus predetermined?
This problem occupied Saint Paul and Saint Augustine and
the debate which they began, was renewed by Luther and
Calvin, only to flare up again during the 17th or the 18th
Century leading to the most violent controversies. The philosophical investigations of Pascal, Malebranche and Leibniz
brought into focus the most central paradoxes of existence, all
of them closely connected with the nature of creative acts –
aesthetic, intellectual or moral. The basic difficulty boils down
to this: that man is free only to the extent to which his actions
can be seen to be rooted in a force which he does not command,
his freedom being something in the nature of a gift. This is what
lies behind the scholastic discussions about predestination and
grace.

The 'epistemological' context: Descartes.   The phenomenology of freedom received a fresh impetus – sometimes in
conjunction with the ideas just discussed – from the reflection
on the nature of error. The inquiry into error is not unconnected
with the earlier meditation on evil. It differs from it in that it
shifts the emphasis from ethics to epistemology. The study of
the problems of the will becomes now merely an aspect of a
larger enterprise the aim of which is to clarify the foundations
of knowledge – knowledge being understood in the sense of
the exact sciences. The theory of judgment is the framework
of this new approach which is given a classical exposition in
Descartes' *Metaphysical Meditations* (*Fourth Meditation*). By
transferring the entire weight of error to the will, Descartes
frees 'the power of understanding' from all suspicion that it
might be responsible for error. 'For by the understanding
alone [he writes] I neither affirm nor deny anything, but only
conceive the ideas of things regarding which I may form a
judgment; nor is any error, properly so called, found in the

understanding thus accurately taken'. Consequently there are no false ideas, no material falsity. This is not to say that the will as such is the cause of error: 'for the power or the will consists only in our being able to do or not to do a thing (that is, to affirm or deny, to pursue or flee), or rather it consists in this only, that in affirming or denying, pursuing or fleeing whatever our understanding proposes to us we act in such a way that we do not feel in any way constrained by an external force.' Thus, as a simple power, will is innocent. In practice, however, it is not. If I happen to be mistaken, it is because I do not restrain my will within the limits of my understanding, 'but extend it even to the things I do not understand; and as the will in itself is indifferent to these things, it is easily led astray'. This indifference of the will, which makes it possible for me to fall into error, is only 'the lowest degree of freedom, and exhibits a defect in knowledge rather than a perfection of the will'. This is the ordinary domain of the will, including all the things that the understanding does not reveal with perfect clarity. It is thus only by a method of abstraction that one knows the will as an active feature linked with the passive features of the understanding. Judgment alone is the object of a complete and concrete experience; this experience, at any rate, allows the separation into two concurrent causes by reason of the disproportion it displays between the limited character of one cause and the limitless extension of the other. However this method of abstraction is not applied in the name of 'psychology', a term which was unknown in this period.

Whereas the Aristotelian psychology of the will formed part of an investigation into ethical issues, the Cartesian psychology of the will formed part of an essentially epistemological investigation. Its aim was to answer the question: Why is there falsehood? Why is there the crack of error in the perfect sphere of truth? A metaphysical explanation of error being impossible (owing to our ignorance of the ultimate ends of the creation) the help is sought from psychology in solving a metaphysical problem – the problem of how it is possible that a nothing, a mere privation, is nevertheless something to us.

The concept of will is henceforth discussed in connection with the problem of the foundations of knowledge and of the act that brings these foundations to the certainty of reflection. It is this certainty of reflection that enables Descartes to speak of 'this indifference of which I am conscious . . .' and to raise the individual self-consciousness to the level of 'objective experience': 'It is the faults of will alone or freedom of choice, which I experience to be so great in comparison with other faults that I can conceive of no other greater or more extensive: so that it is principally my will which leads me to realize that I bear the image of God'.

The 'criticist' context: Kant. In Kant the emphasis is no longer placed on the certainty of reflection which allowed philosophers to speak of an internal experience of freedom. The main thesis of Kant's 'critical philosophy' is that objective knowledge is possible only to the extent to which it conforms to the categories and to the conditions of time and space. I can know the world of nature only to the extent to which it conforms to the laws of causality, that is, to the laws of ordered succession. An 'objective experience' of freedom is hence impossible. Of course, the unity of 'I think', or the unity of apperception is at the basis of all cognitive syntheses that underly our knowledge of objects, but the apperception of 'I think' is not a living experience of our power of choice and cannot serve as a basis from which to infer the existence of a substantial free ego. According to Kant, *rational psychology* made the mistake of drawing this inference. Kant's strictures are aimed not only against the analysis in Descartes' *Fourth Meditation* but against any attempt to constitute a psychology of will on the basis of introspection.

If, however, the will cannot be analysed from the point of view of theoretical reason we must turn our attention to 'practical reason'. I do not know *what* will is but I can determine the practical conditions of *good* will. To do this, it is enough to reflect on the judgments of ordinary moral consciousness, which, in the practical sphere, has an authority comparable to science in the theoretical sphere: 'Nothing that we could think of either in the world or outside it could without restriction be held to be good except good will.' Thus begins Kant's *Groundwork of the Metaphysics of Morals*. The idea of good will as intrinsically good, as absolutely good, irrespective of its 'usefulness' is linked with the view that good will always remains practical and can never become 'knowledge'. To say that will is practical is to say that it lasts only as long as the judgments of good will are held to be valid. Henceforth, philosophy's task becomes, first, to disentangle, by a regressive process, the the concept of free will contained in the concept of good will – this is the analytic path of the *Groundwork* – and then, by a progressive path, as in geometry, to arrive at the theorems that make moral judgment possible – this is the synthetic path of the *Critique of Practical Reason*. It is a *critique* and not a psychology, for it merely defines the necessary conditions of moral judgments, it is not a description of the experience of these conditions.

In this constellation of necessary conditions the ideas of will and duty are rigorously correlative. I have as little cognitive access to a will that represents the power of negation as to a will that represents the power of creating exceptions to rules. I know will only as it is determined by law – the moral law. Free will and moral law are inseparable: free will is the basis of moral law and the moral law is the presupposition of knowing free will.

Does this mean that critical philosophy succeeded in showing that the experience of a will that chooses to ignore duty is philosophically unimportant? Not at all. In the first place, the positing of rational will constantly refers back to its contrary, desire, which critical philosophy banished into the domain of 'pathology'. It is clear that the task of the 'critique' can be carried out only at the cost of instituting various divisions and dichotomies. But this is not all; a division must be introduced within the will itself. Indeed, at each step Kant's critique comes perilously close to the idea of an *arbitrary* will, placed at the crossroads, as it were, between the moral law and desire. It is because of this arbitrary will that the moral law is not encountered simply as a rational determination but as an obligation, as a contraint, in the human experience of duty. It is thus not just will and desire that critical philosophy separates from each other; the will itself is divided into a purely practical will, which is the synthesis of freedom and law, and a simply human will, which is the contingent factor in moral experience. It is this arbitrary will which, in Kant's *Religion within the Limits of Reason*, becomes part of a meditation on 'radical evil', a term which brings to mind the Augustinian reflection on captive freedom. Thus at the boundary of practical reason we are faced with the enigma and the scandal of bad will, brought about by the problems created by the concept of good will.

The 'dialectical' context: Hegel. Hegelian philosophy is an attempt to give a dialectical answer to the series of divisions introduced by critical philosophy: division between the *a priori* and the emprical, theoretical reason and practical reason, moral obligation and desire, rational will and arbitrary will. While the critical philosophy was separating opposites, Hegel, with the help of his dialectic method, tried to show how the 'contradiction' in each case can be transcended and preserved (*aufgehoben*) in a higher unity, making possible a more complete or more adequate understanding of reality.

The dialectical conception of freedom, in Hegel, is not merely one example among others of a dialectical solution of a problem brought to an impasse by critical philosophy; rather, in many respects, it constitutes the dialectical core of the entire Hegelian system.

At the beginning of the *Philosophy of Right*, Hegel describes in abstract terms the dialectical constitution of will. Will is characterized first by a certain indeterminacy; it has the power to set oneself at a distance from any desire and to posit oneself in the pure reflection of an 'I' without content; this initial characteristic of will is that of empty *universality*. At the same time, will involves the ability to determine oneself in respect to a limited end; this second characteristic of will is that of *particularity*; here will becomes something determined. Finally, will is the union of these two moments: 'It is the particularity reflected into itself and in this raised to universality, that is, to *individuality*'. In the concept of individuality the opposition of the universal and the particular is conceived as the source of the power of the will to determine itself.

This dialectical schema is sufficient to show that from Hegel's position freedom is thinkable only if the concept of freedom can be thought dialectically. Freedom is not simply an undifferentiated and ineffable experience; free will is articulated in discourse, the task of philosophy being to extract its underlying logic and to show that this logic is not merely a formal and empty structure but the logic of being.

It is the discourse of the experience of willing that Hegel examines in the successive levels of the *Philosophy of Mind*. At all levels freedom affirms its dialectical character.

The philosophy of freedom, however, cannot be fully developed at the level of the psychology of faculties; it requires a close analysis of a series of institutional forms which mark the passage from the subjective mind to the *objective mind*. The true Hegelian philosophy of freedom is a philosophy of culture culminating in a political philosophy, for there is no will – in the full sense of the word – as long as the initial threshold has not been crossed, the threshold, that is, of *abstract right*, where contract is the basic institution. Contract, however, unites different wills only externally by bringing together the subjects of right who 'internally' remain independent of one another. It is necessary first to internalize contractual obligation and to raise right to the level of 'subjective' morality: this is the Kantian stage described above. But subjective morality is abstract and must be surpassed – and the dialectic of the will embodied, as it were – in the forms of 'objective' morality. These forms include the institution of the family, economic and political institutions, each representing in regard to the one that precedes it an advance towards the ethical whole, the realization of freedom in a world which, if the process were to be carried to completion, would be in the full sense of the word the world of freedom. This world of freedom where will ceases to be merely 'intentional' and becomes real, is seen by Hegel to be at work in the institution of the modern State.

But what becomes of this philosophy of freedom if it is shown, as Marx in his critique of Hegel's political philosophy claimed to have shown, that the Hegelian dialectical synthesis is a synthesis in thought only? Reacting against Kant, Hegel wanted to bridge the divisions of critical philosophy and give a true picture of the 'real'. But what if the 'real' as thought by Hegel, is found to be at odds with empirical reality, the reality of actual political experience? Once again *praxis* collides with *theôria*, but this *praxis* is no longer Kant's practical reason which underlies moral discourse; it is a revolutionary practice, set in opposition to philosophical discourse: 'Philosophers have interpreted the world in various ways, but the point is that the world should be changed.' So states the most celebrated of Marx's *Theses on Feuerbach*. But can one 'change' without 'interpreting'? And can one interpret without grasping the rational structure of reality? Marx questions Hegel and Hegel, in turn, questions Marx.

Explicit phenomenology

At the end of this survey of some philosophical contexts, we might wonder if there is a sense in which we could claim that in each case the same phenomenon is presented to us. It is in order to identify this common *core* that Husserlian phenomenology employs the operation termed 'bracketing' which aims at neutralizing philosophical issues. This bracketing of theories is only a particular case of the general method of 'reduction' which puts out of action the 'natural attitude' and, with it, the consideration of the actual lived experience involved in a historical or cultural context. What remains is a purified 'lived experience' whose structure is accessible to an essential analysis.

However, before proceeding to the description of the 'lived' (the 'experienced') which corresponds to the expression 'free' or 'freedom' it is important to dispel a completely erroneous interpretation of the meaning of the word 'lived' as it appears in Husserlian phenomenology. It in no way suggests an ineffable experience. On the contrary, it suggests an experience that has a meaning, an essentially *expressible* structure and which, by this very fact, lends itself to an *essential* analysis. In this respect, phenomenology and linguistic analysis are not set in opposition to each other but are placed in an inverse relation.

Linguistic analysis maintains that the discourse of action is our best means of access to experience because statements alone are public. By confining themselves to clarifying statements, analysts of ordinary language think they can avoid recourse to intuition, which, besides invoking an unverifiable 'seeing', ties its fate to private – and hence incommunicable – experiences. The phenomenologist answers that ordinary language analysis, according to its own spokesmen, is not limited to a study of the idiomatic expressions of a particular language but claims to be a conceptual analysis. This claim implies that ordinary language is considered to be the depository, through a kind of natural selection, of the most *appropriate* expressions. Now what is the criterion for the appropriateness of our statements if not the very *meaning* of experience? A linguistic analysis is thus possible on the basis of ordinary language only because, underlying language, there exists an articulated experience which is the *referent* of discourse – the private character of experience is not an obstacle to its essential description. Experience can be the object of both a private *observation* and a public *description*. This is possible because the experience of the 'lived' is directly and simultaneously the experience of a 'this-here' *and* of an 'essential structure'. This is what is meant when one says that experience is articulated, that its articulation displays certain essential features. These features are the very ones to which the conceptual analysis in analytical philosophy refers.

I shall thus not oppose phenomenology to linguistic analysis; they seem to arise from two different but convergent strategies. Linguistic analysis, based on the public character of statements, proceeds from the meaning of statements to the experience which is their 'referent'. Phenomenology – maintaining that statements themselves produce nothing but merely expresses certain articulations of meaning which are not linguistic but go deeper into prepredicative structures – proceeds from the meaning of the 'lived' to the language in which it is expressed. However, since one can reach the meaning of the lived only by way of what one says about it, and since one understands what one says only by restoring the meaning of the lived, it is towards a linguistic phenomenology that we must move, following a suggestion by Austin in *A Plea for Excuses*.

Intention. The first feature of the lived which we call *free* concerns *intention*. It is perhaps here that the difference between the two strategies is most apparent. Phenomenology can speak of voluntary intention because it possesses a general term, intention, which first designates the most general feature of the lived – that of being directed towards something. It is this feature that is indicated in language: we say the awareness of . . . , the perception of . . . , the memory of . . . , the desire for . . . , the love of (for) . . . In addition, this general term, intention, designates the unity of a meaning capable of being identified, distinguished from any other, and so of being described and expressed. To be concerned with the phenomenology of voluntary intention is to ask what distinguishes the meaning of the 'willed' from that of the 'perceived', the 'imagined', etc.

The 'willed' can be described as a kind of anticipation, a

project. A project is different from a prediction because here the intended event is an action and moreover an action to be performed not by someone other than the one who anticipates the action, but by the one who, by deciding, commits himself to doing it. This direct involvement of the willing subject in the content of his project is characteristic of volition.

Moreover, volition presents a very complex structure containing many different elements: the perceptual grasp of a situation, the imaginative projection of certain aims to be attained, ethical and other judgments, an estimation of the obstacles and the possible paths, an evaluation of means and ends, a probability judgment of the chances for success, etc. This is why Husserl regards volition as belonging to the level of 'polythetic syntheses', i.e. as belonging to those acts (at the level of judgment) which contain several 'themes' or things posited (in perception, in imagination, etc.). This complex structure finds its expression in a linguistic statement – the very thing that linguistic analysis takes as its starting-point.

As we have said, linguistic analysis follows an inverse path: from statements towards the lived. The *lived* which the phenomenologist deals with becomes the referent of the discourse of action. It is not surprising that the term 'intention' assumes a privileged position here. It is, however, no longer taken as the specification of a more general *concept* of intention. In Husserl this comprehensive concept was not derived from a particular type of statement but was interpreted as resulting from an operation which was itself comprehensive, namely, the operation of 'reduction' or *epoché*, which alone reveals the essential aspects of 'consciousness' and shows it to be through and through the consciousness of . . . For analysts, on the other hand – for example, for Miss Anscombe in her *Intention* – the meaning of the word 'intention' is measured strictly by its use-value in well determined contexts, when one says for example: I *intend to* do this or that; I perform a given action *intentionally*; I do this or that *with the intention of* obtaining such and such result. In these three cases we mention intention only if we also mention an action of a public kind. Analysis is thus centered on the question: what does one add to the designation of an action by calling it 'intentional'? The first of the three expressions – 'I intend to' – is the most bothersome for linguistic analysis: there is not yet any action to show and so to qualify as intentional. The action is completely contained within the intention itself. Does this mean that linguistic analysis refers purely and simply to the description of the project in phenomenological analysis? It seems to me rather that the lived which involves a private observation, calls for a description that is entirely public. I can *warn* another person of my intentions. This declaration and this communication of intention are possible because the verbal expression of intention belongs to the class of speech-acts possessing an 'illocutionary' structure appropriate to communicating intention. What psychologists call willing is indeed stated linguistically in verbal forms closely resembling promising, which Austin, we recall, takes as the model for performatives. To the extent to which volitive intention is fully expressed in a declaration of intention, intention displays all the features of a performative. It is a statement which is neither true nor false but which can fail or fall short, be empty or invalidated. On the other hand, it is a statement that does what it says: to say 'I promise' is in fact to promise; to say 'I intend to . . .' is indeed to begin to try to do . . . It is thus not surprising that the declaration of intention, like the promise, has its illocutionary force and its performative sense only in statements in the first person of the present tense indicative: to say 'I intend to . . .' is to have that intention, It is thus the theory of illocutionary acts that provides the best approach to the first of the three meanings of the word 'intention' distinguished by Miss Anscombe. It is indeed at this level that the discourse of action is distinguished from any other. Volition, in particular, – which so closely resembles a command addressed to another person or a promise made to oneself – appears to be the psychological side of a series of illocutionary acts that have a determined linguistic structure.

A second feature of intention discerned by phenomenology – namely, its complex, hierarchical, 'polythetic' constitution – is widely developed in linguistic analysis. To the polythetic constitution of the 'lived' corresponds, on the level of statements, an eminently *discursive* structure, characteristic of expressions in which one is said to act *with* a given intention. This is the third sense of the word 'intention' retained by Miss Anscombe. Here the intention designates not so much a feature by which one makes intelligible what one does – either by projecting the action or by interpreting it after the event – but a distant aim, that is, an ultimate result posited by an end in relation to all the intermediary actions that are posited as means. An action is intentional in this sense when it is thus placed in the perspective of a chain of means and ends and receives from this concatenation an articulated structure.

In this respect, the statements which describe an isolated action – raising my arm – are scarcely action statements; they lack the discursive character that confers upon action 'the intention with which' one does something. A true action statement contains at least two segments of action, ordered in relation to each other: I raise my arm to signal that I am turning. Two statements joined in this way convey the syntax as well as the semantic structure of action: I do p so that q.

What we call intention in this third sense is much closer to reasoning than to an idea; it is, in fact, formulated in a chain of statements which, together, designate the 'order' of the action. What since Aristotle has been called practical reasoning merely expresses in the formal language of logic the ordering of action through intention. True practical reasoning always takes its starting point from something that is desired; it classifies, orders, stratifies the characteristics of desirability that are connected to successive grades of action. By thus describing his desires in terms of the 'characteristics of desirability', the speaking subject places his desires within a calculus of means and ends. This is a sign of freedom: to be capable not only of 'being tormented by, of yielding to' one's desires but of expressing them in language by stating the characteristic of desirability that is appropriate to them and on submitting the chain of action to the calculus of means and ends. Desire is then no longer merely a sensation; it is placed at a distance, as a distant end in relation to the system of ways and means, of obstacles and instruments that the action must go through in order to 'fulfil' an intention. At this point, a linguistic phenomenology of intention borders upon a *theory of argumentation* (C. Perelman) or even a decision and game theory which makes use of mathematical models. Here, however, we go beyond the bounds of a linguistic analysis of ordinary language as well as phenomenology of the 'lived'. The formal analysis of the strategies used by the economist or the war analyst, in fact, abstracts from real situations, real conflicts, real decisions. Although the word 'decision' still features in the expression 'decision theory', the use of a logical calculus to analyse conjectured situations involves going far beyond any direct reflection on the actual reasoning occasioned by real conduct. Here we find ourselves outside the analysis of ordinary language and outside phenomenology.

Intention and motive.   We return to linguistic analysis and to phenomenology by considering the second use of the term 'intention' in expressions such as: I have performed a given action *intentionally*, on purpose, inadvertently, etc. The notion of intention is no longer taken here in its forward-looking sense. It is an action mentioned in a past tense which we qualify or modify *adverbially*.

While the linguistic analysis of the descriptions mentioned earlier led towards the formalism of the argumentation theory and the calculus of the decision and game theory, this time the phenomenological analysis leads the linguistic analysis towards the interiority of the agent. Let us begin then with linguistic analysis and try to understand the inflexions that phenomenology imposes upon it.

Linguistic analysis is a good introduction to understanding the *adverbial* use of intention. Indeed, linguistic analysis reveals in an entirely straightforward fashion the network-like constitution of our actual discourse. To make the meaning of intention explicit is, in fact, to relate intention to motive. An action done intentionally is one which is explained in terms of motives, attributing to this word the sense of 'reason for acting' rather than that of 'cause'; it is, furthermore, an action attributed to a responsible agent, capable of designating himself as the one who performed the action. We shall ignore for the moment the second implication in order to concentrate on the first. By thus referring the intentional character of the action to a mode of explanation – explanation by motives in the sense of reasons for acting – we also give a sense to the expression 'free act'. The sense we attach to this word is not really different from the sense we attach to the explanation of the intention by motives. To say that an act is free is to include it in the category of acts that are described by a whole network of concepts, each concept referring to all the others: project to motive, motive to agent, etc. Understanding the word 'free' means bringing into play the entire network of semantic links between the key words in this universe of discourse.

In the network of action discourse, the relation intention – motive is particularly noteworthy. We speak of intention only in cases where the answer to the question 'why?' invokes a motive which, for us, has the sense of a reason for acting and not the sense of a cause. To call an act intentional is thus first of all to exclude a certain kind of explanation, explanation by cause. Of course, there are reasons which resemble causes; these are the motives which can be said to 'look back': I take revenge *because* a certain person killed my father; I express my gratitude because a certain person did me a good turn; I take pity because a certain person has fallen on hard times. However, although certain motives 'look back', they do not impel in the manner of causes. It is not the past event as such that produces my current feeling, my present action, but a certain feature of that event, a feature judged bad or good to which the action corresponds. This is why we say: *from* vengeance, *from* pity, etc.; a past event motivates a present action only through the intermediary of a desirable feature, whether positive or negative, which is itself evaluated, interpreted.

This feature is most marked when the alleged motive is neither antecedent nor a consequence of the act, but a way of interpreting the act. I give you such and such a reason for my action; this means: I ask you to consider the action in a certain light, to place it in a certain perspective, to consider it *as*... To allege a motive (in the sense of a reason for acting) is to try to give a meaning which can be communicated to another person and understood by him; the motive makes the action such and such, gives it a certain character, makes it comprehensible from a particular point of view, relates it to psychological, moral, social or cultural meanings which are understood by others; in short, to allege a motive is to *clarify* what one does in the eyes of others and in one's own eyes.

An important approximation to the notion of freedom results from this analysis of the notions of intention and motive in ordinary language. An action is considered free if one can account for it, to others and to oneself, by alleging motives which have the meaning of 'reason for' and not the meaning of 'cause'. We say of actions that they are 'compelled' or done 'under constraint' when we cannot explain them by reference to motives in the sense of 'reasons for' but can in the sense of 'causes'. Between the actions explicable in terms of 'reason for' and those explicable in terms of 'cause', there is a large number of actions representing a variety of intermediary stages between free and constrained. In this respect, for ordinary language, freedom and constraint are not separated by an unbridgeable gulf; they are two poles between which there are various degrees of what is free and what is less free, what is constrained and less constrained. The art of conversation is superior to any philosophy in this play of degrees and nuances (cf. Austin, *A Plea for Excuses*).

But can linguistic analysis justify the distinction between motive and cause? To my mind this distinction is valid only if it can be referred back to a prepredicative structure of experience. The relation motive – project is one of these structures. In fact, it is the prime structure of the phenomenology of will; but this link between motive and project is revealed in its specificity only when the sphere of the lived is clearly distinguished from the sphere of 'natural phenomena', where the causal connection is the dominant feature.

The separation between motive and cause is thus, like the notion of intention, taken in its fullest scope, the result of the 'reduction' applied to the natural attitude. 'Motivation' then appears as a necessary feature of anything that is characterized by intention and purpose.

Phenomenology, however, does not only bring a justification to linguistic analysis; it also adds a rectification. We have seen the tendency of linguistic analysis to identify motive and reason for acting. If the term 'motive' is taken to have the same extension as the term 'intention', it must also be accepted that this term has a wider extension than the term 'reason for acting'. Language, it seems, lays a trap here that should be exposed. Motives, in fact, have a privileged expression in language when they take on the canonical form of an argument, a justification, a defence; they are then stated as 'reasons for' doing this or that. But if the motivation is expressed in language in the form of 'reasons for', this can only be a rationalization, in the psychoanalytic sense of the word, that is, a kind of screen or mask. Linguistic expression must be referred back to the meaning of the lived. A detailed phenomenology of 'motives' shows that rational justification is only one of the modalities of the general function of motive, which is to give 'support' to willing; this general function of support was well described at the beginning of this century by Pfänder in his *Phenomenology of Motivation*.

It allows us to cover an entire spectrum of concrete possibilities, of which motive in the sense of 'reason for' constitutes only one pole. At the other end of the spectrum of forms, there are drives in which the attraction towards the end is indistinguishable from the force of the impulse. Here meaning and force are fused; this we see in the Freudian theory of 'drives' where an 'economy' of cathexis is combined with the dynamics of motives and projects. It is because the roots of motivation reach deep down to the layer of instinct and instinct-inspired desire that the split between motive and cause retains a purely methodological meaning. Here the phenomenological analysis shows the lived to be anchored in my body, at the limit of all discourse. In turn, the lived body appears as the *total field of motivation*, as a place where meaning and force coincide.

The act and its agent. The prepredicative structures that underly action statements cannot be reduced to motivation. We have seen that projects also included belief – the belief that doing depends on me and that I can act. Here again language is a good guide, but only up to a certain point. Let me give an example. In English one says: to decide *something* and to decide *because . . .* , and in French: *se décider*. The reflexive form of the verb is one of the grammatical means used in certain languages to designate a noteworthy characteristic of action terms, namely, that they mention at once the thing done or to be done, the reasons for doing, the act which distinguishes the possible alternatives and, finally, the agent, he who acts: the language of action is, one might say, *self-referential*. He who acts refers to himself in stating his action; this 'self-reference' of the agent of action in the action statement expresses a fundamental feature of human action: that it can be ascribed or imputed to someone. In the same way that the discourse of action implies the distinction between action and movement, between the performative and the declarative, between motive and cause – so, too, this same discourse implies the distinction between an agent who is a person and the constant antecedent of an event which brings about the event but does not 'act'. That action is ascribed to someone is at the root of our understanding of responsibility. It is because action can be ascribed to an agent that action statements can always be reformulated in such a way that this ascription is placed in the foreground. It is always possible to say: *It is I who* did this, or *It is you who* did that. This can be called the judgment of imputation; only an action can be imputed not a movement. This characteristic of being able to be imputed to someone is one of the things we understand and presuppose when we hold an action to be 'free'.

Among the most noteworthy expressions, we must place those that express the *power* of doing. These are the expressions that bring linguistic analysis close to phenomenology. These expressions refer to power not in the sense of a logical possibility, a causal contingency or an epistemological certainty but in the sense of a capacity experienced directly as my own. In this respect, the use of conditionals – 'I could have done otherwise' – in connection with a clause introduced by *if* – 'if I had chosen', 'if I had wanted', etc. – has given rise to an entire literature in linguistics on the subject of 'ifs and cans'. The question arising here concerns the reference of these expressions. This question invites us to explore the phenomenological difference between physical capacity and human aptitude.

In this investigation phenomenology most certainly allows itself to be guided by the 'self-referring' linguistic expressions of the agent. But, just as it resists the temptation to identify motive and reason for acting, phenomenology resists the tendency to see the experience of a power or capacity to act as something that requires merely an analysis of the *judgment* of imputation; to give this experience a purely *juridical* interpretation, as if the entire meaning of the notion of agent were included in the *argumentation* by which one attributes to an agent his 'share' of the action, as one might attribute a right to someone. Of course, the most reflective forms of ascribing an action to someone, and of imputing responsibility, do set in motion the processes of defence and refutation of a juridical character, as the language of excuses so amply shows. However an analysis of prepredicative structures brings to light what we earlier called *belief*, the belief that acting depends on me and that I can act. It is here that statements of the form 'I could if I wanted', much more than argumentative forms by which one ascribes an action to its agent in the way one ascribes a right to him, have an immediate proximity to the phenomenological core of 'I can'. These expressions indeed refer immediately – that is, go beyond any mediation of an argumentative type – to a practical conviction, which reaches without an intermediary the lived link between 'I will' and 'I can'.

Another experience of the lived body is found here, an experience which is no longer that of the whole field of motivation but that of the whole field of power. Indeed, the credit given to my powers connects my will not only with the desires that incite it to act but also with the corporeal aptitudes, the acquired abilities, the routine responses by which willing is extended into 'moving'. Maine de Biran centred his entire philosophy of will on this experience of passing from idea to movement in the production of a voluntary movement. A century later, Maurice Merleau-Ponty, extending the analysis of perceptual experience to volitive experience, showed that in both these kinds of experience the body is presupposed as a cluster of powers which are more or less available to us. The body is not then known as object but grasped as lived body, as my body. It is the 'I can' of the 'I will'. At the same time, it is also the field of absolutely involuntary 'actions'; everything that occurs in me without my direct control and helps to maintain the basis of life out of which all my powers arise. This obscure basis of life is no longer the domain of a phenomenology of the lived but of biological science, which objectifies it in natural knowledge.

Conclusion.   Phenomenological analysis and linguistic analysis partially overlap. On the one hand, the 'lived' described by phenomenology displays certain articulations, an essential structure which in turn is reflected in the structure of statements for which linguistic analysis constructs the theory. On the other hand, linguistic analysis carries us back to phenomenological experience in so far as what is said in these statements is experience itself. Linguistic analysis and phenomenology thus operate at two different strategic levels: the level of the meaning of the lived and that of the articulations of discourse. Phenomenological analysis shows in addition, however, that the lived is rooted in my body, at the limit of all discourse.

Does this mean that a combination of phenomenology and linguistic analysis in a kind of linguistic phenomenology could be substituted, without any loss, for a philosophical reflection of the kind we have been evoking in the above analysis? This does not seem to be the case. The abstract character of analytic efforts cannot be forgotten. To see this clearly, it is enough to compare the concept of volition as isolated by phenomenology and by linguistic analysis, with the concept of praxis as it has come down from Aristotle to Marx.

Consider, for example, the topics covered by a theory of praxis: the relationship between one will and another will in conflict, in cooperation, in contract, etc.; the problem of norms that give a rational character to human action; action within an institutional framework, e.g. action performed within a technological context where it acquires the sense of work; within an economic or social context where desire becomes human need as it relates to work and to money, or within a political context where an individual is confronted with various forms of organized political power within a given constitutional framework.

A theory of praxis has a much wider scope than a mere psychology of will and fully reveals the complexity of the problem of freedom. A philosophy of practice involves a philosophical inquiry of an order very different from that of an analysis of action-terms of ordinary language. The topic of such an inquiry is the problem of *realization of freedom*. This involves an investigation of how one will is related to another and of the role of norms and institutions. It is these problems which ultimately lead the phenomenology of will to the philosophy of freedom.

Is There a 'Problem of Freedom'?

ANTONY FLEW

The paper begins by indicating what the philosophical problems here are. It then considers the general line of Sartre, who urges that we do have alternatives on a great many occasions when we pretend that we do not. The conclusion is that this contention is as true as it is important. Indeed we only say that someone had no choice, or could not have done otherwise, when, in a more fundamental sense, he did, and he could. Nevertheless Sartre exaggerates; and the truth in what he says is obscured by, rather than derived from, its Heideggerian integuments.

Antony Flew is Professor of Philosophy at the University of Reading. He is the author of *A New Approach to Psychical Research* (1953), *Hume's Philosophy of Belief* (1961), *God and Philosophy* (1966), *Evolutionary Ethics* (1967), *An Introduction to Western Philosophy* (1971), and *Crime or Disease?* (1973); the editor of *Logic and Language* (First and Second Series), *Essays in Conceptual Analysis, Body, Mind and Death*, and *Malthus On Population*; and joint editor of *New Essays in Philosophical Theology*.

(1) Our Editor has assigned to me the task of tackling the title question, considered as a question about what Sartre had to say in the chapter on 'Being and Doing: Freedom' in *Being and Nothingness*[1]. This chapter is Chapter I of Part II. My short answer to the question thus set is that there is, of course, a philosophical problem of freedom; or, rather, that there is a large collection of related problems traditionally so labelled. What is not so evident is that Sartre has either an adequate appreciation of the nature of these problems or much to offer towards their solution. Yet what he says has, I think, to be seen in this perspective; and not as a wrestling with some different problem not compassed by the professionally 'cool practitioners of philosophical analysis'.

(a) The traditional philosophical problems of freewill are very frequently mischaracterized, not only by philosophically uninstructed laymen, but also by many of those paid to know better. The endemic error is prejudicially so to specify the problem that one of two rival kinds of solution is taken as given. The question is then put as that of 'Freewill *or* Determinism?' But if that is indeed what the issue is, then what remains to be investigated is: not at all a philosophical question of 'the relations of ideas'; but instead a psychological 'matter of fact and real existence'. The logically prior and more truly philosophical question can be put, a little awkwardly, as that of 'Freewill *and* Determinism' *or* 'Freewill or Determinism?'

In this understanding the traditional philosophical problems of freewill are seen as problems of the logical analysis of, and of the logical relations between, members of two ranges of terms and expressions; focussing upon the big divisive question whether the presuppositions and the implications of the application of members of the one set are or are not compatible with those of the application of members of the other set. On the one hand we have all the notions which are apparently essential to the ascription and repudiation of responsibility: 'He acted of his own freewill', for instance, 'He had no choice',

---

[1] Translated by Professor Hazel Barnes of the University of Colorado (New York and London: Philosophical Library and Methuen, 1956 and 1957, respectively). The original French was first published in France under the German occupation (Paris: NRF, 1943). For the benefit of those unable, or for reasons of 'racial' or party loyalty unwilling, to read French all quotations in the text will be given in the English translation. But I shall in the notes, after providing the page references to this, give also those to *L'être et le néant* (Paris: NRF-Gallimard, 1966).

or 'He could have done otherwise'. On the other side we have the ideas embraced in such claims as that everything which happens has a cause, or that everything which happens could – in principle, of course – be subsumed under universal laws of nature. (In this secular and scientific age we may, I think, properly confine to a parenthesis mention here of what for us must now be the special case: namely, the problems generated by the basic theist claim that the universe is the creature of an omnipotent and omniscient God – 'He's got the whole world in his hands'.)[2]

The big divisive question arises because it looks as if the assumptions and the implications of the two sets of notions, both of which we seem to have the strongest of justifying reasons for employing, are in conflict. What we take to be our everyday knowledge of human beings appears to show that it is often truly said that someone could have done differently than he did. Yet the presuppositions and achievements of deterministic science seem to involve that nothing ever could have been other than it was, is, or will be; and that everything which happens occurs as the necessary and inevitable result of antecedent causes. One kind of answer to the big question is to contend that the two sets of notions are largely, or even completely, compatible. Such contentions are now usefully labelled Compatibility Theses. The opposite response is to urge that, on the contrary, they are incompatible. Contentions of this kind are now called, correspondingly, Incompatibility Theses.

It is too rarely noticed that most of the classical philosophers who published in this area were Compatibilists of some stripe. This was certainly true of Hobbes, of Leibniz, of Locke, of the later Hume, and of John Stuart Mill; to say nothing of Aquinas and Luther, of Calvin and Jonathan Edwards. Heaven forbid that we should try to settle a philosophical dispute by appeal to any sort of authority. But anyone unaware that Compatibilism has been thus most respectably defended necessarily disqualifies himself from trying to meet the Compatibilist case at its strong-

---

[2] Anyone who therefore infers that I myself want to minimize the importance of this special case, or to deny its possible relevance to the contemporary secular discussion, may be referred to three other contributions: 'Divine omnipotence and human freedom' in A. Flew and A. MacIntyre (eds.), *New Essays in Philosophical Theology* (London and New York: SCM Press and Macmillan, 1955 and 1956, respectively); 'Compatibilism and the free will defence', in *Philosophy* 1973; and Part III of *Crime or Disease?* (London and New York: Macmillan, and Barnes and Noble, 1973).

est. Immediately to the present point this innocence increases his temptation to misrepresent the traditional problem as presupposing Incompatibilism; and also – if he is, reasonably, reluctant to deny either of the two putative rivals – his temptation simply to repress that problem.

You are bound to get it all wrong if you insist upon first introducing a technical libertarian sense of 'freewill', and then forthwith mistaking it to be without any argument obvious that freewill, in this philosophers' sense, either is or is presupposed by freewill, in the ordinary lay sense (in which we typically contrast actions done of a person's own freewill with actions done under compulsion). Since this technical sense of 'freewill' is defined in terms of uncaused causes it must indeed be immediately obvious that any such libertarian freewill could not but be incompatible with any universal causal determinism. What is certainly not obvious – and what, surely, the well-girded Incompatibilist should (not simply assume but) argue against the Compatibilist – is that this libertarian notion of freewill is contained in the very idea of action; and hence that Incompatibilism is after all true.[3]

(b) The hesitation in my assessment of the subject chapter is in the main a product of the extreme and – as it seems to me – gratuitous, and therefore scandalous, obscurity and mystification of so much of Sartre's philosophical writing and, presumably, thinking. The long suffering mind of any student of *Being and Nothingness* must boggle when he reads Mary Warnock's comparative comment on *The Critique of Dialectical Reason*. She speaks

of the almost impossible difficulty of reading the latest book, in which all the worst features of French and German philosophical writing seem to have come together to produce a book which must tax the perseverance of the most enthusiastic, and in which, of his earlier philosophical style, only the deliberate obscurity is left. I believe that it is positively *wrong* to write in such a way.[4]

---

[3] For a fuller representation of the classical philosophical problems of freewill in the understanding sketched in the text see, besides the discourses mentioned in note 2 above, ch. vii of my *Introduction to Western Philosophy* (London and Indianapolis: Thames and Hudson, and Bobbs-Merrill, 1971).

[4] *The Philosophy of Sartre* (London: Hutchinson, 1965), p. 12. The italics were introduced by Mrs Warnock herself.

There was an older time when they ordered these things better in France. For it was not thus with Descartes or with Bayle in the seventeenth century. And in the eighteenth among the *Maxims* of the Marquis de Vauvenargues we find waiting uncopied for the copy book of Sartre: 'Obscurity is the kingdom of error'; 'Clearness is the ornament of deep thought'; and – straight to the heart – 'For the philosopher clarity is a matter of good faith'.

(2) The most exciting thing in our subject chapter, and indeed for my money the most exciting thing in all Sartre, is the dramatic conclusion: 'that man, being condemned to be free, carries the weight of the whole world on his shoulders; he is responsible for the world and for himself as a way of being'. Sartre glosses this as involving responsibility 'in its ordinary sense as "consciousness (of) being the incontestable author of an event or of an object"';[5] and such authorship must, surely, always involve that in some crucial and fundamental sense the author could have done otherwise.

My main aim in the present section is to show that no such conclusion can be derived from those distinctive notions from which, I think, Sartre thinks that he has derived it. In the following section I shall try to show how the thing which is both important and true here might have been, and should be, justified.

(a) The first part of our chapter is called 'Freedom: the First Condition of Action'. It begins:

It is strange that philosophers have been able to argue endlessly about determinism and freewill, to cite examples in favour of one or other thesis, without ever attempting first to make explicit the structures contained in the very idea of action ... We should observe that an action is on principle intentional. The careless smoker who has through negligence caused the explosion of a powder magazine has not acted.[6]

---

[5] P. 553: p. 639. This conclusion reads splendidly in the French: 'La conséquence essentielle de nos remarques antérieures, c'est que l'homme, étant condamné à être libre, porte le poids du monde tout entier sur ses épaules: il est responsable du monde et de lui-même en tant que manière d'être. Nous prenons le mot de "responsabilité" en son sens banal de conscience (d') être l'auteur incontestable d'un événement ou d'un objet'.

[6] P. 433: p. 508.

This is not a promising start. For the first statement apparently takes it as obvious that determinism and freewill must be incompatible, and that the philosophical problem therefore is that of discovering which of these two rival doctrines is in fact true. Despite a philosophical training which ought to have taught him better Sartre thus begins by putting forward precisely the misconceptions described in 1(a), above. The second sentence expresses what is for him a fundamental. It was, therefore, sloppy to offer nothing to meet the obvious if perhaps easily surmountable objection that people are often truly said to have acted unintentionally. The third statement is, surely, just plain false. For although the careless smoker had no intention of causing the explosion he presumably was acting, and acting negligently, when he dropped his unextinguished cigarette end and failed to tread it out.

(b) Having thus to his own satisfaction established that the key concept is action, and that this is always and essentially intentional, Sartre proceeds at once to deduce that

action necessarily implies as its condition the recognition of a '*desideratum*'; that is, of an objective lack or again of a '*négatité*' . . . This means that from the moment of the first conception of the act, consciousness has been able to withdraw itself from the full world of which it is consciousness and to leave the level of being in order frankly to approach that of non-being.

Warming to this heady Heideggerian work Sartre continues: 'Consciousness in so far as it is considered exclusively in its being, is perpetually referred from being to being and cannot find in being any motive for revealing non-being.'[7] After a short discussion of two interesting historical examples Sartre concludes: '(1) No factual state whatever it may be . . . is capable by itself of motivating any act whatsoever. For an act is a projection of the for-itself towards what is not, and what is can in no way determine by itself what is not. (2) No factual state can determine consciousness to apprehend it as a *négatité* or lack.'[8]

The first of these last three sentences is, I am sure, to be construed and defended as a made to measure necessary truth:

[7] Pp. 433–4: pp. 508–9.
[8] Pp. 435–6: pp. 510–1.

like Hume's 'Reason is . . . the slave of the passions'. The point is that it must be impossible to deduce from even the fullest wholly neutral and detached description of a man's environment what that man will want to do in that environment, as he perceives and structures it as his situation. Thus interpreted as a tautology what is said is illuminating. This is what Sartre is after when he argues, for instance, that 'it is in and through the project of imposing his rule on all of Gaul that the state of the Western Church appears objectively to Clovis as a cause of [a motive for] his conversion'.[9]

But the second utterance, which is offered as a reason for the first, will not do at all. The high metaphysical assertion that 'what is can in no way determine what is not' is falsified whenever today's causes produce tomorrow's effects. Much more important to us here is that this second statement expresses a crucial and quite unwarranted shift: from questions of what can, or cannot, be deduced from propositions about the environment only; to questions whether prior states of the agent could in any way determine either the consciousness or the behaviour of that agent. The argument which is sufficient to support the first claim, that no description of a man's environment is by itself adequate to determine any conclusion about what he will decide to do, does not even begin to justify any philosophically libertarian contention that there are and can be no physiological or other determinations within the man himself.

The third statement can be satisfactorily defended when it is read as a variation on the first. But we have now to distinguish – as Sartre never, it seems, does distinguish: between, on the one hand, such properly a priori claims about deducibility and non-deducibility; and, on the other hand, contingent contentions that there could not be physiological sufficient conditions of – say – his seeing the head of that spectacular pass as just the place to put his projected bistro.

If you do not appreciate this distinction you may well misconstrue these non-deducibilities as warranting Incompatibilist conclusions; and hence, if you also believe that motivation and decision are realities, as showing that many claims which have been and will be made by psychologists and physiologists must

---

[9] P. 448: p. 524 – 'apparait objectivement à Clovis comme un motif de se convertir'.

be false. Since Sartre satisfies both protases we ought not to be surprised by his drawing precisely this conclusion. If we were to admit, he says, 'that human reality can be determined to action by a prior state of the world . . . Then these acts disappear as acts in order to give place to a series of movements. Thus the notion of conduct is itself destroyed with Janet and with the Behaviourists. The existence of the act implies its autonomy.'[10]

(c) A few sentences after the three discussed in the previous sub-section Sartre further concludes: that 'as soon as one attributes to consciousness this negative power with respect to the world and itself, and as soon as the nihilation forms an integral part of the positing of an end, we must recognize that the indispensable and fundamental condition of all action is the freedom of the acting being'; and 'Thus at the outset we can see what is lacking in those tedious discussions between determinists and the proponents of freewill'.[11]

What the poor bores ought to do is 'to ask how a cause (or motive) can be constituted as such'.[12] For

the motive makes itself understood as what it is by means of the ensemble of beings which 'are not', by ideal existences, and by the future. Just as the future turns back upon the present and the past in order to elucidate them, so it is the ensemble of my projects which turns back in order to confer upon the motive its structure as a motive. It is only because I escape the in-itself by nihilating myself towards my possibilities that this in-itself can take on value as cause or motive. Causes and motives have meaning only inside a projected ensemble which is precisely an ensemble of non-existents.[13]

The key notions, which are what set Sartre off into successive orgies of pretentious verbosity and elaborate mystification, are the harmless necessary truths that a motive for action has to be a desire to bring something about, while what is to be brought about cannot actually be the case unless and until it has in fact been brought about. Sartre seems to think that he

---

[10] Pp. 476–7: p. 556. For a study of the connections and non-connections between motives, evidencing reasons, and physiological sufficient conditions see my 'A Rational Animal', in J. R. Smythies (ed.), *Brain and Mind* (London and New York: Routledge and Kegan Paul, and Humanities Press, 1965).

[11] P. 436: p. 511.

[12] P. 437: p. 512. The key phrase in the French is 'un motif (ou un mobile)'.

[13] P. 437: pp. 512–13.

may derive the important conclusion 'that the indispensable and fundamental condition of all action is the freedom of the acting being' from these favourite notions. This is strongly suggested by the dark saying that 'we must recognize' that conclusion 'as soon as we attribute to consciousness this negative power with respect to the world and itself, and as soon as the nihilation forms an integral part of the positing of an end'. It appears to be confirmed by Sartre's statement of the outcome of the preceding discussion: 'either man is wholly determined (which is inadmissible, especially because a determined consciousness – i.e. a consciousness externally motivated – becomes itself pure exteriority and ceases to be consciousness) or else man is wholly free'.[14] And, of course, since Sartre proposes to make a great song and dance around the idea that desire is a sort of directedness at what is not presently the case, there is no doubt but that he ought to be looking for some real work for that idea to do.

Whatever the difficulties of determining what Sartre did actually want to say, it is quite clear that no kind of consciousness could by its mere occurrence logically necessitate the crucial and fundamental possibility of action, and hence of acting alternatively in either one way or another. Unless the key word 'consciousness' is to be arbitrarily so redefined as to make this sentence the expression of a worse than futile necessary truth, it is false to say that 'a consciousness externally motivated . . . ceases to be consciousness'. For it just is not contradictory to suggest that some unfortunate might be totally – but totally – paralyzed while nevertheless possessing, if not exactly enjoying, every kind of consciousness. This nightmare supposition is, it may be recalled, one of the recurrent themes of the stories of Edgar Allen Poe.

Sartre is much given to alluding to Descartes, at least so long as this can be done without requiring any precise reference to the actual words of the master.[15] He might here have learnt from Descartes' example the dangers of assuming that con-

---

[14] P. 442: p. 518.

[15] Especially remarkable is his frequent talk of 'le cogito'. The first edition of the *Discourse* in fact reads: not 'Cogito ergo sum' but 'Je pense donc je suis'; which, since Descartes was writing in the vernacular, is what one would expect. 'Le je pense' would of course be even worse French than 'le cogito'. But reluctance to employ so barbaric a phrase might have served as a salutary check on alluding to that most famous paragraph without first determining precisely what the point of the allusion is to be.

sciousness is logically connected with things with which it is
not so connected. For it was, surely, partly as a result of mistaking it that thinking, in his peculiar sense of consciousness,
necessarily embraces thinking, in the ordinary sense of ratio-
cination, that Descartes became committed to the scandalous
contention that the brutes must be insensible.

(3) The reason, I suggest, why Sartre may have believed
that such necessary connections do obtain is that he does from
time to time introduce into his ecstatic contemplations of
nihilating consciousness the more pedestrian notion of acting
to realize one project as opposed to alternative possible projects.
But, of course, by thus conjoining the idea of acting with that of
consciousness he has done nothing to demonstrate that any
element of the former can be derived from the latter alone. If
we are to provide some justification for even a qualified version
of the desired dramatic conclusion, then we need to sober down
from the verbal intoxications of nihilating and not-being. We
have on the morning after to remember what Sartre himself
said at the very beginning: it is essential 'first to make explicit
the structures contained in the very idea of action'.

(a) So consider the archetypal Protestant hero: 'Here I
stand. I can no other. So help me God.' When Luther said to
the Diet of Worms that he could no other, he was not to be
construed – as the French would say if only they spoke English –
at the foot of the letter. He was not claiming to be the victim
of a sudden general paralysis. For in this perhaps the usual
sense of 'could not do otherwise' to say that I could not do
otherwise is not merely not inconsistent with but presupposes
the truth of the claim that – in what at the beginning of the
previous section I called 'the crucial and fundamental sense' – I
could have done otherwise. What, as we all know, Luther
meant – and said – was: not that his legs were paralyzed and
that the words were pouring from his mouth uncontrollably;
but that none of the alternative courses of action open to him
were to him acceptable.

Again, consider the people who do something not of their
own freewill but under compulsion. It may be the Bank Manager who opens the safe and hands out its contents in face of the
threatening machine guns of Mr 'Legs' Diamond and his business associates. Or it may be my elder daughter who says

something rude to her teacher because a horrid boy threatened to spoil her pretty new frock if she did not. The excuse that they acted under compulsion does not imply that there was no alternative possible course of action which they might have chosen. There was in each case a very obvious alternative available. It is precisely that alternative to which their respective excuses refer. The point is: not that the agent had no alternative; but that, although there was an alternative, it was one which the agent could not properly be blamed or punished for not choosing.

Both the person who does something of his own freewill, and the person who does the same thing under compulsion, act. There therefore must have been some alternative which they might have chosen. It is for this reason, and for this reason only, reasonable that we should – as we do – require more formidable alternatives to excuse more serious offences. Had our Bank Manager been able to plead only that 'Legs' Diamond had threatened to spoil the Manager's natty executive suit, his excuse would even in our softer and more permissive period have been unacceptable. Nor on the other hand would the fact that the alternative was his own death necessarily be sufficient. For it is not obvious that we ought to receive as a full excuse, as opposed to a weighty extenuation, your plea that you assisted the SS at Auschwitz, or the NKVD in the Katyn Forest, only because they would have killed you had you, like too few others, refused.

The cases where a person acts, or refrains from acting, under compulsion are totally different from cases where the person does not act at all. Suppose that I am overpowered by a team of skilful strong arm men, who throw me willy nilly out of the window. Suppose too that I fall through the roof of your greenhouse, and that your treasured orchids are ruined by that fall. Then, however excusable in the excitement of the moment, it would be incorrect for you to demand to know why I did such damage to those precious orchids; or for me to explain that I acted only under compulsion. For there is no conduct to be explained. I did not do or refrain from doing anything. I did not act under compulsion. I did not act at all. The responsible agents were the defenestrators. I was simply a missile victim.

(b) The previous subsection is a mere sketch for the prolegomena to the analysis of the concept of action. Yet even that is enough to indicate the sound and simple justification for a qualified and weakened version of Sartre's own dramatic conclusion. For it is both true and enormously worth saying that wherever people are agents they chose to do what they did do, and they always could have done other than they did. If they do nothing where as agents they could do something, that too is part of their conduct: 'Not to choose is, in fact, to choose not to choose'.[16]

It would, therefore, even be correct to say that every agent is as such abandoned; if only that meant only that he cannot help making some choice – perhaps the final choice of suicide. 'I am abandoned in the world . . . I bear the whole responsibility without being able, whatever I do, to tear myself away from this responsibility . . . and suicide is one mode among others of being-in-the-world.'[17]

All this is true because in the intended senses of the words it is necessarily true. It is enormously worth saying because there are truths which we are forever concealing from ourselves under too easily misunderstood excuses: 'I could not have done otherwise', 'I had no choice', and so on. For just as it would be inept to claim that, in the superficial sense, you could not have done otherwise unless, in the fundamental sense, you could; so when we say, in the correspondingly superficial and usual sense, that we had no choice, we are taking it for granted that, in a fundamental sense, we had. When members of the family of *The Godfather* make someone 'an offer which he cannot refuse', and when that someone says he has no choice but to accept, he surely does have a choice. He is in this unlike the rival mafioso gunned down without warning.

To insist in this way upon the inescapable responsibility of the agent as such has point and value. Compare the more particular

---

[16] P. 481: p. 561. The 'en effet' translated 'in fact' might perhaps here for once have been better rendered as 'in effect'.

[17] Pp. 555–6: p. 641. Anyone so donnishly austere as to prefer to take his philosophy unspiced by references to nothingness, facticity or even abandonment, can be referred to a decisive paragraph in Locke's great chapter 'Of the Idea of Power'. For there, all of a quarter of a millenium before Sartre, that archetypal Anglo-Saxon John Locke wrote: 'It is unavoidably necessary to prefer the doing or forebearing of an action in a man's power . . . a man must necessarily will the one or the other of them; upon which preference or volition, the action or its forebearance certainly follows, and is truly voluntary. But the act of volition, or preferring one of the two, being that which he cannot avoid, a man, in respect of that act of willing, is under a necessity, and so cannot be free . . .' (*Essay* ii (xxi) 23).

case of responding to the excuse of a general and chronic lack of time by insisting, equally tautologically, that everyone's day contains no less and no more than the same twenty four hours. So if I have time for this but not for that it can only be: not because I have less time in the days of my life than other people do; but because I choose to spend my time not upon that but upon this.

(c) I have been trying to show that part of the conclusions of Sartre must be true of all agents as such. But part is not all; and there is also the question of how often, if ever, we in fact are agents. Since it is essential to this notion that any agent qua agent must in the fundamental sense have been able to do otherwise, anyone who like Sartre wishes to make much of our agency owes it both to his public and to truth herself to try somehow to come to terms with suggestions that science can make no room for such possibilities.

Sartre is, as I indicated earlier, ruinously inhibited by his combined ignorance of and contempt for his boring predecessors.[18] It may indeed be true that 'the notion of conduct is itself destroyed with Janet and with the Behaviourists'. It certainly is true that, in some sense, 'The existence of the act implies its autonomy'.[19] But we are, especially in so long an essay, entitled to at least a reference to some other work in which the errors of this alleged denial of the reality of conduct are dealt with more fully and at closer quarters. And furthermore, since there are and will be other psychologists and physiologists besides Janet and the Behaviourists, we have to know more about this autonomy. Does it, for instance, imply that there can be no contingently sufficient physiological conditions even for the performance of one particular action taken on one particular occasion?[20]

[18] Not for the first or the last time it has to be said that no one has any business to plunge into print with a discussion of philosophical questions about freewill unless they have subjected themselves to the propaedeutic of some catholic course of classical reading. One good but still entirely manageable programme would be to read both Schopenhauer's prize *Essay on the Freedom of the Will* and the relevant portions of all the earlier works mentioned therein. An edition by K. Kolenda of that *Essay* is included in the excellent Library of Liberal Arts (Indianapolis and New York: Bobbs-Merrill. 1960).

[19] Quoted in 2(b), above (reference in note 10).

[20] For an explanation of the type/token distinction see, for instance, pp. 249 and 352 of the *IWP* of note 3.

If it really does, then Sartre – and, of course, not only Sartre – is going to be in a lot of trouble. Given any analysis of this sort no one, surely, has any business to be as sure as most people are that he truly is an agent. For if this is indeed part of what being an agent implies, then to know that one was would be to know the truth of some very bold negative claims.[21] We should, therefore, perhaps not be surprised, although it is still permissible to be scandalized, to notice how unforthcoming Sartre is upon this crucial point.

Apart from the short way with Janet and the Behaviourists we appear to have only one text:

Does this mean that one must view freedom as a series of capricious jerks comparable to the Epicurean clinamen? Am I free to wish anything whatsoever at any moment whatsoever? . . . Inasmuch as it has seemed that the recognition of freedom had as its consequence these dangerous conceptions which are completely contradictory to experience, worthy thinkers have turned away from a belief in freedom.[22]

The subsequent pages giving Sartre's answer are characteristically opaque. My own best guess, as unconfident as it is unflattering, is that his reply is in effect to maintain that these *clinamena* do not have to be happening all the time; although his account of our freedom is surely supposed to apply not just to a few spectacular make or break conversion decisions but to the every day and all the time life of any agent whatsoever.

(d) Besides maintaining, somewhat dogmatically although I believe correctly, that we are agents Sartre also makes what seem to be quite reckless claims about the massive scope of that agency:

man being condemned to be free carries the weight of the whole world on his shoulders; he is responsible for the world and for himself as a way of being. We are taking the word 'responsibility' in its ordinary sense as '. . . being the incontestable author of an event or of an object'. In this sense the responsibility of the for-itself is overwhelming, since he is the one by whom it happens that there is a world. Since he is also the one who makes himself be, then whatever may be the situation in which he finds himself, the

---

[21] See, for instance, on the obstacles to such knowledge G. J. Warnock's 'Every event has a cause', in A. Flew (ed.), *Logic and Language*, Vol. ii (Oxford: Blackwell, 1953).
[22] P. 452: p. 529.

for-itself must wholly assume this situation with its peculiar co-efficient of adversity, even though it be insupportable.[23]

It is magnificent. But it is not the truth. Nor is it, if I understand it, even consistent either in itself or with many of the considerations urged in its support. It is not consistent, since if there is a 'situation in which he finds himself', then it surely cannot be the case that 'he is the one by whom it happens that there is a world'. Nor is it true that 'he is the one by whom it happens that there is a world'. For, even if the word 'world' is charitably read as referring to the world as seen in terms of his projects, still those projects themselves, as Sartre himself frequently remarks, involve and indeed embrace intransigent objective facts.

Nor will it do to say that 'the situation, the common product of the contingency of the in-itself and of freedom, is an ambiguous phenomenon in which it is impossible for the for-itself to distinguish the contribution of freedom from that of the brute existent'. Sartre the for-himself appears to be making precisely this supposedly impossible distinction a few sentences later, when he admits that 'whether the rock "to be scaled" will or will not lend itself to scaling . . . is part of the brute being of the rock'. He makes it again in another way when later on the same page he utters the reckless falsehood: 'The rock will not be an obstacle if I wish at any cost to arrive at the top of the mountain'.[24] The most press-on regardless assault may simply, and perhaps fatally, be defeated; while, if it succeeds, its success will have been precisely in overcoming (what were by the very attempt chosen) obstacles.

[23] Pp. 553–4: p. 639.
[24] P. 488; pp. 568–9.

Hegel's Conception of Phenomenology

WALTER KAUFMANN

While Hegel wrote his *Phenomenology of Spirit* his conception of the book changed drastically. The term 'phenomenology' was an afterthought. In this paper the 'scientific' conception of phenomenology, which hinges on the claim that a particular succession of stages can be shown to be necessary and complete, is contrasted with a 'poetic' conception which, though never expressly formulated by Hegel, is nevertheless implicit in his *Phenomenology of Spirit*. In his later work we encounter a third, 'restricted' conception of phenomenology based on a contrast between phenomenology, on the one hand, and anthropology and psychology, on the other. I argue that the 'poetic' conception is the most interesting and fruitful of the three.

Walter Kaufmann is Professor of Philosophy at Princeton University. His books include: *Nietzsche* (1950; 4th ed., revised and enlarged, 1974); *Critique of Religion and Philosophy* (1958); *From Shakespeare to Existentialism* (1959); *The Faith of a Heretic* (1961); *Cain and Other Poems* (1962); *Hegel* (1965); *Tragedy and Philosophy* (1968); *Without Guilt and Justice* (1973).

At least since World War I, the term 'phenomenology' has increasingly brought to mind Hegel as well as Husserl and his followers. Actually, the term had been used before Hegel by J. H. Lambert, Herder, Kant, Fichte, and Novalis.[1] Hegel was the first writer to use the term in the title – or at least the subtitle – of a book. The original title-page calls it *System der Wissenschaft* (in large print) and *Erster Theil, die Phänomenologie des Geistes* (in small print, below the author's name). The book is often cited as 'Hegel's *Phenomenology*' and I shall use that abbreviation here. It was first published in 1807 and has been regarded by many, particularly in this century, as Hegel's most interesting work and as a philosophical classic.

One might suppose that the nature of 'Hegel's conception of phenomenology' would have assumed importance as soon as Husserl began to use the term for the new direction in philosophy he was taking. But Husserl's whole enterprise seemed to be so clearly antithetical to Hegel's that philosophers were initially interested in one or the other, if either, but not in both. Jean-Paul Sartre created a new perspective by honoring Hegel as well as Husserl among his philosophical ancestors, when he included a long section 'Husserl, Hegel, Heidegger' in his *L'être el le néant* (1943). Seven years later, Heidegger included an essay on 'Hegels Begriff der Erfahrung' in his *Holzwege*. Eventually it became necessary for students of the phenomenological movement that began with Husserl to take note not only of those by whom Husserl had been influenced but also of Hegel, because the French phenomenologists could not be understood without reference to him.[2]

One might suppose that the use of the same term by Husserl and Hegel points to some common elements; and after all, both men stressed their determination to make philosophy a rigorous science. But an attempt to analyze Hegel's conception of phenomenology encounters several surprises.

First, one might assume that Hegel scholars had long ago

---

[1] See Johannes Hoffmeister's informative introduction to his edition of Hegel's *Phänomenologie des Geistes* (Philosophische Bibliothek: Hamburg, 1952), pp. vii-xxviii, for a detailed discussion of these authors. Cf. also Hoffmeister's article on *Phänomenologie* in his *Wörterbuch der philosophischen Begriffe*, 2nd ed. (Hamburg, 1955), pp. 463–5; Rudolf Eisler, *Handwörterbuch der Philosophie* (Berlin, 1913), p. 486; and Herbert Spiegelberg, *The Phenomenological Movement*, Vol. I, 2nd ed. (The Hague, 1971), pp. 7–19.

[2] See Spiegelberg, *op. cit.*

defined Hegel's conception of phenomenology. But most Hegel scholars, including those who have dealt at length with Hegel's *Phenomenology*, have avoided this problem. Hegel himself was a generalist, but generalism is out of favor in our universities, and most of those who write about Hegel prefer questions of detail.

Secondly, Hegel's own ideas about what he was trying to accomplish changed while he was writing his *Phenomenology*, and the book is not based on any clear conception of 'phenomenology'. The subtitle of the book, *die Phänomenologie des Geistes*, was an *afterthought*, and the half title on page 1 of the original edition still reads: *Erster Theil. Wissenschaft der Erfahrung des Bewusstseyns* (Part One: Science of the Experience of Consciousness). The interesting introduction to the book is tailored to *this* subtitle and does not contain any mention of phenomenology. Nor is the word 'phenomenology' mentioned anywhere in the book, except for about three references to *The Phenomenology of Spirit*. That term puts in a belated appearance four pages from the end of the volume,[3] and then also twice[4] in the 91-page preface which Hegel wrote in January 1807 after most of the book, which had been finished in October, had already been printed. In the six-page table of contents, which was composed last of all, the preface is divided into nineteen unnumbered sections, and here 'Phenomenology of Spirit' is mentioned twice. But the table of contents obviously represents an attempt to impose upon the book an order that Hegel had not had in mind while writing it. Not only does it contain all sorts of subdivisions that are not marked in the text but, more significantly, the text is divided into eight parts, each headed by a Roman number and title, beginning with 'I. Sense certainty; or *This* and Opinion', and ending with 'VIII. Absolute Knowledge'. But the table of contents lumps together I, II, and III under '(A) Consciousness', then inserts '(B) Self-consciousness' before IV, and finally lumps together V, VI, VII and VIII under '(C)' without any title. This last part which has no title to parallel 'consciousness' and 'self-consciousness' comprises pages 162–765! For no good reason, it is subdivided into '(AA) Reason', '(BB) Spirit', '(CC) Religion', and '(DD) Absolute Knowledge', a

[3] On p. 762 of the first edition.
[4] Pp. xxxii and xliv.

series of headings that is redundant and pointless because they are simply inserted above, respectively, 'v. Certainty and truth of reason', 'vi. Spirit', 'vii. Religion', and 'viii. Absolute knowledge'. Moreover, these titles are not commensurate with each other and with the preceding four titles. The inclusion of art under the heading of '(cc) Religion, vii. Religion, B. Die [griechische] *Kunst*-Religion' is eccentric; nor are we offered any reason why in a 'Phenomenology of Spirit' Chapter vi should be distinguished from the rest by the heading 'Spirit'. This table of contents is evidently a product of haste, and several of the page numbers in it are wrong. Hegel's conception of the book changed in the course of writing, and then again after the whole manuscript, except for the title page, table of contents and preface, had gone to the printer. The idea of calling the work a 'phenomenology of Spirit' came to Hegel only when the book was almost finished and much of it already printed.[5]

Adding to the confusion, Hegel used 'phenomenology' in an altogether different way when he published his system in outline form in his *Encyclopedia* in 1817,[6] without however repudiating the Phenomenology of 1807. A radically revised and greatly expanded edition of the *Encyclopedia* appeared in 1827, and another revision in 1830; and in both of these 'Phenomenology' appears in the table of contents, as it did not in 1817, as one small subpart of the system. Yet when Hegel died in 1831, he was working on a new edition of his *Phenomenology* and, as far as he got, had made no substantial changes whatever.

Thus, the question about Hegel's conception of phenomenology raises such complex and important issues that a discussion of it might serve as an introduction to the study of his whole thought and development. But here it must suffice to consider briefly six questions:

1. What did Hegel say about phenomenology in the preface of 1807?

2. How does his introduction to the *Phenomenology* illuminate his conception?

---

[5] Regarding the first appearance of the words 'phenomenology of spirit', see Kaufmann, *Hegel: Reinterpretation, Texts, and Commentary* (1965), pp. 110f. (hereafter cited as Kaufmann, 1965).

[6] *Encyclopädie der philosophischen Wissenschaften im Grundrisse. Zum Gebrauch seiner Vorlesungen* (Heidelberg, 1817).

3. What did Hegel actually do in his *Phenomenology?*

4. What did Hegel say about phenomenology between 1807 and 1817?

5. What conception of phenomenology do we find in the *Encyclopedia?*

6. How, in view of all this, can one sum up Hegel's conception of phenomenology?

Something would be gained if one could devote as much space to each of these questions as can here be given to the whole lot. But something would be lost, too. Even these introductory observations may go further toward establishing an untraditional view of Hegel[7] than a lengthy monograph on one of the first five questions. Such monographs must always stop short of telling us what 'Hegel's conception of phenomenology' really was.

What did Hegel say about phenomenology in the preface of 1807?

The preface is divided into sections only in the table of contents, which provides nineteen unnumbered headings, each followed by a page number but running on without a break. The seventh section is called 'The Sphere of Knowledge', the eighth 'The Ascent into this Sphere is the Phenomenology of Spirit', and the eleventh 'In what respect is the Phenomenology of Spirit Negative or contains what is False'. In the text the word phenomenology is introduced in the first sentence of section 8.[8]

In sections 6 and 7 Hegel claims that 'The spiritual alone is the actual . . . The spirit that, so developed, knows itself as spirit is science . . . Pure self-recognition in absolute otherness . . . is the ground and basis of science or knowledge in general. The beginning of philosophy presupposes or demands that consciousness finds itself in this sphere. But this sphere itself receives its perfection and transparence only through the movement of its becoming.'[9] A little later, section 8 begins: 'This becoming of science in general or of knowledge is what

---

[7] For a much fuller account of this untraditional view see Kaufmann, 1965.

[8] The nineteen headings are listed *ibid.* p. 367, and section 8 begins on p. 400. In the two-volume paperback edition, see Kaufmann, *Hegel: Texts and Commentary* (Garden City, N.Y., 1966), pp. 5 and 42 (this edition hereafter cited as 1966).

[9] Kaufmann, 1965, pp. 396–8 (1966), pp. 38–40 (the facing right pages are given over to the commentary).

this Phenomenology of the Spirit represents [as the first part of the same]'. The words here placed in brackets were struck out by Hegel when he began shortly before his death to prepare a second edition. The word 'same' was intended to refer to science. In German book titles are not printed in italics, and in some cases it is arguable whether 'phenomenology of spirit' means the book or the concept. Here, however, where it matters most, Hegel is clearly speaking of his book.

The passages quoted here suggest that science, alias philosophy, requires the spirit's realization that what is actual is also spiritual[10] and thus the spirit's 'self-recognition in absolute otherness'. Hegel also says expressly that philosophy cannot begin before this realization. Yet the development of this insight, which is the subject of the *Phenomenology*, is said to give philosophy its 'perfection and transparence'. Transparence? Hegel implies that the *Phenomenology* is *not yet* philosophy, which he equates with knowledge and science, but then goes on to say that this book, which deals with the 'becoming of science', is in fact the first part of his *System of Science*.

In section 7 Hegel deals with this problem as follows: 'Science, on its part, demands of self-consciousness that it should have elevated itself into this ether [of pure self-recognition in absolute otherhood] . . . Conversely, the individual has the right to demand that science should at least furnish him with a ladder to this standpoint . . .' Thus the *Phenomenology* is presented as a ladder on which the reader can climb up from the most unsophisticated 'sense certainty' to 'absolute knowledge'. So understood, it is not yet scientific philosophy but a mere introduction. Yet Georg Lasson warned the readers of his edition of the book in 1907, in his excellent 100-page introduction, that 'it is a complete misunderstanding to see in the *Phenomenology* something like a propaedeutic for philosophy'.[11] And in section 10 Hegel himself says: 'The way in which the Concept of knowledge is reached thus also becomes a necessary and complete becoming. Hence this preparation ceases to be a fortuitous bit of philosophizing. . .'[12] What is thus intended

---

[10] Cf. the famous formulation in Hegel's preface to his *Philosophy of Right* (1821): 'What is rational, is actual; and what is actual, is rational.' This idea was not developed in Berlin to please the King of Prussia, as has often been claimed; it is central in the preface of 1807. See also 1965, p. 380 (1966), p. 20

[11] Philosophishche Bibliothek: Leipzig, 1907, p. xcvii.

[12] Kaufmann, 1965, p. 410 (1966), pp. 52–4.

to make this preparation scientific and 'the first part of science' is the alleged *necessity* of the progression from the first stage to the last, and the account is even said to be 'complete'. Claims like these have sent generations of interpreters to look for some sort of necessity in the transitions from stage to stage in Hegel's *Phenomenology*.

In his *Phenomenology*, Hegel explains neither his conception of necessity nor his choice of the word 'phenomenology'. As for 'necessity' and 'necessary', he uses both words loosely, as do many German writers, as inclusive antonyms of 'caprice' and 'capricious'. This is always a fault, but it is a truly fateful error in a philosopher whose avowed ambition it is 'to contribute to this end, that philosophy might come closer to the form of science'[13] and who associates science so closely and crucially with necessity. *Hegel systematically overlooks the difference between demonstrating that something is necessary and merely giving a reason for it.*[14]

How does the introduction illuminate Hegel's conception of phenomenology?

Here the word 'phenomenology' is not mentioned at all because Hegel had not yet thought of this label when he wrote the introduction. But he said some things here that help us to understand why he liked this label when it did occur to him.

'Science, as it emerges, is itself an appearance [*eine Erscheinung*] . . . the presentation of the appearance of knowledge [*des erscheinenden Wissens*] shall be attempted here.'[15] Hegel goes on to call 'the path of natural consciousness that reaches true knowledge . . . the path of the soul that migrates through the sequence of its forms as if these successive stages were prescribed to it by its nature so that it may purify itself and become spirit by attaining, by means of its complete experience of itself, the knowledge of what it is in itself [i.e., implicitly and not yet, in the beginning, for itself, for its own consciousness].'[16]

---

[13] Kaufmann, 1965, p. 372 (1966), p. 12.
[14] See Kaufmann, 1965, p. 85, indeed the whole of section 17; also p. 371 (1966), pp. 9–11; also Kaufmann, *From Shakespeare to Existentialism*, 2nd rev. ed. (Garden City, N.Y., 1960), pp. 158f.
[15] Lasson's ed., pp. 52f (reference in note 11); Hoffmeister's ed., p. 66 (reference in note 1).
[16] Lasson, p. 53; Hoffmeister, p. 67.

The soul progresses by realizing the inadequacy of its earlier stages and by coming to see again and again that its supposed knowledge was not actual knowledge. Its progress is 'the way of doubt' (*Zweifel*), the 'way of despair' (*Verzwei-flung*).[17] Hegel refers to his own account of the progress as 'the detailed history of the education of consciousness itself for science'.[18] And near the end of the introduction he says: 'By virtue of this necessity [*sic*] this way to science is itself already science, and regarding its contents it is the science of the experience of consciousness'[19] which was, as mentioned earlier, the originally contemplated subtitle of the book and still appears in the half-title of the first edition.

Now 'the science of the experience of consciousness' and 'the phenomenology of the spirit' are not synonyms. The former suggests a rigorous investigation of the various forms of consciousness, all the way from sense certainty to the recognition of spirit in whatever is actual. The latter suggests a study of the manifestations of spirit. The former focuses on the subject, the consciousness whose experiences are studied, while the latter calls attention to what appears, the spirit. It is only from the point of view of 'absolute knowledge' that *both* labels are applicable because both the stages of consciousness and that which appears in each are manifestations of spirit. It is a central point in the book that the subject–object dichotomy is transcended. This is also implicit in the famous first sentence of section 5 of the preface: 'everything depends on this; that we comprehend and express the true not [only] as substance but just as much as subject'. This claim, says Hegel, 'can be justified only by the presentation of the whole system'.[20]

What did Hegel actually do in his Phenomenology?

Chapter I, 'Sense certainty; This and Opinion' comprises about 15 pages in the first edition; chapter II, 'Perception; or Thing and Illusion', 20; chapter III, 'Force and Understanding, Appearance and the Suprasensible World', over 40. In this part of the book, which the table of contents subsumes under

---

[17] Lasson, p. 54; Hoffmeister, p. 67.
[18] *Ibid.*
[19] Lasson, p. 60; Hoffmeister, p. 64.
[20] Kaufmann, 1965, p. 388 (1966), p. 28.

' (A) Consciousness', the approach is reminiscent of traditional, especially Greek, epistemology.[21] Chapter IV, 'The truth of certainty of oneself' (60 pages) is altogether different. In the first half, A., we encounter Hegel's famous and influential reflections on master and slave, while B. deals in turn with stoicism, skepticism, and the unhappy consciousness. More and more, the illustrations gain a life of their own, and Hegel becomes absorbed, for example, in his constant allusions to the 'unhappy' spirituality of medieval Christianity.

It will have been noted that every chapter is longer than the preceding one. If the chapters had averaged about 20 pages each, then the whole introduction to the system, even if it had comprised eight chapters, might have been printed in the same volume with Hegel's Science of Logic, as Hegel had anticipated when he started writing the book in 1806. But in chapter V he got carried away entirely and dealt with 'Certainty and Truth of Reason' in more than 210 pages. The early portions of this mammoth chapter represent at least some attempt to link the discussion to the original plan; here we read, for example, about the observation of nature and about description in general. But Hegel's prefatory claims of scientific rigor and necessity become more and more astounding as one reads on. One might think of complimenting him for being so full of surprises, so utterly unpredictable, so richly imaginative, so irrepressibly *geistreich* or ingenious, but not for the qualities on which, according to his own programmatic preface, everything depends.

Even so, some scholars find the break between chapters V and VI still greater than between IV and V. 'VI. Spirit' runs on for about 250 pages and deals at length with ancient Greek ethical notions, largely in terms of rather fanciful allusions to Antigone, but without any express analysis, not to speak of a rigorous or scientific discussion, of Sophocles' play or of Plato's or Aristotle's ethics; it deals at greater length with the alienation involved in modern life, with the enlightenment, and with 'the absolute freedom and the terror' of the French Revolution, and finally proceeds to a critique of modern *Moralität*.

---

[21] Wilhelm Purpus, *Zur Dialektik des Bewusstseins nach Hegel* (Berlin, 1908), has dealt at length with Hegel's debts to Plato and Aristotle.

When Hegel had reached this point (p. 624), the notion that all this might be an introduction to his Science of Logic which might be developed in the main part of the same volume had obviously become absurd. Indeed, the remaining two chapters simply could not be as long as vi, or any thought of publishing all this material, even without the Logic, in a single volume, would have to be abandoned. There is no need here to recount Hegel's difficulties with his publisher.[22] Suffice it to say that he managed to keep 'vii. Religion' down to 115 pages, and the last chapter, on 'Absolute Knowledge', remained short (just under 25 pages).

Obviously, all of this can be subsumed under either 'experience of consciousness' or 'manifestations of spirit'. But having completed such a book as this, how could Hegel claim in his preface that the way in which the final stage is reached is necessary and that for this reason it represents the first part of science?

Thus we have *two very different conceptions of phenomenology*. The 'scientific' conception hinges on the claim that the succession of stages that are exhibited is necessary and complete, and also shown to be both. This claim is essential for Hegel's claim that the *Phenomenology* is a scientific and philosophical work in his own sense of these terms. The other conception of phenomenology is not stated by Hegel but is implicit in the book. The *Phenomenology* is a loose series of imaginative and suggestive reflections on the life of the spirit. This second conception would have been anathema to Hegel and still is repugnant to most of his admirers. Let us call the first conception 'scientific' and the second 'poetic'.

Hegel was not a serenely rational professor who was able to prove to his own satisfaction what needed to be done and who then set about to do it, painstakingly grinding out his text. He was a tormented spirit, full of ideas and erudition, eager to write a major work; but when he was 35 and his friend Schelling, five years younger than he, had already published ten books, Hegel had not been able to write a single one. Now, in utter turmoil, deeply divided against himself, he began a major work under the pressure of printer's deadlines, had to send in the manuscript in instalments, and wrote almost as

---

[22] See Kaufmann, 1965, pp. 111f.

fast as it might take another person to copy his manuscript. In the process the book turned out to be quite different from anything Hegel had planned or anticipated. But after it was finished, barely in time to meet the publisher's ultimatum, Hegel sat down once more and wrote a long prefatory essay – again in record time – and did not tailor it to the finished product. Instead he developed his ideas about what needed to be done, attacking the romantics and the notion that one could fashion a sound philosophy out of intuitions, aphorisms, and scattered insights; he insisted that philosophy must become a science, and that meant being rigorous and systematic. He said much more, some of it brilliant; but he was at a loss how to explain in what way what he had actually written was related to his 'System of Science'. He called it 'Part One: The Phenomenology of Spirit', but used the word 'phenomenology' only to refer to his book and did not discuss the term. Nor was he *ever* able to give any consistent account of the relation of this book to his system.

'Science of the Experience of Consciousness' would have been a less poetic title and therefore less appropriate. 'Spirit' is much more poetic than 'consciousness'; it is also a wonderfully rich and ambiguous word; and 'phenomenology' – particularly if one did not bother to explain this strange term – had a saving vagueness, too. Certainly, the study of the appearances of the spirit is a poetic conception. The term is introduced very near the end of the book; and the book ends with an undeniably poetic vision: 'The goal, absolute knowledge, or spirit that knows itself as spirit, is reached by way of the memory of the spirits as they are in themselves . . .' Hegel then contrasts history, whose domain includes the accidental, with the 'science of the appearance of knowledge', and concludes:

both together, history comprehended, form the memory and the Golgotha [*Schädelstätte*] of the absolute spirit, the actuality, truth, and certainty of his throne, without which he [the absolute spirit] would be lifeless and lonesome; only
> from the goblet of this realm of spirits
> his infinity foams up for him.

Thus ends the book. The absolute spirit is actual only in the series of finite spirits, and we, if we want to behold the absolute spirit, must look at finite spirits. This vision owes more to

Herder and Goethe, Schiller and Hölderlin than it does to any philosopher; and the final quotation *is* from Schiller, with the weighty 'only' added by Hegel.

What did Hegel say about phenomenology between 1807 and 1817?

First, there is Hegel's own description of his book which appeared in the Jena cultural supplement on 28 October 1807.[23] Such *Selbstanzeigen*, 'advertisements for oneself', generally appeared *before* the book.

Hegel's *Selbstanzeige* runs about one page in length, from which I quote:

The Phenomenology of the Spirit is to replace psychological explanations as well as the more abstract discussions of the foundation of knowledge. It deals with the *preparation* for science from a point of view that makes a new, and interesting, and nothing less than the first science of philosophy. It includes the various *forms of the spirit* as stations on the way on which it becomes pure knowledge or absolute spirit . . . The wealth of the appearances of the spirit, which at first glance seems chaotic, is brought into a scientific order which presents them according to their necessity. . . A *second volume* will contain the system of Logic as speculative philosophy, and of the other two parts of philosophy, the *sciences* of *nature* and the *spirit*.'

The conception of phenomenology as a new and interesting science is not found in Hegel's works, and the claim that it is to replace psychology conflicts with Hegel's later views. The *second volume* never appeared. When the *Science of Logic* did appear, it alone took up three volumes (1812, 1813, and 1816). Hegel's *Encyclopedia*, however, fits the description of volume 2 and might well have been presented as such. Instead, as we shall see, Hegel called one small part of the *Encyclopedia* 'phenomenology'.

Next, there are some relevant letters. When he read the proofs of the book, Hegel wrote to Niethammer on 16 January 1807: 'Reading it for the last time to find misprints, I often wished, of course, that I might be able to clear the ship here and there of ballast to make it fleeter. – In the second edition which is to follow *soon – si diis placet?!* – everything shall become better;

[23] It is translated in Kaufmann, 1965, p. 366 (1966), pp. 4f.

this comfort I shall commend to myself and others.'[24] But it did not please the gods; when Hegel finally did start preparing a second edition, he died before he had finished revising the preface; and the revisions he made there were, without exception, microscopic and in many instances anything but improvements.

A week later Hegel wrote a former student, C. G. Zellmann: 'Science alone is theodicy: it keeps one both from looking at events with animal amazement, or ascribing them, more cleverly, to accidents of the moment or of the talents of one individual – as if the destinies of empires depended on an occupied or not occupied hill – and from lamenting the triumph of injustice and the defeat of right.'[25] Hegel's insistence on demonstrating some *necessary* links in his books was not inspired solely by a dubious conception of science and rigor; it was also born of deep suffering.[26]

On 1 May, Hegel wrote Schelling about the

unfortunate confusion . . . that has affected the whole process of publishing and printing, and in part even the composition itself . . . Getting into the details has damaged, as I feel, the synopsis of the whole; but . . . even if it had been formed better, it would still take me a lot of time before it would stand there clearer and more finished. – That single parts, too, would require a lot more work in many ways to be really mastered, I need not say as you will discover this for yourself only too clearly. – Regarding the greater deformity of the later parts, be considerate also because I finished the editing around midnight before the Battle of Jena . . .[27]

While Hegel would have denied that the course of history, including the history of philosophy, could be changed *in the long run* by 'accidents of the moment or of the talents of one individual', he conceded that the form and contents of his *Phenomenology* had been influenced importantly by such accidents.

Finally, one of Hegel's friends, Isaak von Sinclair, wrote him that he had got lost in the chapter on self-consciousness and 'that you seemed to me to have been misled into adopting a

---

[24] Kaufmann, 1965, p. 317.
[25] *Ibid.* p. 318.
[26] See *ibid.* the chapter on 'Hegel on History', especially sections 60–2; also section 12.
[27] *Ibid.* p. 319.

point of view that is too historical and even, if I may express myself this way, too pathological, being guided more by your gift of combination than by the calm observation that prevailed in the beginning'.[28]

So much for letters. In 1808 Hegel moved to Nürnberg to become Rektor of a boys' secondary school (*Gymnasium*). He also taught his pupils philosophy. During his first year there

he wanted to teach pneumatology or doctrine of the spirit together with logic as a kind of introduction to philosophy; he divided this pneumatology into . . . phenomenology and psychology. A surviving disposition shows that initially he meant to present his whole Phenomenology, but he subsequently broke off at some point in the chapter on Reason – evidently because the students were not able to follow him. During the following years he limited Phenomenology to 'Consciousness, Self-Consciousness, Reason'.[29]

This proved to be a turning point in the birth of a new conception of phenomenology that is encountered in the *Encyclopedia*.

What conception of phenomenology do we find in Hegel's Encyclopedia?

The book is divided into three main parts: Science of Logic, Philosophy of Nature, and Philosophy of Spirit. Philosophy of Spirit also has three divisions; and each of these is subdivided further. In the first edition of 1817 the contents of Philosophy of Spirit is as follows; omitting some of the subheads:

First Part. *Subjective* Spirit
  A. *Soul*
  B. *Consciousness*
    a. Consciousness as such
    b. Self-consciousness
    c. Reason
  C. *Spirit*
    a. *Theoretical* Spirit
    b. *Practical* Spirit
Second Part. *Objective* Spirit
  A. *Right* [or *Law*: Das *Recht*]

[28] Otto Pöggeler, *Die Komposition der Phänomenologie des Geistes*, in *Materialien zu Hegel's Phänomenologie des Geistes*, ed. H. F. Fulda and D. Henrich (Frankfurt a. M., 1973), pp. 336f.
[29] *Ibid.*

B. *Morality* [Die *Moralität* : morality of the Kantian type]
C. *Ethics* [Die *Sittlichkeit*]

Third Part. *Absolute Spirit*
  a. Religion of art
  b. Revealed religion
  c. Philosophy

The last three subheads are inconsistently preceded by *small* a, b, and c; and printed in smaller type, not only in the table of contents but also in the text. Art still appears, as it did in the *Phenomenology*, only as a type of religion – Greek religion. But *Sittlichkeit*, which in the *Phenomenology* appeared long before *Moralität*, because Hegel associated *Sittlichkeit* with Antigone, is now considered a higher stage because Hegel associates it with Goethe and Schiller. 'Universal history' appears rather oddly as the third subdivision under *Sittlichkeit*, because *Sittlichkeit* culminates in a discussion of the state and political life, and world history here means political history, while the history of religion and philosophy, and later also art, belongs in the realm of absolute spirit.

The *Phenomenology* of 1807 had represented an attempt to cover the whole 'Philosophy of Spirit', Now, however, the opening paragraph of 'Subjective spirit', which is followed by 'A. Soul', makes a curious suggestion, not taken up either in the text or in the table of contents. We are told that

subjective spirit is a) the immediate spirit or *spirit of nature* – the subject of what is usually called *athropology* [*sic*] or the *soul* ; b) spirit as identical reflection into itself and into what is other, relations or specification; *consciousness*, the subject of the *phenomenology* of the spirit; c) the spirit that is for *itself* or spirit as subject; the *subject* of what is usually called *psychology*.

Here, in §307, we find a radical break with the *Phenomenology* of 1807. One is led to wonder why Hegel could not have used some other term to interpose between anthropology and psychology. In 1817 he depicts psychology as a higher stage and simply ignores the fact that this new conception of phenomenology is utterly different from that of 1807 which had included Spirit, Morality, Ethics, Art-Religion, and Philosophy. He does this without comment or argument.

Hegel had come to feel that his first book had become much too long and he had discovered in teaching secondary school students that it was better to stop somewhere in the chapter on reason. But what Hegel does in 1817 remains perplexing. Down through the reflections on master and slave, the highly condensed paragraphs of the *Encyclopedia* bear some relation to the *Phenomenology* of 1807, but stoicism, skepticism, and the unhappy consciousness are no longer mentioned, and the topic of 'Reason', to which Hegel had devoted almost 250 pages in 1807 – almost twice as much space as he had allotted to the preceding four chapters taken together – is now taken care of in half a page. It is dealt with before psychology, which now represents a higher stage.

Ten years later, in the second edition of the *Encyclopedia*, a great deal has changed. But in the lay-out reproduced above Hegel made only two alterations. The three divisions of Subjective spirit, are now A. Anthropology, B. Phenomenology, and C. Psychology; and the first division of Absolute spirit is now 'a. Art'.

The third and last edition of 1830 contains thousands of changes, but the only change in the lay-out reproduced here is that 'Psychology' which in the second edition still had only two subparts (a. Theoretical spirit, and b. Practical spirit) is promoted to equality with all the other subheads in the Philosophy of Spirit by the addition of 'c. The free spirit'.

Thus we have found a third conception of phenomenology in Hegel, in addition to the *scientific* and the *poetic* conceptions: the *restricted* conception, which limits phenomenology to the study of consciousness, self-consciousness, and – nominally – also reason. Having published a Phenomenology of Spirit, Hegel now reserves the study of *spirit* for psychology, of which one might think that it was the study of the *soul*, and he defines anthropology as the study of the soul. Yet he offers no reasons for any of this, and occasionally cites his *Phenomenology* of 1807 as if nothing had happened.

How, in view of all this, can one sum up Hegel's conception of phenomenology?

We have found three conceptions, and anyone with a penchant for small distinctions could adduce more. The restricted conception is much the least important of the three; few but Hegel scholars are even aware of it; and it has never excited much interest. This is as it should be. But the implications should be noted. If Hegel had really been a systematic philosopher, and if his system were his major achievement, then the way in which he worked phenomenology into his system should take precedence over the book of 1807. In fact, phenomenology, about which he had thought so long, was incorporated into his system in an ill considered and arbitrary fashion.

The *Encyclopedia* was written in great haste, just as the *Phenomenology* had been. It was conceived, as the title pages of all three editions remind us, as a syllabus for Hegel's students. A professor was required to assign a text; Hegel had no wish to base his lectures on other men's books; and he knew from his experience at Nürnberg that his *Phenomenology* was not suitable. When he finally obtained a chair of philosophy, he therefore quickly published an outline of his system that could be used as a text for almost any course that he might choose to give. The *Encyclopedia*, which contains Hegel's famous system, was never meant to be more than a text *zum Gebrauch seiner Vorlesungen*, for the use of his students in connection with his lectures. One could read the whole book (originally, 477 numbered sections on 286 small pages with wide margins) and, without necessarily understanding everything, gain some sort of overview or orientation that would then prove helpful in connection with the lectures.

It is to Hegel's credit that he kept revising the book and made as many changes as he did. It is also understandable that, having once published a system in outline form, he did feel somewhat comitted to it and hence did not make more changes. But his son, who later edited the second posthumous edition of his father's lectures on the philosophy of history, pointed out to 'those who identify the rigor of thought with a formal schematism . . . that Hegel clung so little to the subdivisions he had once made that he changed them every time he gave a course.'[30]

After Hegel's death, his students interlarded selections from their lecture notes into the third edition of the *Encyclopedia* and thus made it into a three-volume work that few people could ever be expected to read through. More recently, an English translator has taken the second and shortest of the three major parts of the *Encyclopedia*, the philosophy of nature, and by the addition of erudite commentaries has made that alone into three volumes. One can appreciate so much devotion and be

---

[30] Kaufmann, 1965, p. 234. The whole section (53) is relevant.

grateful for the addition to our knowledge; but it becomes more and more difficult for anyone to recall the original fluidity of Hegel's thought and to see his works as he himself saw them.

The trouble with much recent scholarly and editorial work on major German philosophers is not that such work is 'destructive'[31] but, on the contrary, that it is too constructive; so far from dissolving what was once whole, it freezes up what was fluid. Fleeting thoughts and doubtful notions that pass through a great mind and are put on paper to be re-examined in the light of day, words once spoken in a lecture and perhaps not even recalled by the speaker afterwards – sometimes even phrases that were misheard or misread – find their way into volumes in which they look no different from ideas that were carefully considered and polished to perfection.

This process began with Hegel himself. He wrote his *Phenomenology*, and later also his *Encyclopedia*, under circumstances and pressures that did not allow for much weighing and recasting, and especially in his first book came to write at such a pace that he put fleeting thoughts and doubtful notions on paper and then had to send them to the printer without an opportunity to re-examine his own work. Before he had finished the book, half of it was printed, and it was too late to treat the finished version as a first draft.

This makes a mockery of the scientific conception of phenomenology. One might protest that even though Hegel's book falls short of that, the scientific conception remains tenable despite the book he actually wrote. But any such claim would have to depend on showing that *any* single series of stages leading from sense certainty to absolute knowledge *could* be both necessary and complete. It would be more to the point to show why *no* such series could be necessary and complete.

That leaves us with the *poetic* conception. Opponents of such an interpretation of Hegel may plead that it is not 'philosophical' and 'rigorous' enough,[32] and at first glance it may indeed seem to be 'soft' compared to the 'tougher' scientific conception. A philosopher, it may be supposed, should be satisfied with

---

[31] See Pöggeler, *op. cit.* (reference in note 28 above).
[32] See, e.g., Klaus Hartmann in a review in *Hegel-Studien*, Vol. 7 (Bonn, 1972), p. 399. Engels offers some brilliant formulations that go well with my view; see Karl Marx, Friedrich Engels, *Werke* (Dietz Verlage, Berlin), Vol. 20, p. 477, and Vol. 38, pp. 129, 204 and 269.

nothing less than solid arguments. But anyone who knows what a rigorous, 'scientific' argument about Antigone or *Sittlichkeit* would look like must retort: the 'scientific' interpretation of the *Phenomenology* is anything but 'tough'; it depends on a very *feeble* conception of 'science', rigor, and argument. One really has to put on blinkers and immerse oneself in carefully selected microscopic details to avoid the discovery that the *Phenomenology* is in fact an utterly unscientific and unrigorous work.[33]

This does not, of course, mean that the book is not philosophical. In philosophy rigor is not the only criterion. For example, consider three memoirs inspired by great love and admiration for two very remarkable recent philosophers who might almost be called patron saints of 'analytical' philosophy. George Pitcher observes in his memoir of J. L. Austin:

I was ready to follow him to the moon. There were others, too, just as willing. Ideally, perhaps, this effect should have been brought about by means of overwhelming philosophical arguments, but in fact it was not, for Austin produced none. Indeed, I cannot recall anything I ever heard, or read, of Austin's that contained a straightforward, old-fashioned philosophical *argument* . . . It is certain that we would not have reacted . . . as we did but for the quite extraordinary . . . authority that seemed uncannily to still all critical doubts while he spoke . . .[34]

Norman Malcolm says in his memoir of Wittgenstein: 'one had to attend [his lectures] for quite a long time (at least three terms, I should say) before one could begin to get *any* grasp of what he was doing'.[35] Surely, that is a way of saying that he did not offer rigorous arguments in which conclusions were derived from stated premises. And in the 'Biographical Sketch' that appears in the same volume, Georg Henrik von Wright remarks about Wittgenstein: 'He once said that he felt as though he were writing for people who would think in a quite different way, breathe a different air of life, from that of present-day men'.[36]

Hegel did not think along such lines. He operated with a

---

[33] For a critique of Hegel's treatment of Antigone – one of the most celebrated parts of the *Phenomenology* – see Kaufmann, 1965, sections 30 and 36. For my own treatment of Sophocles, see Kaufmann, *Tragedy and Philosophy* (Garden City, N.Y., 1968), chs. IV and VII.

[34] Sir Isaiah Berlin *et al.*, *Essays on J. L. Austin* (Oxford, 1973), pp. 20f.

[35] *Ludwig Wittgenstein: A Memoir* (London, 1958), p. 28.

[36] *Ibid.* p. 2.

dubious conception of science and felt that he ought to be rigorous in a way in which he palpably did not manage to be. But he *was* developing a new way of thinking. He did not do this very adequately by any standards, certainly not by his own; but that may be generally true of philosophers who try as much.

The new way of thinking that we encounter in Hegel's *Phenomenology* cannot be described adequately in a few words; but one could call it, in one word, *developmental*. Views and positions, theoretical as well as moral, small as well as comprehensive, must be seen (a) in relation to the person who holds them; (b) as marking a stage in that person's development and thus in relation to what comes before and after; and (c) in relation to opposing views that help us to see their partiality and inadequacy. This is one of the most fruitful suggestions ever made by a philosopher and has had repercussions in the study of art and literature, religion philosophy, psychology, history, and economics.

Hegel fancied that he could construct a single comprehensive sequence in which every stage could be shown to be necessary, and he expended much effort in pseudo-demonstrations. His anti-pluralistic bias was rooted in Biblical monotheism with its single sequence from the Creation to a Revelation and finally a Messianic Kingdom. But the idea that there might be some typical sequences that recur frequently, if only under certain conditions – perhaps some few alternative patterns – remains fruitful.

It has become fashionable for scholars to copy the ways in which minor scientists cough and spit, and to overlook the human centre even in the humanities, in psychology, and in history. In spite of his absurd pretensions and confusions, our age could still learn a great deal from Hegel's *Phenomenology*.

Phenomenology and Marxism

WOLFE MAYS

This paper concerns itself with the attempts to establish a common ground between Phenomenology and Marxism. It examines critically (1) Sartre's Marxist writings: his extension of the dialectic beyond the narrow confines of dialectical materialism; (2) Merleau-Ponty's approach to a philosophy of history; and (3) the attempt by Tran-Duc-Thao and some Italian philosophers to relate phenomenology and Marxism through Husserl's concept of the *Lebenswelt*. The paper concludes (a) that there is a radical difference between existentialist and Marxist *praxis*, and (b) that Husserl, unlike Marx, is more concerned with the history of ideas than with socio-economic history.

Dr Mays is Reader in Philosophy at the University of Manchester and Editor of *The Journal of the British Society for Phenomenology*. He is the author of *The Philosophy of Whitehead*, *Études d'Épistémologie Génétique* Vols. I and IV (with others), and has edited (with Stuart Brown) *Linguistic Analysis and Phenomenology*.

Introduction

At a first glance there may seem to be little common ground between Phenomenology and Marxism, since Marxism, especially in its professed philosophy of dialectical materialism, has always prided itself on its objectivity – the tracing of objective laws in history, whilst phenomenology together with existentialism, which both emphasise individual consciousness, have been criticised by Marxists as being varieties of idealism, as exemplifying the Robinson Crusoe mentality and as a product of Western Capitalism in the decline.

Nevertheless, it is certainly possible to find some similarities between Marxism and Existentialism, especially its Kierkegaardian variety. Both doctrines represent a reaction against the Hegelian system and both emphasise concrete existence rather than abstract essence. It is, however, somewhat more difficult to see the connection between Marxism and Husserlian Phenomenology, in view of the latter's a historical character and transcendental form. However, in the work of the early Marx certain Hegelian concepts are still manifest, and these bear some resemblance to such Husserlian concepts as intentionality and intersubjectivity.

Sartre and Merleau-Ponty, who have both in varying degrees been influenced by existentialism and phenomenology, and might be termed 'existential phenomenologists',[1] have endeavoured to incorporate Marxist themes in their respective philosophies. In doing this they both reject the doctrines of dialectical materialism accepted by the more orthodox (or vulgar) Marxists who base their beliefs on those of the later Marx, and Engels' interpretation of them, in which man is regarded as a product of material and social evolution, and human nature assumed to be largely determined by economic forces. Spiegelberg[2] notes that Sartre has never hesitated to call this objectivist philosophy 'absurd', the latter believing

---

[1] Cf. Paul Ricoeur, *Husserl: An Analysis of his Phenomenology*, trans. Edward G. Ballard and Lester E. Embree (Northwestern University Press, 1967). Ricoeur has Sartre and Merleau-Ponty in mind when he talks of 'the works, particularly the French ones, which are situated at the confluence of the phenomenological method derived from Husserl and the existential problem-set received from post-Hegelian philosophy'. (p. 203).

[2] Herbert Spiegelberg, *The Phenomenological Movement*, Vol. II (Martinus Nijhoff: The Hague, 1960), pp. 419–20.

that his existentialism of freedom and liberation is a much more adequate foundation for a revolutionary programme.

Spiegelberg remarks on the peculiar picture of Marx as a philosopher held by some French thinkers, a picture which differs from that held of him elsewhere, where he is rather seen as the Marx of *The Communist Manifesto* and *Das Kapital*. The new French Marx, he goes on, stems from his early post-Hegelian writings where he appears as a philosopher for whom 'man is the root of everything'. It is this kind of Marxist humanism which lends itself to an existentialist interpretation. Spiegelberg does not, however, believe that the political writings of the existentialists exhibit many phenomenological features: that at best one might find in Sartre and Merleau-Ponty the rudiments of a phenomenology of class-consciousness. Otherwise, he concludes, the connections between phenomenological existentialism and Marxism are merely incidental, explained by the concrete situation of the French intellectual – in particular the political and social existence of the Resistance and Liberation.

The increased interest in the young Marx has led to the consequence noted by Spiegelberg and others,[3] that Marx means different things to different people, depending on whether they refer to the doctrines of the early Marx of *The Economic and Philosophical Manuscripts*, or the theses of the later Marx as developed, for example, by Engels in his *Dialectics of Nature*. For the latter, Marx is seen as a historical determinist – the process of history being governed by laws comparable to natural laws, whereas the former emphasise the essentially humanistic quality of Marx's early writings, where history results from the way in which man as a free agent, albeit a social one, comes to terms with his situation.

It is worth looking at some of the doctrines of the early Marx to see what affinities they have to the existential phenomenological position. O'Malley notes that for the early Marx philosophy is the activity of criticism, namely, a grasp of the existential and ideal through a study of what exists. For Marx, the historical world of human institutions has its own rational and

---

[3] Cf. Shlomo Avineri, *The Social and Political Thought of Karl Marx* (Cambridge University Press, 1968), pp. 1–2.

ethical content, and it is the task of philosophy to grasp this content and to criticise the world for the purpose of improving it.[4] There seems to be a marked phenomenological streak in all this: it certainly does not sound materialistic or deterministic. If theory is only an aspect of philosophy – the other being *praxis* – and if essential structures can be grasped (by theoretical reason) only within the concrete and actual situation, then Marx (at this stage) seems very far from wishing to claim knowledge of laws determining the course of history.

Marx in his early work takes over from Feuerbach the notion of a *species being*,[5] which specifies man as a conscious being, one who is able to conceptualise, and who at the same time has an awareness of himself as sharing a common nature with others, i.e., an awareness of the self as being a member of a species, which is the basis for the existence of a specifically human society. Existing political institutions are for Marx to be judged according to whether or not they allow the individual to realise the universal moral dimension of his nature, which is the realm of freedom (and which seems to resemble the Kantian Kingdom of Ends). In modern society, however, man as a result of being alienated from his ends, cannot develop as a *species being*.

For the early Marx reality does not exist independently of human consciousness, a doctrine which superficially, at least, resembles the Husserlian concept of intentionality. Marx as Avineri notes,[6] derived from Hegel's *Phenomenology of Mind* his view that reality is shaped by man through consciousness, which exhibits itself through man's practical activities: reality is therefore always human reality. The productive forces exhibited in man's daily economic actions are therefore, Avineri goes on, not objective facts external to human consciousness. Conscious human activity enters both the material or economic infrastructure, where we are concerned with maintaining and improving the material conditions of life, and into the ideological constructions (or superstructure) in terms of which we rationalise and justify the social formations (the family, civil society and the state) which our economic activity takes.

[4] Cf. Karl Marx, *Critique of Hegel's Philosophy of Right*, ed. with an introduction and notes by Joseph O'Malley, p. xxi.
[5] *Ibid.* p. xli.
[6] Avineri, *The Social and Political Thought of Karl Marx*, cf. pp. 68–72.

Sartre and Marxism

Perhaps the most significant of Sartre's early writings on Marxism is his 1946 paper 'Matérialisme et révolution'[7] in which he criticises the materialist philosophy held by the French Communist Party, i.e., Stalinist neo-Marxism. This, he says, attempts to eliminate subjectivity, reducing the world including man to a material system of relationships between things which are studied by science. Since science is analytical and not dialectical, it is unable to deal with human history, purpose and value. Sartre regards this form of vulgar Marxism, with its belief in determinism and the inherent beneficience of the natural order, as a form of bad faith. For Sartre it is really a social myth, suitable for the revolutionary attitude, since it tries to show that the so-called higher activities of man (including moral values) are dependent on economic factors.

In *The Problem of Method*,[8] the dialectic is extended by Sartre beyond the narrow confines of the dialectical materialism criticised in 'Matérialisme et Révolution', and is taken as a method for investigating the situation of a period. By this he refers to the set of material conditions which give that situation its specific character, and which may be studied, among others, by sociological and psycho-analytical techniques. But as against the Marxist, Sartre believes that to obtain a proper understanding of a historical period, we also need an understanding of the human condition which existentialism attempts to provide. Thus, for example, the emotion of love is not simply the product (or reflection) of social factors, but is intrinsic to our being. And in order for man to be able to control his future, his ideas and projects need to be something more than the reflection of social processes. Sartre maintains that it is only when man decides to change society in the light of his revolutionary project that he can come to terms with it.

Sartre now shows a more tolerant face to Marxism than he did in his 1946 paper. He here considers Marxism to be the

[7] Jean-Paul Sartre: 'Matérialisme et révolution', *Situations III* (Gallimard: Paris, 1949), pp. 135–225.
[8] Jean-Paul Sartre, *The Problem of Method*, trans. Hazel E. Barnes (Methuen, 1963). See particularly ch. II, 'The Problem of Mediations and Auxiliary Disciplines'. *The Problem of Method* was originally published in French as 'Question de Methode', the prefatory essay in *Critique de la Raison Dialectique*, Vol. 1, by Jean-Paul Sartre (Gallimard, 1960).

philosophy of our time and existentialism its parasitical appendage. By emphasising the uniqueness of each particular person and of each particular event, he believes that existentialism may make a valuable contribution to Marxist thought. The method of integrating man as an existential being (i.e., as defined in terms of his project) into the philosophy of Marxism and thus completing it, Sartre calls the progressive–regressive method. He argues that the day in which Marxism would have filled the 'lack' for which one reproaches it, existentialism will cease to be separate.[9]

In his *Critique de la Raison Dialectique* Sartre takes the concept of *praxis* as a fundamental principle in his explanation of individual and social action: need and *praxis*, are connected with the concept of 'lack' or 'scarcity':[10] it is to satisfy his needs that man acts. Marx, says Sartre, did not understand the element of negativity which because of scarcity is built into man. As we live with our fellow-men in a field of scarcity, there is both a dependence on the other and, as may be seen in rivalry, a negation of the other. History then implies the *praxis* of men who through their projects wish to overcome and reshape their environment towards certain ends.

One of the key concepts of early Marxist thought is that of alienation, where the relation of the individual to society or to himself is inconsistent with his welfare as a human being. Marx stated it in the form of man being alienated from his *species being* by the economic system, and this alienation manifests itself in the individual in the form of class-consciousness. Since for Sartre, society is made up of individuals rather than classes, and the relations between individuals are always characterised by conflict (i.e. the Hegelian master-slave relation), the individual is then alienated by not being able to realise his own ends (or his freedom) through the existence of the other. The antagonism between classes because of conflicting economic interests is then for Sartre a special instance of the conflict between the 'for-itself' and the other.[11]

In his account of alienation in *The Problem of Method*, Sartre

---

[9] Cf. *The Problem of Method*, ch. IV, 'The progressive–regressive method'. See also Sartre's preface to this work, pp. xxxiii–xxxv.

[10] *Critique de la Raison Dialectique*, cf. pp. 200–24.

[11] Cf. *Being and Nothingness*, trans. Hazel E. Barnes, (Philosophical Library: New York, 1956), pp. 413–15, and his statement 'The being-for-others precedes and founds the *being with* others' (p. 414).

brings in psycho-analytic themes which are of some interest. Psycho-analysis, he tells us, discovers the point of insertion for man and his class – i.e., the particular family which mediates between the universal class and the individual. He goes on to argue that today's Marxists are only concerned with adults. They assume that men experienced their alienation first in their own work, whereas in fact, each one lives at first as a child in his parents' work. He believes that existentialism aided by psycho-analysis can study today only situations in which man has been lost since childhood in a society founded on exploitation.[12] Sartre employs a similar method in his most recent book *L'Idiot de la famille*,[13] where he studies Flaubert and his work as a novelist in relation to the historical and political characteristics of the times in which he lived.

Critics of Sartre's Marxism

Lukács in his *Existentialisme ou Marxisme?*[14] gives a critique of Sartre's approach to Marxism. But as this work was first published in 1948, the criticism is confined to Sartre's earlier writings. Lukács accuses him of putting forward a caricature of Marxism. He argues that Sartre's criticism of Marxism, as accepting a conception of matter existing independently of consciousness, applies only to vulgar Marxism, which concerns itself with the changing scientific concept of matter and not with what Lukács terms the philosophic concept. Nevertheless, Lukács considers that there is an element of truth in Sartre's position insofar as he emphasises the importance of individual action, which bourgeois determinism and vulgar Marxism habitually underestimate. Marxism does not, he continues, as Sartre claims, eliminate subjectivity since it regards historical events as made up of human actions, having their direct origin in human decisions, which are always taken in concrete situations.

Lukács contends that for Sartre society is made up of isolated individuals, and that he overlooks the influence of material conditions on the individual and society. The Marxist analysis

---

[12] *The Problem of Method*, pp. 62–5.
[13] Cf. Jean-Paul Sartre, *L'Idiot de la famille: Gustave Flaubert de 1821 à 1857*, Vols. I and II (Gallimard, 1971).
[14] Georges Lukács, *Existentialisme ou Marxisme?*, 2nd ed. 1961 (1st ed. 1948), (Nagel: Paris). See Parts I and II, particularly III 2, 'Sartre contre Marx'.

of history, he goes on, then begins precisely where existentialism abandons it. To understand history Marxist analyses go back to the natural (i.e. economic) foundations of life. Marxism discerns historical laws – objectively existing general tendencies, but it does not because of this deny the role of subjectivity in history. Although the central tendencies of social evolution are perfectly clear, it would, he says, nevertheless be ridiculous to deduce from them exactly how Peter and Paul will make their decisions in particular circumstances.

For Lukács as opposed to the vulgar Marxists criticised by Sartre, in order to understand the concrete, historical and social concept of man, we need to grasp that the economic categories are forms of existence and determinations of our being. The individual is not, he goes on, to be understood in terms of a personal project, but rather in the degree in which he has assimilated the objective realities of society. The existentialist's ahistorical, abstract human condition, which posits an unlimited freedom, he believes to be a universalisation of the plight of the bourgeoisie during the decline of capitalism.

For the Marxist, on the other hand, Lukács says, authentic liberty is only recognised necessity: to the degree in which we discover the laws of nature, science puts the natural forces at the service of mankind. This is the true freedom which permits us not a choice, but effective action. Lukács also argues that in his account of the contingency or ambiguity of a situation, Sartre misuses the probability concepts of modern physics, which far from making physics more subjective introduce greater precision into it. However, Lukács is perhaps a little unfair to Sartre here. For Sartre the concrete reality is the individual man in the world, but his freedom is not unlimited since it is committed freedom. Further, as against Lukács, Sartre could argue that the physicist's conception of probability is based on our experienced contingency of the everyday events around us, i.e., our situation.[15]

Whether the Marxist approach is to be considered as objective and the existentialist subjective, does to some extent depend on whether one takes the historical process as being purely objective in character. For both Sartre and Merleau-Ponty our understanding of history involves an element of

[15] See Sartre's criticisms of Lukács in *The Problem of Method*, pp. 21, 28, 31–2, 37–9, 52–3.

interpretation and this may change at different periods: in other words, a historical enquiry is essentially a hermeneutical one. In such an enquiry one goes beyond the directly given to the discovery of meanings not immediately manifest in the observations: as in Freudian psycho-analysis one discovers the latent content of a dream under its manifest content. Sartre also applies this approach to the varying interpretations of a work of art at different periods. Speaking of Flaubert's *Madame Bovary*, he says that the objective meaning of the work is the result of a comparison between what the reader brings to it from his own historical perspective, and what the author offers to it from his own.[16]

Another critic of Sartre's attempt to reconcile existentialism with Marxism is Adam Schaff.[17] Most of his criticisms follow along the same lines as those of Lukács, but he is also critical of some of Sartre's later views. It is Schaff's contention that Sartre in his discussions of individual responsibility treats the individual and his responsibility as abstractions, since he removes the problem of the freedom of choice from its social and historical context. For the Marxist, on the other hand, he goes on, the individual in making decisions and in a certain sense in choosing between given attitudes and activities, always does so socially in the sense of the social conditioning of the personality.[18] Schaff is also critical of Sartre's attempt to make the concept of 'Scarcity' the foundation of social development, and he identifies Sartre's position with Social Darwinianism and Malthusianism.[19]

As against Schaff one might say that it does not seem to be the case, that our personality and the decisions we make are largely the product of the society and historical period we live in – the individual has, as Sartre contends, also an important part to play. Indeed one of Schaff's and Lukács' criticisms of existentialism – that it is the product of a decadent society, seems to have the character of an *ad hominem* argument. Sartre is, however, open to a similar charge when he says 'A philosophy

---

[16] *Ibid.* p. 64.
[17] Adam Schaff, *A Philosophy of Man* (Lawrence and Wishart, 1963).
[18] *Ibid.* cf. Part One 3, 'The Problem of the Individual'.
[19] *Ibid.* cf. Part One 4, 'Existentialised Marxism'.

is first of all a particular way in which the "rising class" becomes conscious of itself'. But he also believes that the philosopher as a person has a part to play in working out his ideas in a particular historical situation.[20] Further, Sartre would argue that Malthusianism, paternalism and human engineering give us a more meaningful understanding of the historical process than does economics.

A characteristic of Sartre's Marxism is its relative unconcern with the economic theses of Marx as developed in *Das Kapital*, and its emphasis on the concepts of alienation and *praxis* of the early Marx.[21] Hartmann notes that there is nevertheless a difference between Sartre's use of these concepts and Marx's. Whereas in Marx's early economic scheme, man becomes alienated through his work insofar as that work serves to maintain private property, for Sartre in his *Critique* alienation is explained by pre-economic factors. It is traced back to individual *praxis* in relation with society. In view of increasing scarcity man's social relations are alienated. And this, Hartmann remarks, is a much more abstract explanation than that provided by private property. For Sartre then we judge whether social formations are free or unfree (i.e., whether they alienate me) largely in terms of individual *praxis*. But, as Hartmann goes on to note, since freedom is a normative principle it cannot itself be an individual *praxis*.[22]

Hartmann then brings out an interesting confusion in Sartre's thought, namely, that even an existentialist philosophy priding itself on its concreteness, and its appeal to the particular, nonetheless makes use of general normative principles like freedom. This principle is implicit in Sartre's conception of the human condition which exhibits itself in individual *praxis*. One might therefore ask whether the existentialist slogan 'existence precedes essence' is not really deceptive.

[20] *The Problem of Method*, cf. pp. 3–4 and 4n.
[21] Another criticism of Sartre and also Merleau-Ponty is to be found in, Raymond Aron, *Marxism and the Existentialists* (Harper and Row, 1969). He notes, 'Perhaps the most characteristic trait of the Marxism of the French existentialists (and of Lukács too, for that matter) is their indifference to the economic and perhaps even to the sociological doctrines of Marxism' (p. 10).
[22] Klaus Hartmann, 'Praxis: a ground for social theory', *The Journal of the British Society for Phenomenology*, Vol. I, no. 2, pp. 47–58.

Merleau-Ponty and Marxism

Merleau-Ponty was already under the influence of Marxist thought in the early 1930s; and this is to be seen in his *Phenomenology of Perception* footnote, in *Humanisme et Terreur* and in his essays in *Sens et Non-Sens*.[23] Like Sartre he finds it difficult to accept the position of orthodox Marxism: that man is the final result of a material process of evolution and that there is a deterministic factor in human history. Although both would admit that the economic aspect of society exercises a powerful influence on our lives, they do not believe that it determines all aspects.

Merleau-Ponty exhibits considerable sympathy for the writings of the early Marx, where man is conscious of himself as a *species being* – as having a social dimension.[24] He points out that the materialism of Marx is the view that all the ideological formulations of a given society, morals, conceptions of law and of the world, are synonymous with or complementary to a certain type of *praxis*, i.e., the manner in which society has established its fundamental relations through human productivity. It is the view, he says, that economics and ideology are internally connected in the totality of history, like the matter and form in a work of art or a perceived thing. The ideological factors of a society are therefore not an illusion, appearance or error, but just as real as the economy with which they are internally connected.[25]

Merleau-Ponty therefore argues that Marx, at least in his early work, was endeavouring to integrate the subjective and objective aspects of our experience. Marx, Merleau-Ponty goes on, introduced the notion of the human object which phenomenology has taken up and developed. 'The classical philosophers', he continues, 'have fragmented this notion: the field, the house, were for them complexes of colours in all respects comparable to natural objects, and only clothed with human meaning by a secondary judgment. Marx in speaking of human

---

[23] Maurice Merleau-Ponty, *Phenomenology of Perception* (1945), trans. Colin Smith (Routledge and Kegan Paul, 1962), pp. 171n–173n; *Humanisme et Terreur* (Gallimard, 1947); *Sens et Non-Sens* (Nagel, 1948).
[24] *Sens et Non-Sens*, cf. pp. 227–8.
[25] *Ibid.* p. 231.

objects wished to say that meaning adheres to the object as it present itself in experience.'[26] The spirit of a society is then for Merleau-Ponty realised, transmitted and perceived through these cultural objects.

For Marx according to Merleau-Ponty, a philosophy of history presupposes that human history is not simply a collection of juxtaposed facts – individual decisions and happenings, ideas, interests and institutions, but that it is rather a meaningful totality.[27] After rejecting the great man theory of history he explains this further by saying that history only has a meaning 'if there is, as it were, a logic of human co-existence, which . . . as if by natural selection, eliminates in the long run those experiences which diverge from the permanent needs of man'.[28] Merleau-Ponty seems here to be putting foward something like a Hegelian or holistic theory of history in which he emphasises both historical laws as well as individual decision making. Man, he says, cannot opt out of history and his own age. Although Merleau-Ponty opposes historicism, he clearly does not repudiate the idea of historical trends, but rather the view that these trends must conform to an *a priori* analysis.

Merleau-Ponty's two works *Humanisme et Terreur* and *Les Aventures de la Dialectique*,[29] have been said to be contributions to the phenomenology of history – the historical dimension of human existence. In *Humanisme et Terreur* he was concerned among other things with analysing the Moscow trials of the 1930s, and emphasising the ambiguity of the accused's behaviour in confessing to acts of sabotage, etc. The condemned, he says, are in a sense both guilty and innocent. It is possible that they may be rehabilitated at a later date and their actions vindicated when a new phase of history has changed once more the meaning of their conduct: they may be shown to have been trying to save the Russian people from tyranny. Since history is then ambiguous for Merleau-Ponty, our evaluations of historical events will change from period to period. This 'ambiguous' interpretation of history differentiates Merleau-

[26] *Ibid.* p. 232.
[27] Maurice Merleau-Ponty, 'The Yogi and the Proletarian' in *The Primacy of Perception*, ed. James M. Edie (Northwestern University Press, 1964), cf. pp. 213–14.
[28] *Ibid.* p. 214.
[29] Maurice Merleau-Ponty: *Les Aventures de la Dialectique* (Gallimard, 1955).

Ponty from the more orthodox interpretations of Marxism which assume a determinacy in history.

In *Les Aventures de la Dialectique*, where among other things, Merleau-Ponty gives a critique of dialectical materialism, he is also highly critical of Sartre's Marxism[30] (largely of the pre-*Critique* period) which, he argues, is Marxism with its basis not in the dialectical movement of history, but in the Cartesian *cogito*. For Sartre, he goes on, Marxism is built around the myth of the gaze, history being reduced to a simple moral choice. Although both Sartre and Merleau-Ponty repudiate the idea of historical necessity and try to enlarge the implications of Marxism, they exhibit differences in their philosophical approach, which is one of the reasons, apart from personal ones, for their disagreements. For example, for Merleau-Ponty the social relationships between individuals occur at a pre-personal level: we become aware of them in our experience (i.e. the *Lebenswelt*) in the form of intersubjectivity. On the other hand, for Sartre, conflict is inevitable between the 'for-itself' and others, and class-consciousness is seen as an extension of this conflict. Further, Merleau-Ponty cannot accept Sartre's argument that we are either totally free, hence totally responsible for our actions or not free at all, since our actions are limited by past events and our situations.[31] Simone de Beauvoir, however, in her reply to Merleau-Ponty's critique of Sartre, quotes passages to show that Sartrian freedom is always engaged freedom: that the view of Sartre is in no way different from that of Merleau-Ponty – who refuses to acknowledge this.[32]

Merleau-Ponty follows up his critique of Sartre by an *Epilogue*.[33] Here he seems to move away from his earlier position which exhibited considerable sympathy to Marxism, even though it was an *attentisme Marxiste*. He now elaborates a liberal rather than a revolutionary view of politics, a liberalism which seems to resemble the 'heroic' liberalism of Max Weber.

[30] *Ibid*. cf. ch. v. 'Sartre et l'ultra-bolchevisme', pp. 131–271.

[31] On the differences and disagreements between Sartre and Merleau-Ponty, see Graham Daniels, 'Sartre and Merleau-Ponty: an Existentialist Quarrel', *French Studies*, 24 (Oct. 1970), pp. 379–92.

[32] Simone de Beauvoir, 'Merleau-Ponty et le psuedo-sartrisme', *Les Temps Modernes* (1955), pp. 2072–122.

[33] *Les Aventures de la dialectique*, cf. pp. 273–313.

He now calls for a non-Communist Left. In *Signes*,[34] a later work, Marxism is seen by him rather as a secondary truth: it becomes a cultural object like Cartesianism, but no longer viable as a political doctrine.

Lukács' criticism of Merleau-Ponty,[35] like his critique of Sartre, is limited to the discussion of his early writings, where Merleau-Ponty showed considerable sympathy for Marxism, Although Lukács is of the opinion that Merleau-Ponty is better acquainted with Marxism than any other existentialist, he asserts that Merleau-Ponty's Trotskyist sympathies prevent him from obtaining a true understanding of Marxism.

For Marxism, Lukács says, history exhibits an objectively determinate direction, whereas for Merleau-Ponty history is both rational and fortuitous. For example, in his account of the Moscow trials, Merleau-Ponty says that the true and the false only distinguish themselves *post factum*. But for Lukács, it is in very large measure the objective content and real direction of history which determines whether the characters of the histor-ical personages are heroic, ignoble, tragic or comic. Although he recognises that for Merleau-Ponty history does manifest definite trends, Lukács goes on to say that we can never for him be certain which line of privileged facts will finally dominate history. This is especially to be seen in Merleau-Ponty's con-clusion that the justice or error of a political conviction can only be crystallised out *a posteriori* in the light of later events. Merleau-Ponty then, Lukács says, sees history under the guise of a designing and capricious female, who only exhibits her intentions at the last moment or after the event. Lukács dubs this conception of history 'historical agnosticism'.

In answer to Lukács one might say that history is never regarded by Merleau-Ponty as being so ambiguous as to make him give up the desire to understand the contemporary political scene.[36] Merleau-Ponty is ever ready to criticise political doctrines and attitudes which he feels lack logical cogency, whether they belong to the Capitalist West or Soviet Russia. For Merleau-Ponty there are two kinds of confusion or am-

---

[34] Cf. Maurice Merleau-Ponty, *Signes* (Gallimard, 1960).
[35] *Existentialisme ou Marxisme?*, Part III 5, 'L'éthique existentialisme et la responsabilité historique', pp. 187–236.
[36] Cf. 'Propos', *Signes*.

biguity: one which comes from the natural order of events and an intellectual one which we can, if we try, correct or at least clarify. He therefore believed that political man when making a choice required to have at his disposal adequate information and guidance. In this way he could in some measure come to terms with the first kind of ambiguity, although by the very nature of things he cannot entirely circumvent it.

Other attempts at reconciliation

Despite the criticisms of Lukács and others, philosophers, especially on the continent have continued to attempt to reconcile phenomenology with Marxism. Starting from the Marxist position that class-consciousness arises from the conflict of the superstructures, i.e., political, religious, legal, ideological, etc., with the infrastructure or material conditions of life, they have gone on to argue, as Merleau-Ponty, for example, does, that such superstructures are just as real as the economic productive forces.[37]

Tran-Duc-Thao[38] stresses this point, when he notes that the autonomy of the superstructures (or ideological factors) is as essential to the comprehension of history as the movement of productive forces. For Thao, to say that the ideological form of the Reformation is merely a reflection of material interests is to refuse to understand history. This ideological form can, he asserts, be explained as the 'rationalised translation' of really lived experience, of the new conditions of life brought in by the actual development of the bourgeoisie. Hence, our ideological constructions are relative to the mode of production not because they reflect it, but because they draw their meaning from a corresponding experience in which the spiritual values are lived and felt. In other words, economics and ideology are both manifestations of human nature. Or as Merleau-Ponty puts it, the notion of economics has to be expanded so as to bring into it 'besides the process of production and the struggle of economic forces against economic forms, the constellation

---

[37] Cf. Jean-F. Lyotard, *La Phénoménologie* (Presses Universitaire de France, 3rd ed., 1959), especially pp. 110–21.
[38] Cf. Tran-Duc-Thao, 'Marxisme et Phénoménologie', *Revue Internationale*, Paris, 1946 (no. 2), pp. 176–8.

of psychological and moral forces which combine to determine the struggle'.[39] The revolutionary problem as Thao sees it, is not only to organise and establish a new economy: it is the realisation by man of the very meaning of the future. In this sense, he believes that Marxist theory is not a dogma but a guide to action.

Although Marxism like the later phenomenology of Husserl with its emphasis on the life world refuses to separate being from meaning, nevertheless, as Thao points out,[40] Husserl's concept of the life world is different from the 'material world' of the Marxist. The life world is defined in terms of the con- stituting subject, and is arrived at by a reflective act – the *epoché* – in which the concept of an objective world is put on one side. Thao regards the life world as an abstract aspect of reality, since reality for him is nature itself or matter in dial- ectical movement. Because of this, he argues, phenomenology cannot grasp the 'material content' of the experienced life. Thao like Lukács identifies 'material content' with objective historical existence, rather than with the matter postulated by the physicist.

Despite his interest in both Marxism and phenomenology, Thao concludes that they are irreducible to one another as phenomenology is at present conceived. It is only by identifying *originary subjectivity* with matter, that he believes that Marxism can conserve phenomenology by surpassing it. By thus en- deavouring to put phenomenology on to an objective material basis, Thao arrives at a realism in which historical and product- ive forces are taken as objective and as in nature.

A more recent approach to this problem may be found in the work of Paci[41] and his colleagues, who starting from Husserl's last work *The Crisis of European Sciences*, put forward what has been called the new phenomenology of the Left (as opposed to that of the Right which emphasises the more intellectualist side of Husserl). Although agreeing with Thao that ideologies have a real character they would not, however, wish to identify reality with 'matter', but would like Merleau- Ponty rather stress the concept of intersubjectivity. For Husserl

---

[39] Cf. *Phenomenology of Perception*, p. 172n.
[40] Cf. Tran-Duc-Thao: *Phénoménologie et materialisme dialectique* (Minh-Tan: Paris, 1951).
[41] Enzo Paci, 'Towards a New Phenomenology', *Telos*, no. 5, Spring 1970, pp. 58–81.

in his *Crisis,* Paci tells us, the task is the description of the *Lebenswelt* (i.e., the lived world) in which the Cartesian distinctions (of subject and object) are not yet made.

The *Lebenswelt,* Paci says, is a basic structure upon which all the sciences rest together with all culture and civilisation. Following the Sartre of the *Critique,* he states that we must notice as primary among the various aspects of intentionality, the lack of something or the need for something. The *Lebenswelt,* he continues, is the region of what is lacking, and at the same time the struggle for the satisfaction of needs. However, without live economic needs economics as a science is impossible. These needs are dependent upon the operation of concrete subjects who can be phenomenologically reached by the reflection of every subject upon himself.[42] The world of production is the intersubjective world of these subjects in which each subject lives in privation with respect to the other. Paci therefore sees as a basic possibility in the *Lebenswelt,* a revolutionary activity which lived by the rebelling subjects leads them to form new associations and new modes of intersubjective solidarity.[43]

Paci clearly recognises that his approach involves a radical reinterpretation of the Husserl of the *Crisis,* since, as he says, Husserl does not penetrate into the life of intersubjective relationships that constitute society.[44] Rovatti too notes that by making this move – from a way of studying phenomenology to a way of doing it – one finds Marxist themes. Phenomenology 'is no longer a science of *eide* in the sense of logic, but it becomes a science of human *praxis* whose ideal of *eidos* is the revolutionary task'. He concludes, that if the *epoché* is not taken as ethical action with man as a person having ends and goals, it becomes a form of pure intellectualism.[45] Paci and his colleagues have then injected into Husserl's more intellectualist and critical approach an element of *praxis* – an emphasis on decision-making directed towards the ethical rather than the logical sphere. In doing this they stress the subjective side of the economic equation – human needs rather than economic productive forces.

[42] *Ibid.* cf. pp. 63–4.
[43] 'Towards a New Phenomenology', cf. p. 74.
[44] *Ibid.* cf. pp. 75–6.
[45] Pier Aldo Rovatti, 'A phenomenological analysis: the return to the subject and to the dialectic of totality', *Telos,* no. 5, p. 161.

Commenting on the attempt by Paci and others to reconcile Husserl's later philosophy and dialectical materialism, Shmueli[46] states that although Husserl's vision of man, both of the individual as of the collective, may have some superficial resemblance to, it has no real common ground with Marx's image of man and society. The life world, he goes on, is still very remote from Marx's concept of social reality formed by the class struggle. Further, Husserl's philosophy is a critical philosophy and one concerned with the analysis of every actual and possible experience. 'Husserl's *telos* of intersubjective activity, a ratio-liberal society guided by philosophical principles which makes science possible, is eschatologically different from the dialectics of historical materialism.'[47]

Ricoeur, however, warns us not to take the contrast between Husserl's and Marx's thought too rigidly if Marxism is not to be reduced to its positivist caricature. He points out that 'a dialectical conception which remains open to the return shock of ideas upon the infrastructure of societies cannot fail to reflect on the very origins of human capital equipment'.[48] One must remember that our modern industrial techniques which for Marx comprise such an important element in capitalist economy, proceed from the scientific revolution set in motion by Galileo, among others, and the very project of a natural science is something which Husserl is much concerned with in his *Crisis*. The difference is that the early Marx is concerned with natural science insofar as it arises as a response to human needs, whereas Husserl is concerned with obtaining an intellectual understanding of the possibility of science itself. And this no doubt is what Shmueli has in mind when he remarks that 'there is a colossal difference between the full constructive impact of ideas in history and the return shock of ideas upon the infrastructure of societies.'[49]

Conclusion

What can be said about the attempt to reconcile Phenomeno-

---

[46] Efraim Shmueli, 'Pragmatic, existentialist and phenomenological interpretations of Marxism', *Journal of the British Society for Phenomenology*, Vol. 4, no. 2., May 1973, p. 145.

[47] *Ibid.* p. 149.

[48] *Husserl: An Analysis of his Phenomenology*, p. 168.

[49] 'Pragmatic, existentialist and phenomenological interpretations of Marxism', pp. 146–7.

logy and Marxism? We can find, as we have seen, two approaches among phenomenologists and existentialists interested in Marxism. In the first, one may like Thao move from phenomenology and the *epoché* towards a material world interpreted historically rather than scientifically, and say that phenomenology, in order that it may be reconciled with Marxism, needs to be given a realistic interpretation. In the second, you may as with Sartre proceed in the reverse direction, and argue that the (vulgar) Marxist materialist position must be completed by existentialism.

There are obvious similarities between the existentialist *praxis* of Sartre and Merleau-Ponty, and Marxist *praxis*. Yet it seems a different sort of *praxis*, at least in Sartre's case, since he emphasises the individual and the concrete situation rather than referring to the totality of historical reality as the Marxist does. Merleau-Ponty in his Marxist period would seem to take up an intermediate position, since he accepts individual *praxis*, but gives it a historical dimension, although of a contingent character.

Further, for Sartre the subjective need or 'lack' is more basic for economic behaviour than are Marx's productive forces or objective work. In the *Critique*, a need or 'lack' is connected with scarcity, and the decisions individuals make in competing for rare resources. Economic behaviour is then based on individual decisions arising from our projects, rather than on the feelings of pleasure and pain of the classical utility theory of economics: feelings which were said to arise in the course of attempts to satisfy our material wants and were taken to be the origin of our objective exchange value. In some ways despite its subjective character, Sartre's theory seems to have more in common with the modern conception of economic theory as a logic of decision making, than with the Marxian theory of value.

The similarity between phenomenological existentialism and Marxism shows itself most clearly in the early post-Hegelian Marx. Sartre's philosophy as developed in *Being and Nothingness* exhibits such Hegelian themes as the master-slave relation and the negative element implicit in the dialectic. Indeed the very meaning of the term phenomenology is related to the Hegelian concept of the transcendental, which refers to the attempt to relate the conditions of the appearance of things to the structure of subjectivity. This is an approach from which the early Marx, despite his attempt to stand Hegel 'on his feet', does not seem to have entirely emancipated himself: reality, at least on his early view, does not exist independently of consciousness.

In the case of Husserl's later work there is an increasing concern with the relation of the individual with history. As Ricoeur notes 'in the later Husserl we can observe transcendental phenomenology turning towards an investigation of man's insertion into the world'.[50] However, it is doubtful whether intersubjectivity, which still emphasises the individual, can be completely equated with the social dimension implicit in the concept of a *species being*. History for Husserl tends to be much more the history of ideas, rather than the history of ordinary and extraordinary events studied by the working historian, or the tracing of historical trends which the Marxist considers to be the function of historical materialism. Hence, although one strand of Husserl's later thought is sympathetic to the Hegelian position and that of the early Marx, through its attempt to understand the history of scientific thought and our culture, another strand is not – namely, the attempt to base this understanding on our individual life world.

It is worth ending with a glance at Merleau-Ponty's later position, in which there is a marked tendency to separate philosophy from politics. He now believes that the 'politics of philosophy' is something no one puts into practice, and that philosophers can speak of many other things with greater certainty. In returning to a philosophical reading of our age, he describes it as a philosophy not tied down by philosophical responsibilities, and hence freer in character. It 'does not play the game of passions, of politics of life . . . but reveals precisely the Being that we inhabit'.[51] This cooler, reflective way of looking at things is coupled with Merleau-Ponty's move away from Marxism, and his acceptance of a liberal view of politics: a view which interestingly enough resembles Husserl's goal of a 'rational liberal society guided by philosophical principles'.

[50] Cf. Paul Ricoeur, *Husserl: An Analysis of his Phenomenology*, p. 203.
[51] *Signes*, cf. p. 20.

The Life-world and Role-theory

PHILIP PETTIT

This is a critical analysis of a thesis central to Alfred Schutz's idea of the life-world: that people understand one another only because they enact 'roles'. On analysis the thesis breaks down into three propositions, all of them concerned with understanding behaviour, though not to common effect. The first proposition says that if people are to find one another's behaviour 'interpretable' then it must fit a 'standardised description'. The others say that if, beyond this, people are to find one another's behaviour 'explicable' or 'justifiable' then it must fit a 'standardised story'. The first proposition expresses a general condition on human behaviour: 'interpretability' is something which agents must always seek. It makes a fair claim to be a true proposition but we see this only when we see that it does not rule out the 'novel' behaviour which is usually a part of social change.

Philip Pettit is a Research Fellow, Trinity Hall, Cambridge. He is author of *On the Idea of Phenomenology* (Scepter Books, 1969) and *The Concept of Structuralism* (Gill Macmillan, 1975).

The phenomenological idea of the life-world is now common currency in social thought, due mainly to the work of Alfred Schutz.[1] Roughly, it is the idea, akin to the analytical idea of forms of life, that each society generates its own categories and, with them, its own criteria of what is intelligible and what rational. To social thinkers like Schutz the idea has suggested that people only make themselves intelligible to one another by taking on established 'roles'; this view I take to be the main thesis of a certain sort of 'role-theory'. My concern in the present essay is to sketch the idea of the life-world and to scrutinise the thesis about roles which Schutz draws from it.

The essay is in three sections. In the first I discuss the idea of the life-world, situating it in the work of Husserl and Schutz. In the second I crystallise the thesis about roles, coming down to one proposition contained in it which seems to express a general truth. In the third I raise a problem confronting this proposition, consider Schutz's response to it and argue for a resolution which would bring the analytical idea of the 'desirability characterisation' into the discussion.

I.   Husserl published his first extended discussion of the life-world in the *Crisis* of 1936.[2] He put it in contrast there to the

[1] My thanks are due to Martin Hollis, Mary Kelly, Joel Kupperman, John Maguire, Edo Pivčević and Denys Turner whose comments have improved this essay. I am also grateful for the comments I received when I read an earlier version of the essay at the Cambridge Seminar in philosophy of social science organised by Gary Runciman and Quentin Skinner.

The relevant writings of Schutz are contained in:

The Phenomenology of the Social World, (1932), (Northwestern, 1967).

Collected Papers, I, II, III (The Hague, 1962, 1964, 1970).

Reflections on the Problem of Relevance (Yale, 1970).

The Structures of the Life-World (London, 1974).

I refer to the first of these in the text as *1932*, the year of its publication in German. I refer to the *Collected Papers* as *CP1*, *CP2* and *CP3* and give the year in which the paper was first published or, if it was only published posthumously, its year of composition. Dating the references may help to justify an assumption on which I have worked, that the development in Schutz's thought is not significant for my purposes. The other two works – both posthumous – I refer to as *1970* and *1974*. For a useful collection of some relevant writings see H. Wagner (ed.), *Alfred Schutz on phenomenology and social relations: selected writings* (Chicago, 1970).

I offer some account of Schutz's ideas in section 1 and, to a lesser extent, in sections 2 and 3. My analysis of his role-thesis in section 2 should not be taken as an interpretation of what he meant by the thesis so much as an interpretation of what such a thesis can rightly be taken to mean.

[2] See Edmund Husserl, *The Crisis of the European Sciences and Transcendental Phenomenology* (Northwestern, 1970). See also the posthumously published *Experience and Judgement* (London, 1973).

world of science. The life-world was the world given in concrete experience, the world of science – say, the mathematicised world of Galileo – a thought construct; the one was relative to human subjects, the other claimed an ideal objectivity.

The contrast between the subjectivity of the life-world and the 'objective', the 'true' world, lies in the fact that the latter is a theoretical-logical substruction, the substruction of something that is in principle not perceivable, in principle not perceivable in its own proper being, whereas the subjective, in the life-world, is distinguished in all respects precisely by its being actually experienceable.[3]

In *Crisis* and his other late writings Husserl argued that scientific procedures and concepts had their roots in the life-world.[4] They were developments of everyday procedures and concepts and the world to which they gave rise was an idealisation of the everyday world.

Objective science, too, asks questions only on the ground of this world's existing in advance through prescientific life. Like all praxis, objective science presupposes the being of this world, but it sets itself the task of transposing knowledge which is imperfect and prescientific in respect of scope and constancy into perfect knowledge – in accord with an idea of a correlative which is, to be sure, infinitely distant, i.e., of a world which in itself is fixed and determined and of truths which are *idealiter* scientific ('truths-in-themselves') and which predicatively interpret this world.[5]

Until this was realised, until it was seen that science had a non-technical motivation, Husserl felt that the meaning of science in human life would not be understood. Science would remain in crisis, alienated from everyday concerns.

Already in its Galilean conception, the exact world was from the first substituted for the world of our experience, and men entirely neglected to question the original sense-bestowing activities by means of which the exact space of geometry developed from the space of intuition, with its vague and fluent typification. Such a reflection would have shown that it is not a phantasy-like simulation of intuitive spatial forms which leads to the exact forms of geometry but only a method of idealisation of the intuitively given; and so also for all the determinations of natural science which are

[3] *Crisis*, p. 127. On 'experienceable' see the note to this passage p. 127.
[4] *Crisis*, p. 130.
[5] *Crisis*, pp. 110–11, Cf. *Experience and Judgement*, p. 43.

attributed to existents as determinations which they have in themselves. It was thereby overlooked that this method of idealisation in
the end accomplishes nothing other than an anticipation, infinitely
extended, of what is to be expected in experience.[6]

Four years before the appearance of *Crisis*, Alfred Schutz, a
young disciple of Husserl's, had published *The Phenomenology of
the Social World*. (Here mentioned in references as *1932*: see note
1). One of his main theses was that in its procedures and its
concepts social science – he was thinking particularly of Weber's
'interpretative' social science – derived from everyday procedures and concepts and gave rise to an idealised version of the
social world. In particular he maintained that the construction
of ideal types so favoured by Weber was to be found already in
everyday life. (See *1932*, ch. 5) After the appearance of *Crisis*
Schutz recognised publicly that his thesis was identical with
Husserl's; probably in fact it was inspired by him. 'Idealisation
and formalisation have just the same role for the social sciences
as the one which Husserl has stated for the natural sciences,
except that it is not a question of mathematicising the forms but
of developing a typology of "fulnesses"' (*CPI* 1940, p. 138: on
mode of reference see note 1).

In Schutz's work life-world and social world became the one
thing. He accepted in its main features Husserl's account of that
world. Husserl had written:

The life-world, for us who wakingly live in it, is always already
there, existing in advance for us, the 'ground' of all praxis whether
theoretical or extratheoretical. The world is pregiven to us, the
waking, always somehow practically interested subjects, not
occasionally but always and necessarily as the universal field of all
actual and possible praxis, as horizon. To live is always to live-in-
certainty-of-the-world.[7]

As described here the life-world has three main features, each
of which Schutz also ascribed to it: it is the given world, the
practical world, and the social world.

The world is given in the sense that it is pre-theoretical and
prepredicative; how anything appears to an individual does not
depend on his theorising or even on his judgment. Thus people
do not have to judge individually that Rex and Fido are alike

---

[6] *Experience and Judgement*, p. 44. Cf. 'The Origin of Geometry', published as an appendix
to *Crisis*.
[7] *Crisis*, p. 142.

in features *a*, *b* and *c* before seeing each as a dog. 'By a series of common sense constructs they have pre-selected and pre-interpreted this world which they experience as the reality of their daily lives' (*CP1* 1954, p. 59). The life world is practical in the sense that which features are given significance by these constructs is determined by people's practical interests (see *CP3* 1959, p. 98). Finally, the world is social in the sense that each individual assumes, as a matter of practice, that the constructs which shape how he sees things also shape how others see them (see *CP1* 1951, p. 75).

We now have a rough sketch of the phenomenological idea of the life-world. But one element deserves emphasis: that of the typification involved in 'common sense constructs'. Husserl had argued that it is of the essence of the life-world that everything experienced within it is assumed to be of some established type, so that our first contact gives us a clear expectation about what more is coming; we see a physical object in one profile and we expect to see it in a complementary profile if we move. 'Thus, our pregiven surrounding world is already "pregiven" as multiformed, formed already according to its regional categories and typified in conformity with a number of different special genera, kinds, etc.'[8]

Schutz took up the refrain. 'The world, the physical as well as the sociocultural one, is experienced from the outset in terms of types: there are mountains, trees, birds, fishes, dogs, and among them Irish setters; there are cultural objects, such as houses, tables, chairs, books, tools, and among them hammers; and there are typical social roles and relationships, such as parents, siblings, kinsmen, strangers, soldiers, hunters, priests, etc.' (*CP2* 1955, p. 233). On at least one occasion Husserl had taken types to mean broad categories like the animate and the inanimate.[9] Schutz restricted them more usually to concrete characterisations. He took the terms of the characterisations to be given in the everyday vocabulary. 'We may interpret the pre-scientific human language as a treasure house of preconstituted types and characteristics, each of them carrying along an open horizon of unexplored typical contents' (*CP1* 1950, p. 285).

On one point concerning typification Schutz made a break with Husserl explicit.

---

[8] *Experience and Judgement*, p. 38.
[9] See *Crisis*, pp. 226–7; cf. *CP3* 1959, p. 106.

Husserl has shown that, from the outset, the pre-predicative experience of the life-world is fundamentally articulated according to types . . . What Husserl has not explained in his published writings, however, is that this typification takes place according to particular structures of relevancy. In pre-predicative typification I can perceive my dog Fido in his typical behaviour as healthy or sick, as an individual, a German shepherd dog, a typical dog in general, a mammal, a living creature, a thing of the external world, a 'something at large' (*CP3* 1953–8, p. 125).

Here Schutz is saying that everything in the life-world has a set of typifications, each answering to an aspect under which it may be found relevant by an individual or group. He devoted a good deal of his time to examining the 'structures of relevance' which vary between individuals and groups within a life-world, but this work does not concern us in the present essay (see *CP3* 1953–8, pp. 116–32; *CP2* 1955, pp. 226–73; *1970*; *1974*).

With typification in place the sketch of the life-world idea is almost complete. It remains to show how Schutz uses the idea in his social writings to analyse the experience which people have, not of an impersonal world, but of one another. Schutz assumes that the life-world gives 'constructs in terms of which men in the reality of daily life experience their own and their fellow-men's behaviour' (*CP1* 1953, p. 6). The question now is, what are those constructs, what are those typifications?

In order to appreciate Schutz's answer to this question it is necessary to understand an argument which he invokes concerning the requirements of intersubjective understanding. The argument is that such understanding requires, precisely, typifications of behaviour; I shall call it, 'argument *A*'. Before giving the argument I must mention a distinction which occurs in the statement of it: Schutz's distinction between the 'in-order-to motive' and the 'because motive'. The in-order-to motive is the intention with which the agent acts, something on which he is taken as authority; it defines what it is he does, the act he performs. A because motive is a factor – say, an experience of the agent, or perhaps a disposition of his – which leads the agent to form that intention and perform that act (see *1932*, pp. 86–96).

Argument *A* can be stated from the point of view of the agent or from the point of view of someone trying to understand his action, the 'audience'. We will take it from the point of view of the audience. The first premise is that as audience I must know the agent's motives, both the in-order-to motive and the because motives. 'I am interested above all not in the overt behaviour of others, not in their performance of gestures and bodily movements, but in their intentions, and that means in the in-order-to motives for the sake of which, and in the because motives based on which, they act as they do' (*CP2* 1940, p. 15). The second premise is that I can only know the agent's motives if I can rightly assume that we are alike in how we express our motives in overt behaviour. 'More or less naively I presuppose the existence of a common scheme of reference for both my own acts and the acts of others' (*Ibid.*). The conclusion is that as audience of another's action, as someone trying to understand it, I must bring the action under a typification which I would be prepared to have applied to a similar action of mine. Argument *A* from the agent's point of view gives the complementary conclusion that as agent I must fit my action to a common typification if I am to allow my action to be understood by another. 'On the one hand, I have – in order to understand another – to apply the system of typifications accepted by the group to which both of us belong. . . On the other hand, in order to make myself understandable to another, I have to avail myself of the same system of typifications as a scheme of orientation for my projected action' (*CP2* 1955, p. 237).

But, to return to our earlier question, what are the typifications in which we see our own actions and those of others? Schutz distinguishes between two kinds of typifications or, in Weber's phrase, 'ideal types'. The one is the typification of the action itself, the other is the typification – say, in terms of character or function – of the agent. They give two ways of understanding another, and of being understood.

When I seek to understand another's behaviour in ideal-typical fashion, a twofold method is available to me. I can begin with the finished act, then determine the type of action that produced it, and finally settle upon the type of person who must have acted in this way. Or I can reverse the process and, knowing the personal ideal type, deduce the corresponding act *1932*, p. 188).[10]

This account of behavioural typifications makes them sound like 'roles', in the popular sociological sense. Schutz recognises this too. 'It can be explained why we interpret the actions of our

---

[10] The qualification 'in ideal typical fashion' is understandable in the light of what I say about Schutz in the third section.

fellow-men in terms of course-of-action types and of personal types, and why we have to undergo a self-typification in order to come to terms with them by establishing a universe of communicative comprehension. The social sciences study this problem under the heading of "social roles"' (*CP1* 1959, pp. 148–9).

We may take the word 'roles' to describe the constructs in terms of which Schutz thinks we see our own behaviour and that of others. The conclusion of argument *A* – that roles are required for intersubjective understanding – I shall call Schutz's 'role-thesis'. This thesis is the part of the life-world theory in which our interest centres in this essay.

II.   The significance of the idea of the life-world in Husserl's thought was that it provided a new way of defining the phenomenological project. The project was to uncover the 'constitutive intentionality' at work in every experience; this intentionality I discuss in the next section. In his earlier work Husserl had given a 'Cartesian' account of the project, conceiving of it as a return to the immediate data of consciousness, the materials on which intentionality had to work. After *Crisis* he could give another account, considering the project as an investigation of the 'products' of intentionality to be found in the life-world.[11]

The significance assumed by the idea of the life-world in Schutz's thought, and in social thought generally, was not that which Husserl gave it. The idea was used, not to define the phenomenological project, but to define the project of social science: this was to be the empirical study of life-worlds. Husserl was concerned with the 'general structure' of all life-worlds but he was not unaware of the important differences there might be between them. 'When we are thrown into an alien social sphere, that of the Negroes in the Congo, Chinese peasants, etc., we discover that their truths, the facts that for them are fixed, generally verified or verifiable, are by no means the same as ours.'[12] If life-worlds differ, then this would suggest that there is interest in the empirical study of any particular life-world, present or past, local or exotic.

If we restrict ourselves to the study of the present, local life-world – that is, to social science as distinct from history and

[11] See *Crisis*, pp. 154–5.
[12] *Crisis*, p. 139; cf. p. 147.

anthropology – we find that the idea of the life-world leads in two directions. It can lead us to define a new type of social science or it can lead us to define social science, traditionally conceived. We go in the first direction if we ask about what in the given life-world makes intersubjective understanding possible. 'Man is capable of understanding his fellow-man. How is this possible?' (*CP1* 1951, p. 95). We go in the second if we ask about how the idealised world of social science – say, the world of economically rational men – relates to the actual life-world. 'Can and does the social scientist refer to the same reality of the social world that appears to the actor? And if so, how is this possible?' (*Ibid.*, p. 96). Schutz spent a good deal of his time on the second question, arguing for a 'humanistic' philosophy of social science (see *1932*, ch. 5; *CP2* 1942, pp. 81–8; *CP1* 1953, pp. 34–47). The question which interests us however is the first.

We know already, from the first section, what Schutz's answer is to this question. The answer is given, in abstract form, in his role-thesis. This thesis has guided the 'new social science' which looks for the concrete features of role play that enable us to understand one another.[13] In this section I want to clarify the role-thesis, crystallising it into its constituent propositions.

The question to which the role-thesis provides an answer is not specific about what it is for people to understand one another. A first step in clarifying the answer must be to clarify the question. To understand another person may mean to understand his behaviour in a general sense or it may mean to understand the specific part of his behaviour consisting in his beliefs – or, more properly, the profession of his beliefs. This is a first important distinction. A second comes as readily to mind. To understand may mean to find intelligible in a general sense or, again more specifically, to find rational or justifiable. Thus the problem of intersubjective understanding breaks down into four problems: those of the intelligibility and justifiability of beliefs specifically and of behaviour generally.

---

[13] For some varieties of this 'new social science' see Erving Goffman, *The Presentation of Self in Everyday Life* (1959; Harmondsworth, 1969); Peter L. Berger and Thomas Luckmann, *The Social Construction of Reality* (1966; Harmondsworth, 1967); Harold Garfinkel, *Studies in Ethnomethodology* (New Jersey, 1967). See also R. Harré and P. F. Secord, *The Explanation of Social Behaviour* (Oxford, 1972). This 'New Social Science' has historical links with Schutz but in most of its varieties goes well beyond some of his intentions and falls short of others.

But 'intelligibility' remains ambiguous. A belief may be intelligible in the sense that we know what is believed; here 'intelligible' means 'interpretable'. It may or may not be intelligible however in the further sense that we know why it is held; here 'intelligible' means 'causally explicable'. The same distinction holds, though it is less often drawn, for behaviour. A piece of behaviour is interpretable when we know what is done – on this we shall have more to say; it is explicable when we know why it is done. Thus, in all, we have six problems hidden in the problem of how people understand one another: the problems of the interpretability, explicability and justifiability of belief on the one hand, behaviour on the other.

The basic point to be made in clarification of the role-thesis is that it does not have much to say specifically about beliefs. The counterpart in the analytical tradition to the phenomenological idea of the life-world would seem to be Wittgenstein's idea of forms of life. It is curious that this idea has bred a thesis about belief which corresponds in some way to the role-thesis about behaviour. The thesis is that we understand one another's beliefs by rules of interpretation, explanation and justification specific – in all likelihood – to our society. The thesis has been used to a relativist effect in the philosophy of history and anthropology.[14] Our concern is not with this thesis but we may mention that it is a thesis we would expect to appear, side by side with the role thesis, in a full development of the idea of the life-world.

As a thesis about how people understand one another's behaviour the role-thesis must be broken down into three propositions: proposition 1 about interpretability, proposition 2 about explicability and proposition 3 about justifiability. The propositions maintain in each case that if his behaviour is to exhibit the feature in question then the agent must ensure that it falls under some role description: one that is immediately obvious or one at least for which he can successfully 'negotiate'. I want to argue now that proposition 1 differs substantially in sense and in status from the other two propositions. Before I do so however I must give a better account of what is involved in interpreting, explaining and justifying behaviour.

---

[14] For a version of the thesis see Peter Winch, *The Idea of a Social Science* (London, 1958) and 'Understanding a primitive society' in Bryan R. Wilson (ed.), *Rationality* (Oxford, 1970). For criticism of the thesis see Steven Lukes, 'Some problems about rationality' and Martin Hollis, 'The limits of irrationality' and 'Reason and ritual', all in Wilson; also Roger Trigg, *Reason and Commitment* (Cambridge, 1973).

We suppose that we are dealing with intentional action: roughly, action for which there is an answer to the question 'What was the agent meaning to do?' I wish to differentiate the following elements in intentional action: the agent's *intention* in the sense of what he is after and, derivatively, in the active sense of his being after it; the agent's *grounds* in the sense of what he is aware of that prompts him to act – without compelling him, like a fright, and making the action unintentional – and, derivatively, in the active sense of his being aware of it; the agent's *disposition* in the sense of what disposes him to take a given grounds into consideration, to form a given intention – this corresponds properly to Schutz's because motive and can be a trait, a policy, a creed, an office, an emotion or whatever. (Schutz's because motive probably also includes our grounds; his in-order-to motive is our intention.)[15]

To interpret an action for our purposes is, as Schutz says, to give the agent's intention, his in-order-to motive: for everyday purposes it will often be more than this, including mention for example of serious unintended consequences. Intention is not well defined because it may cover, roughly speaking, a short term or a long term plan. Schutz is happy enough with this but I want to distinguish between these two (see *CP1* 1953, pp. 23–4). Only the short term plan specifies an action concretely and I call it the agent's 'intention'; it is what is ordinarily sought in the interpretation of an action. A long-term plan, which suggests only an abstract description of the action, I call the agent's 'policy', and I count it as a dispositional factor.[16]

---

[15] Notice that the hoary old 'motive' does not appear among these elements. This is because the motive explanation – by which one acts, for example, out of jealousy, gratitude, revenge, fear or patriotism – does not mention a distinctive explanatory element so much as make a claim about the operative – the 'real' – intention and grounds. If the motive were a distinctive element it would count as a disposition but one can act out of the motive of jealousy without being of a jealous disposition; one's action may be exceptional. See D. S. Shwayder, *The Stratification of Behaviour* (London, 1965), pp. 185–200.

Notice, secondly, that the scheme, being an idealisation, is not altogether in line with ordinary usage. Thus we should not ordinarily say that in every case of intentional action the active sense of 'intention' is applicable. I may have intentionally brushed a fly from my forehead but did I actively 'intend' to do it? Perhaps we would not ordinarily say I did. What we would say, however, is that I realised a short-term plan, and this is enough to make applicable the active sense of intention, as defined in our ideal scheme.

[16] There are two cases where we characterise a short term plan abstractly, thus making it look like a policy. One is the 'motive' case mentioned in note 15. The other is the case discussed in the third section where we are forced to describe an intention in a 'desirability characterisation'.

To explain an action is to say what, in the circumstances, was the significant factor responsible for bringing it about. To justify the action is to find the intended effect unobjectionable; to find the means for realising it not ineffective; and to find the predictable side-effects tolerable in the circumstances. This account at least will do for our purposes.

I wish to distinguish now between what I will call the explicit interpretation of an action, which is implicitly an explanation and justification, and the explicit explanation or justification, which is implicitly an interpretation. The explicit interpretation is provided by mention of the action's intention or by mention of its grounds, the grounds indicating what the intention is. Thus an explicit interpretation of why someone went for a walk might be that he wanted to take the air or that it is a fine day. Such an interpretation will usually constitute an implicit justification – there were no other relevant factors – and an implicit explanation – the action was brought about by the agent's intention or grounds, in the active sense.

The explicit explanation of an action is provided by mention of the disposition which led the agent to perform the action. These might be examples of explicit explanations of why someone went for a walk: 'He is athletic' (trait), 'He is anxious to lose weight' (policy), 'He is a nature worshipper' (creed, perhaps), 'He is on police duty' (office) or 'He is upset about something' (emotion). The explicit explanation is primarily concerned to show what brought about the action though it is an implicit interpretation: it presupposes some account of what was done – at least that one which is felt to require further explanation. A similar story can be told about explicit justification as that told here about explanation: I will take it as told and consider explicit explanation and justification together.

We may return to the three propositions in the role-thesis. Since interpretability, explicability and justifiability do not come apart as cleanly as we first thought we must revise the propositions slightly. I propose that we take proposition 1 to deal with what is required if my action is to be explicitly interpretable, and propositions 2 and 3 with what is required if it is also to be explicable and justifiable in explicit terms. Taking the propositions in this sense I now want to show that proposition 1 differs in sense and status from the other two. Where I say simply 'interpretable' I mean 'explicitly interpretable'; similarly with 'explicable' and 'justifiable'.

Proposition 1 is distinctive in sense because the role which it says is required for interpretability is a different sort of role from that required for explicability and justifiability. What is required if I am to be able to interpret someone's action, to know what he is doing? A first requirement is that the action fall under a description which I understand. This however is not enough. Suppose I know that someone in reading about war horrors intends to worry himself. Suppose indeed that this is really all he has to say about what he is doing. The action would in this case fall under an understandable description but, in one sense at least – the sense suggested by Schutz – I could scarcely claim to know what he is doing.

The further requirement, if I am to be able to interpret someone's action, is that it fall under a standardised description. I mean by this, a description which I understand by reference to a standard case, which is of the category in question – here, a standard case of intentional action. I suggest that what Schutz means by typification and role in the sense in which they are required for interpretability is, precisely, standardised description. What I must do as agent if my action is to be interpretable is allow the action to fall under a standardised description: one that is obvious or one for which I can plausibly negotiate. This is what proposition 1 says.

This proposition is not only distinctive in sense but in status. It has the status of a general condition on human behaviour because interpretability is something which an agent must always ensure in his behaviour: otherwise he makes himself radically incapable of engaging with other men, a condition which amounts to total idiocy. Every action of mine is a potential interaction and every interaction supposes that I fit what I do to a standardised description so that the other person can understand it and know how to react. 'I posit meaningful acts in the expectation that others will interpret them meaningfully, and my schema of positing is oriented with respect to the others' schema of interpretation' (*CPI* 1940, p. 135; see also *CPI* 1953, pp. 22–3).

The difference between proposition 1 and the other two propositions contained in the role thesis is that the other propositions require roles in a sense other than that of standardised description and do not require them as a general condition on human behaviour. If I am to ensure that my behaviour is explicable, and this in terms other than those supplied by its interpretation, then I must fit what I do to a story about its motivation, which I present in my style of behaviour or in speech. Further, the story must be standardised in the same sense as the description: it must be capable of being understood by reference to a standard case of motivation and cannot invoke just any producing factor. To explain oneself under challenge – or, I will assume, to justify oneself – is usually to negotiate in speech acceptance of such a story: one was angry or upset, had such and such a goal in mind, was taking a hard line, and so on. In the idea of a standardised story, we have a different sense of role from that given by the idea of a standardised description.

The difference in status between proposition 1 and the other two propositions is that explicability and justifiability – in the sense in question – are not factors which an agent must always ensure in his behaviour; thus the other propositions do not express a general condition on human behaviour but only a condition which must be met in certain circumstances. I do always have to behave in such a way that my behaviour falls under a standardised description but I do not always have to fit it to a standardised story. I will always want to be interpretable in what I do – even if my aim is to beguile – but I may not choose, or I may not be called, to be explicable and justifiable. Suppose I am a lecturer who spends a good deal of his time criticising his colleagues. I may take on the style or the speech of the pure scholar to explain and justify my behaviour. Or again I may not: I may prefer to run the risk of being taken as spiteful, perhaps in the hope of remaining inscrutable.

We have now reached the point where we can see that as a general thesis about intersubjective understanding Schutz's role-thesis comes down to proposition 1. It says, simply, that as a condition of being mutually interpretable people must fit their actions to standardised descriptions. I believe that it is a true proposition but in order to bear this out I must show how it can deal with a problem raised by social change.

III.   The problem is that in a particular sort of case it appears that agents succeed in getting 'novel' actions understood by their fellows. I am thinking of those actions of radical or eccentric individuals or groups which can, in appropriate circumstances, generate or promote social change. Such actions may be unprecedented in the sense that there seem to be no standardised descriptions to fit them. Or they may be pre-empted, in the sense that the only appropriate standardised descriptions would present the agents as morbid or grossly immoral. It is a fact of social change that agents can negotiate an interpretation of their novel actions in terms of hitherto unstandardised descriptions.

It should be noted that novel actions in this sense are not just difficult to explain or justify like everyday examples of crazy behaviour; they are difficult to interpret, at least consistently with the assumption that the agents are not just being morbid or immoral. I assume that the strike weapon or the student occupation was once a novel action, the action of the pacifist in objecting conscientiously or the action of the hippy in dropping out. I assume that banking was a novel action on its interpretation as something more than usury, co-habitation on its interpretation as something more than fornication. I assume, finally, that in our society there are examples every day – not significant ones perhaps – of novel actions: 'streaking' is the best recent instance.

The problem now is that it is hard to see how novel behaviour and novel interpretation of behaviour is possible, granted proposition 1. Schutz makes this general comment on how we deal with a novel fact of experience. 'We first define the new fact; we try to catch its meaning; we then transform step by step our general scheme of interpretation of the world in such a way that the strange fact and its meaning become compatible and consistent with all the other facts of our experience and their meanings' (*CP2* 1944, p. 105). The problem is, how do we do this – particularly when the new fact consists in how others behave.

What Schutz has to say on the problem is not of much help, mainly because of his failure to distinguish proposition 1 from propositions 2 and 3. He thinks of our freedom to drop roles in the sense of motivational profiles and takes it as the freedom not always to fit our actions to standardised descriptions. 'We keep – even in the role – the liberty of choice, as far as such liberty exists at all within the scope of our human and social conditions. This liberty embraces the possibility of taking off our disguise, of dropping the role, of recommencing our orientation in the social world. We continue to be subjects, centres of spontaneous activities, actors' (*CP2* 1942, p. 82).

According to Schutz we are free of roles in the private world in which we communicate with our friends; here argument *A* does not carry. It is only in the public world where we deal with strangers that we use roles to understand and be understood. In the private world of friends we relate I to thou, in the public world of mere contemporaries we have only 'they-relationships'. 'A social relationship between contemporaries, therefore, consists in this: Each of the partners apprehends the other by means of an ideal type; each of the partners is aware of this mutual apprehension; and each expects that the other's interpretative scheme will be congruent with his own. The they-relationship here stands in sharp contrast to the face-to-face situation. In the face-to-face situation my partner and I are sensitively aware of the nuances of each other's subjective experiences' (*1932*, pp. 202–3).

It is worth mentioning that the individualism to which Schutz here retreats is a natural product of his phenomenology. The key phenomenological idea is that of intentionality, the idea that in every experience the individual is actively putting form and flesh on the bare materials of sense. Take the visual perception of a physical object. The argument is, roughly, that the object is seen as an object continuing in time because the percipient associates the object perceived with an object remembered; it is seen as an object occupying space because he assumes that it has other profiles than that which he registers from any particular perspective; it is seen as an object of a definite type because he puts it in a category and class with certain other objects.

It is true that Husserl, especially after introducing the life-world theme, insisted that as a matter of fact people exercise intentionality on the same lines in any society. It remains the case however that this is only as a matter of fact, not necessity; it is still the individual, in isolation, who is responsible for how he sees things. This epistemological individualism leads naturally to an ethical individualism – specifically, to an existentialist exaltation of individual creativity; here Sartre is an object lesson.[17] Very likely, it is such an existentialist tendency in his

[17] See J.–P. Sartre, *Being and Nothingness* (London; 1957). On Sartre's 'epistemological individualism' see my 'Parmenides and Sartre', *Philosophical Studies* (Ireland), Vol. 17, 1968. Husserl tried to argue for a 'transcendental intersubjectivity' in *Crisis* but the obscurity of this doctrine may excuse Sartre for finding individualism in Husserl. Schutz disapproves of Sartre's interpretation in 1970, ch. 1.

thought which motivates Schutz to argue in the last analysis for the dispensability of roles.

To return to the problem facing proposition 1, we must explain how novel behaviour and the interpretation of novel behaviour is possible. I propose to offer an explanation whose interest is that it may revive an analytical concept now fallen into disuse – the idea, in Elizabeth Anscombe's phrase, of the 'desirability characterisation'. I mean to argue that desirability characterisations are standardised descriptions which serve in crucial cases to interpret otherwise unintelligible behaviour; this, despite the fact that they are abstract rather than concrete typifications (see note 16).

The theory of desirability characterisations, as originally put forward by Anscombe, is that the only thing that necessarily puts a stop to the question 'What do you want X for?' is a characterisation of X in some desirability term like 'exciting', 'dutiful', 'delightful' or 'charitable'; not that it is impossible to fail to want such a thing, only that it is always possible to claim to want it.[18] It is trivially true of whatever I do intentionally that I want to do that action, that I want to bring about the state of affairs which I conceive of it realising; in this sense, as Anscombe says, 'the primitive sign of wanting is *trying to get*'.[19] It apparently follows that giving a desirability characterisation of what one wants in doing something puts a stop to the question 'Why did you do that?'

Two kinds of objection are frequently brought against the theory of desirability characterisations. The best way in which I can show how I want to use the theory in resolving the problem facing proposition 1 is by considering these.

The first objection is that introducing a desirability characterisation does not always put a stop to the question 'Why did you do that?'[20] If the question was seeking an explanation of the action then mention of the desirability characterisation can be met with the challenge 'Do you seriously expect me to believe that you did *that* just because of wanting ...?' If it was seeking justification it can be met with the challenge 'Was wanting . . . a good reason for doing *that*?'

Our distinctions in the second section show how this objection

---

[18] G. E. M. Anscombe, *Intention* (Oxford, 2nd ed., 1963), pp. 70–6.
[19] *Ibid.* p. 68.
[20] See J. C. B. Gosling, *Pleasure and Desire* (Oxford, 1969), pp. 83–5.

is to be answered. Mention of a desirability characterisation gives an interpretation of an action but does not give the special sort of explanation or justification which is required to meet the challenge envisaged in the objection. The characterisation offers a standardised description of the action, it allows the action to be assimilated to a standard case or set of cases. It does not point to a story about the behaviour in terms of which an agent might formulate a searching explanation or justification of his action. The case where mention of a desirability characterisation does not put a stop to the question 'Why did you do that?' is one of those cases where interpretation comes apart from explanation and justification. The question to which mention of the desirability characterisation does put a stop in such a case is 'What's the sense of that?' or, more coloquially, 'What sort of an action is that?' It is natural to reformulate the original theory somewhat and claim that this is a question to which it always puts a stop. Against the reformulated theory the first objection does not carry.

The second objection is that desirability characterisations can be applied to whatever one wishes: anything can be described as exciting because, in principle, anything can be found so. This objection would make the characterisations useless in interpreting actions since it would mean that an agent could negotiate an interpretation for any action at all.[21]

One may hazard a guess at the source of this objection. It is often felt – without good reason, so far as one can see – that to explain why an agent does something one must go back to a quasi-mechanical moving force: usually, his desire. The mechanical thesis has some plausibility because it is true that, as already mentioned, desire or wanting in one sense – that of 'trying to get' – is always present in intentional action. This is a different sense of desire however from that envisaged in the mechanical thesis: here desire means 'anticipating with felt pleasure', something which we would rank as a particular kind of dispositional factor. If the mechanical thesis is accepted, however, whether or not by reason of this confusion, it then seems arbitrary to say that the agent is limited in what he can claim to want – limited, as a matter of principle – by the existing

---

[21] See R. M. Hare, 'Descriptivism' in W. D. Hudson (ed.), *The Is-Ought Question* (London, 1969), p. 249; also A. J. Watt, 'The Intelligibility of Wants', *Mind*, Vol. LXXXI, 1972.

desirability characterisations; such a limitation can only reflect a matter of fact about people's desires. Thus there is no reason to believe that the agent will not have unusual desires – he may find exciting what others find dull, for example – and will not use desirability characterisations exactly as his desires dictate.[22]

Once the mechanist motive for upholding it is put aside the second objection loses its appeal. Take the word 'exciting'. By its socially established use it applies unquestionably in certain standard cases: with respect to such things as taking risks and breaking conventions. Not that one must oneself find all these things exciting; one must know that they are the sort of things that people in general find exciting. When the word is extended to apply to things very different from these the extension must be defended. It is defended by familiar devices that link the new experiences with the old: by pictures, for example – 'being on edge', 'having butterflies in the stomach' – or by similes – 'it's like not knowing what's going to happen', 'it's like a musical crescendo'. It seems quite clear that there are some experiences which no devices can link with the standard cases of excitement: try 'immersing one's elbow in a saucer of mud for the afternoon'.

There is every indication that what is true of 'exciting' is true of other desirability characterisations too. Such characterisations are defined by reference to standard cases and are incapable therefore of being extended to just any novel case. This point reinforces the point made in response to the first objection, that desirability characterisations serve to provide standardised descriptions of the actions to which they are applied. They are ways of interpreting actions, not necessarily ways of explaining and justifying them.

The position we have reached is this. To perform an action which does not put one's status as an intelligent being in question is to fit the action to a standardised description: proposition 1 holds good. In the commonplace case the action will fall naturally under quite a concrete characterisation: something like a typification, in Schutz's sense. In the critical case of a novel action however there may yet be a standardised description – and one acceptable to the agent – under which the action

---

[22] For a critique of such mechanism see Richard Norman, *Reasons for Actions* (Oxford, 1971).

falls. This is likely to be found in one of the traditional desirability characterisations.

My thesis is that these characterisations offer basic terms for negotiating interpretations of what we do. They are the gold of our system of legitimation and are brought out in two cases: when the ordinary currency is under pressure and when it fails. It is under pressure when the question seeking interpretation – 'What's the sense of that?' – is pressed beyond the answer which mentions a commonplace characterisation of it; here – and this is the case emphasised by Anscombe – the desirability characterisation serves to put a definite stop to the question. The ordinary currency fails in the case which interests us most, where the action is novel and there is no commonplace characterisation of it, or at least no acceptable one. In this case the desirability characterisation may save the agent from being put down as mad, morbid or immoral. It can give him a chance of having his behaviour accepted – even to the point of its becoming an established form and receiving within the society a concrete standardised description.

If the thesis about desirability characterisations is correct then there is little to stop us accepting proposition 1 : that is, the core of the role-thesis, which is itself the core of the life-world idea. This is a good place to end but best end with a question.

What about desirability characterisations? I have said what they do and suggested some examples but they need to be better specified in any social context. Some of them may be characterisations natural to men everywhere and useful in historical and anthropological understanding. I suspect that many – perhaps the important ones in social change – are specific to cultures and periods, being produced by particular ideologies. Think of these ideas and the desirability characterisations they allow; 'the freedom of the individual', 'the will of God', 'the duty to "contribute"', 'the need to "be yourself"', 'the claim of the "life-force"', and so on. To recognise the use of such ideas is to recognise an important task in the analysis of ideology.[23] Also it is to see that desirability characterisations do not quite free us from the hold of our actual social situation: proposition 1 still has bite.

---

[23] See Quentin Skinner, 'Some problems in the analysis of political thought and action', *Political Theory*, Vol. II, 1974. Mr Skinner is concerned with strategies whereby social innovators make their behaviour, not just interpretable, but also explicable and justifiable.

Concepts, Phenomenology and Philosophical Understanding

EDO PIVČEVIĆ

In the preceding papers some of the problems that occupy a focal place in phenomenological discussions have been examined. It is clear that the manner in which phenomenologists approach philosophical issues differs considerably from the style of approach more usual in the analytical philosophical tradition; the isolated experiments with the so-called 'linguistic phenomenology' hardly amounting to a serious attempt to bridge the differences between the two methods. I attempt to highlight some of the limitations of both linguistic analysis and the phenomenological approach through a consideration of their respective treatment of concepts. I argue that at least in the case of some concepts a new structural analysis is needed which incorporates features of both these types of approach while going far beyond either.

Edo Pivčević is Senior Lecturer in Philosophy at the University of Bristol. He is the author of *Ironie als Daseinsform bei Sören Kierkegaard* (1960) and *Husserl and Phenomenology* (1970; German translation under the title *Von Husserl zu Sartre*, Munich, 1972).

The problem of philosophical understanding may be seen as a problem of finding an appropriate method for analysing concepts. It is frequently a sense of disappointment at the achievements of linguistic analysis in this respect that makes people look to phenomenology with hope. A mathematician by training, Husserl himself was led to phenomenology largely because of a feeling of disatisfaction with what he saw as the philosophical limitations of logico-linguistic analytic techniques.[1] In a similar way, Descartes spurned the 'philosophically sterile' logico-linguistic techniques of an earlier period and practised what was in effect a phenomenological analysis. More recent forms of logico-linguistic analysis, although incomparably more subtle and penetrating, are none the less afflicted with serious philosophical weaknesses. But I do not believe that Husserl's phenomenology provides an entirely satisfactory philosophical alternative. This, of course, is not to say that the phenomenological method is not a valuable philosophical tool. Quite the reverse. But we must be ready to recognize its limitations.

1.   Let us begin by considering a logico-linguistic approach to concepts. Frege, as is well known, regarded concepts as a subclass of functions; more specifically, as predicative functions, or functions 'whose value is always a truth value'.[2] The general characteristic of functions, he argued, is that they are 'unsaturated' or 'incomplete'. This can be seen by inspecting functional expressions. The expression 'The square root of x' contains a gap in the form of a variable. If an argument (number) is substituted for the variable x, the value of the function can be worked out for that argument. In a similar way, Frege thought, we can regard concepts as being adequately represented by the 'unsaturated' predicative parts of statements, e.g. 'has brown hair' or 'loves'. If proper names are added in appropriate places these predicative functional expressions will yield one of the two 'truth-values', i.e. they will result in truths or false-

---

[1] Husserl had a thorough knowledge of the logical literature of his day and was well versed in the techniques and symbolism of the new 'mathematisierende Logik'. He was familiar with Frege's work and a well annotated copy of Frege's *Begriffsschrift* found among his papers showed that he studied carefully Frege's new 'formalized language of pure thought.' But he never accepted Frege's method. See my book *Husserl and Phenomenology* (London: Hutchinson, 1970), chs. 2 and 3.

[2] *Translations from the Philosophical Writings of Gottlob Frege* (Oxford: Basil Blackwell, (1960), p. 30.

hoods. The difference between such expressions and proper names is that the latter contain no 'gaps' as part of their structure; they are complete in themselves.

It is by such linguistic considerations that Frege sought to explain the *ontological* difference between concepts and objects. He linked concepts with predicates and objects with proper names and designating expressions in general. But the philosophical inadequacy of his linguistic reasoning soon made itself painfully apparent. The hall-mark of concepts, he maintained, is to be found in the 'unsaturatedness' exemplified by predicative expressions. But suppose we wish to assert something about a concept. Suppose we say 'The concept of justice is difficult to define'. Then, according to Frege's criterion, 'The concept of justice' will have to be regarded not as a concept, not even as a name of a concept, but as a name of an *object*. This is what Frege himself admits, speaking obscurely of concepts being 'converted into objects', or being 'represented by objects' in such cases.[3] But if this is accepted, then we can no longer meaningfully say 'The concept of justice is a concept'. It is a consequence of Frege's criterion that such statements must be rejected as ungrammatical. Which seems absurd.

Frege is clearly in difficulties here. The key idea in his analysis of concepts is the idea of 'unsaturatedness'. He finds that he can make this idea clear only by analysing predicative parts of statements. But since we can, and do, talk *about* concepts as well as use them predicatively, the question arises whether predicative 'unsaturatedness' really is the whole story. For there are good grounds for doubting that whenever one says something about a concept one is in effect merely saying something about an 'unsaturated' predicative function. After all, there are concepts – e.g. the concept of identity – which do not lend themselves to a predicative analysis in any case. So what does one talk about when one is making a reference to a concept?

Faced with this question Frege decided that in asserting something about a concept we are really saying something about its extension (which, to him, was a special kind of object). But this is manifestly wrong. When we try to define the concept of justice we address ourselves to its meaning, not to its extension; if we refer to its extension, then only obliquely, *via* its meaning.

---

[3] *Ibid.* p. 46.

The statement 'The concept of justice is difficult to define' is equivalent to the statement 'The meaning of *justice* is difficult to define'. It follows that we must direct our attention to meanings; and conceptual meanings (as the example of identity very clearly shows) must not be too hastily interpreted in terms of the linguistic behaviour of certain predicates.

The problem before us, then, is how we should approach meanings, in particular conceptual meanings; where should we begin our analysis; what method should we use. On this the attitude of the phenomenologists is very different from the attitude of the linguistic analysts. There are objections, however, to both.

2.   The practitioners of linguistic analysis, largely under the influence of Wittgenstein, have come to regard the problem of meaning as a problem of linguistic use. Wittgenstein's idea was that we should regard linguistic expressions as 'instruments characterized by their use'.[4] The meaning of an expression is determined by the use this expression is put to within a language game, or games. The meaning of a chess piece is defined by its characteristic moves within the game of chess. Similarly expressions acquire what meaning they have from their function within a language game or 'linguistic calculus'.

But this idiom is slightly awkward if applied to concepts. A concept may be implicitly applied without the relevant concept-word being actually used. If I say 'I gave him money because I wanted to help him' I give a reason for my action without actually using the word 'reason'; moreover, sentences of this sort will have to feature in any explanation of the meaning of the word 'reason'. We must, therefore, distinguish between application instances of a concept and use of a concept-word. This has far-reaching implications which are not always clearly understood.

I shall take an example from J. Bennett's discussion of concepts in his *Kant's Analytic*. Bennett admits the need to distinguish between '*x* has the concept of. . .' and '*x* knows the meaning of ". . ."',[5] but this distinction does not distract him from taking a strictly Wittgensteinian approach to concepts.

---

[4] 'Think of words as instruments characterized by their use. . .', *The Blue and Brown Books* (1960), p. 67. See also *Philosophische Grammatik*, ed. Rush Rhees (1969), pp. 59–60: 'Die Erklärung der Bedeutung erklärt den Gebrauch des Wortes. Der Gebrauch des Wortes in der Sprache ist seine Bedeutung.'

[5] *Kant's Analytic* (Cambridge University Press, 1966), p. 75.

The question to which he addresses himself is not 'What is a concept?' or 'What are concepts?', but 'What is it to *have* a concept?', and his reply is that to have a concept is to have an *ability*. As he says, 'To have a concept is to be able to do certain things, particularly linguistic things such as answering questions like "Is this a man?" and "Why is that not a man?".'[6] He further writes:

> Someone counts as having the concept of humanity if he can correctly use 'human' and its cognates, or 'menschlich' and its cognates, or 'humain' and its cognates, etc. In saying this I treat concepts as abilities rather than as mental states which may lead to abilities: a man's ability to use a word properly does not merely suggest but *proves that he has the corresponding concept* [My italics – E.P.].[7]

This 'explanation' begs too many questions. Let us look more closely at what is actually asserted.

It is claimed that to have a concept is to have an ability to do certain things. The insistence on 'ability' serves to emphasise that the sense of 'having' in '*x* has the concept of. . .' is not the same as in '*x* has red cheeks' or 'brown hair'. But notice that what is claimed is not that having a concept *involves* an ability to perform in a certain way, but that it is such an ability, that it is the same as having such an ability. But in fact, while it may be that the ability to perform satisfactorily in certain respects is a necessary condition of having concepts, this is not a sufficient condition; or else we might have to say that a clock which always chimes the correct hour knows what it is to keep the correct time.

What precisely does it mean to say that concepts are 'abilities'? Bennett uses 'ability' synonymously with 'linguistic ability' or 'linguistic skill' (although in the first quotation above there is a vague suggestion that concepts might also involve other, albeit, it seems, less essential abilities). However, to call concepts 'linguistic abilities' is of little help unless the meaning of 'language' is reasonably clear. But what exactly is meant by 'language'? We cannot say simply: 'language' is the ability to use language. We must give examples of such ability. But how does one *recognize* given examples as examples of a language? They might be merely scribbles on paper, or random sequences of sounds with no unifying intention behind them. Now, it might

[6] *Ibid.* p. 54.
[7] *Ibid.* p. 71.

be said that we know what a language is by using a language ourselves. We employ a language to transmit messages and are able to receive messages in a similar way. Surely this must be sufficient to give us an idea of what a language is. The answer to this is of course: yes, but only because we are capable of conceptual thought. The ability to use language cannot be identified as a linguistic ability without conceptual thought, and this exposes the fallacy of equating concepts with linguistic abilities.

Consider again the topic of examples. This paperclip on my desk is a spatio-temporal particular distinct from all other spatio-temporal particulars, but it is also an example of the kind of thing known as 'paperclip'. I can look at it from both viewpoints. Similarly, I can look at this plant in the flower pot on my window-sill simply as the plant that was given to me as a present on my last birthday, or as a specimen exemplifying a particularly interesting species. Now suppose that I am confronted with an object that is in every respect unique. I could still distinguish between this object as an individual and its underlying type. This type is not an entity *per se*, a Platonic idea. But it would be useless to pretend that because of this the distinction does not really matter. We can always imagine the possibility of there being other objects of the same kind. Moreover, a conceptual understanding of an object presupposes the logical possibility of there being more than one specimen of the same type. If a given object is the only one of its kind, this can only be an empirical, not a logical fact – or else the object in question is not an object.

Reverting now to our discussion of language, it seems clear that no linguistic performance as such represents an exercise of concepts unless it is accompanied by an understanding of the meaning of such performances; which, in turn, is *not* a linguistic performance. To have concepts is not merely to possess a linguistic ability of a certain kind; it is to be able to understand the possibility of the same *thought* being expressed in different languages in different ways. It is maintained that a correct linguistic performance not only suggests but proves that the person in question has the corresponding concept. But this will not help me in my difficulty, say, with a Chinaman whose language I do not know and whose linguistic performance, consequently, I cannot assess. Of course, I can learn his language, and he can learn mine. But the assumption that we shall both be making when embarking upon such a language-learning enterprise is that we can communicate the same thoughts in a different idiom.

Clearly, to have concepts involves an understanding of the meaning of a linguistic performance, not merely the ability to use a language in a certain way. This is not to suggest that this understanding is something entirely separate, something that one might possess *without* actually having the ability to use any kind of language oneself. All the same, it is crucial to draw a distinction between the two.

Not surprisingly Bennett finds it difficult satisfactorily to explain the term 'linguistic ability'. The difficulty is made more severe by his distinction between a 'concept-exercising language' and languages which are not 'concept-exercising' (such as might be a language that consists merely of linguistic responses to sensory stimuli). He tells us that he is concerned only with the former; but how does he *know* the difference between the two kinds of languages? His reasoning becomes circular at this point. He explains that he uses the phrase 'concept-exercising language' as an abbreviation for 'language of the highly developed kind in connection with which "concept" can be given real work to do, i.e. whose metalanguage can usefully contain the word "concept"'.[8] But 'concept' is a word like any other and it is in the concept that we are interested. 'To abbreviate', as Bennett says, 'is not of course to clarify'. However, when he tries to be more specific things begin to go wrong. This is the explanation he gives: 'The question of whether a language is a concept-exercising one does depend upon what sorts of statements can be made in it: for example, it depends partly upon whether statements of a general or reason-giving kind can be made in it.'[9] A little later he adds to this statements about the past. But in specifying the meaning of the phrase 'concept-exercising language' in this manner he is appealing by implication to our understanding of generality, and hence to our ability to identify general statements for what they are. In other words, he is presupposing a capacity on our part for *conceptual thought*. Without such a capacity the distinction between languages which are 'concept-exercising' and those which are not 'concept-exercising' would be meaningless.

But – it might be objected – why make such heavy weather of

[8] *Ibid*. p. 85.
[9] *Ibid*. pp. 86f.

this. It is perfectly natural and indeed unavoidable to presuppose an elementary grasp of generality and of identity of meaning; and hence the capacity for conceptual thought. Quite so. But the implications of this must be *elucidated* and taken fully into account in an analysis of concepts, and it is precisely this that linguistic arguments do not, and by their very nature, cannot do.

The point is this: linguistic skills are intelligible as concept-exercising skills only against the background of a certain type of *experiences*, i.e. against the background of certain non-linguistic facts. Without the appropriate experiences the term 'concept-exercising language' would make little sense. Indeed it would be impossible to draw a significant distinction between 'concept-exercising' languages and language based on a stimulus/response pattern. By drawing the latter distinction (which he rightly and confidently expects us to understand) Bennett is invalidating his own linguistic premises.

So what explanation should we give? How can we clarify the nature of concepts? It might be said, as a first step towards an explanation, that the concept-exercising capacity is similar to the ability to play a particular kind of instrument; a laboriously acquired skill like playing the flute. But the analogy, though helpful in some ways, can be misleading. For one can know that a person is playing the flute without being able to play it oneself, but one can not know that anyone is using concepts without being able to use them oneself.

But perhaps what is needed is not an explanation but a *demonstration*. I demonstrate my ability to use concepts by asking questions, making statements, etc. I *show* what concepts are by using concepts in the same way in which the flute player might show what flute playing is by playing his flute. But again the analogy is not quite adequate. Whereas the flute player might succeed in demonstrating the nature of flute playing even to his unmusical listeners by simply playing his instrument, one can hardly hope to be able to demonstrate the nature of conceptual thought to anyone by using language in certain ways, unless one's listeners are capable of conceptual thought themselves.

3. The arguments in favour of the view of concepts as linguistic abilities are usually coupled with an attack on mental objects and on what is regarded as the philosophically pernicious

tendency to see concepts as a subclass of such objects. It is argued against mental objects that the assumption of such objects as some kind of mental analogues of physical objects embodies a category-mistake and that consequently their existence cannot be coherently asserted.

The concept of a category-mistake was introduced into recent philosophy by Gilbert Ryle who formulated in terms of this concept his criticism of what he called the 'dogma of the ghost in the machine' – the view, that is, that human mind while in some mysterious way linked with the body (which is held to be merely an intricate machine) has nevertheless an independent life of its own : in short, that there are two separate worlds of objects : one physical, the other mental. Ryle's principal thesis is that this 'dogma' is based on a confusion of logical categories or types. It is mistakenly assumed that we can speak at the same logical level about two ontologically different kinds of existences ; that we can say in the same logical breath, as it were, that there are both minds and bodies, physical processes and mental processes, mechanical causes of bodily movements and mental causes of bodily movements. This, claims Ryle, is absurd. In each of these conjunctions the terms involved belong to different logical categories and require a different type of treatment. The 'dogma' is nonsensical because it conjoins terms of logically different types.

This is not entirely clear. If this means that it is never possible to bring categorially disparate objects under a common denominator without this resulting in a logical absurdity, then this is manifestly false. Whenever we have two objects of different types there is always a higher category under which their differences can be elucidated. Any contrast presupposes some common denominator between the contrasted items, or else the very contrast cannot be made intelligible.

If, however, Ryle's main quarrel with the 'official dogma' is that this dogma is based on the wrong choice of common denominator for the contrasted terms, then his undertaking appears in a somewhat different light. His position, then, may be summed up thus. The concept of an object is inappropriate to serve as a common denominator category in terms of which the distinction between the mental and the physical could be satisfactorily explained. Rather we should rely on the concept of behaviour and discuss the distinction in terms of behavioural differences. Instead of talking in terms of mental objects we should examine the different types of mental capacities as they manifest themselves in observable behaviour and compare them with behavioural manifestations of non-mental capacities.

However, it needs to be shown that the choice of the new common denominator is indeed the correct choice, and if it should turn out – as it well might – that the choice was too restrictive and in certain respects inappropriate, then Ryle himself might be said to be guilty of a 'category-mistake'. Inevitably a failure on his part adequately to justify his own categorial rearrangement would seriously weaken the premisses from which he argues against the 'official dogma'.

It is not possible here to go into the details of his analysis; nor is this necessary for our purpose. We must, however, comment briefly on the restrictive nature of his premisses in regard to concepts, especially higher order concepts. It is clear that Ryle rejects any idea of concepts as mental objects; equally he rejects the idea of concepts as mental-objects-*cum*-abilities. But is it possible to explain concepts solely in terms of abilities to 'do certain sorts of things'; i.e. in *dispositional* terms? Let us see what Ryle has to say about the logic of dispositional statements.

Dispositional statements, he maintains[10], resemble law statements in that they are partly 'variable' or 'open'. At the same time, they differ from law statements in that they refer to the capacities, tendencies, propensities, etc. of *particular* persons or things. They combine the elements of generality and singularity. They are not reports of concrete episodes, they narrate no incidents – although, if they are true, they are 'satisfied' by narrated incidents. They are 'open' in the sense that they may refer to any number of relevant episodes. Thus to say 'John Doe knows French' is to claim that John Doe can demonstrate his ability on different occasions, e.g. by responding pertinently if addressed in French, by translating from French, etc. Dispositional statements, however, may involve time limits. For example, the statement 'John Doe knew French last year' refers to all the relevant episodes within the indicated period. On the other hand, 'John Doe spoke French at breakfast this morning' is a factual statement reporting a concrete incident and is radically different from either of the other two statements which are both dispositional and do not narrate any concrete episodes. According to Ryle, the myth of the 'ghost in the machine' is

---

[10] *The Concept of Mind* (London: Hutchinson, 1963), p. 119.

closely linked with the tendency to ignore this difference; to interpret dispositional words such as 'know', 'believe' etc. as *episodic* words and to regard what are merely dispositional statements about certain capacities as reports of some occult mental incidents, acts, states, objects.

But things are less simple than they seem. For it is not always easy to decide what episodes are evidence for what dispositions. Suppose someone says 'John Doe thinks in French'. How do we decide which particular episodes satisfy this dispositional statement? Can we decide this without actually consulting John and relying on what he says? If we cannot, then we shall have to allow at least the possibility of there being other than externally observable episodes, and, in consequence, we shall not have entirely succeeded in getting rid of the 'ghost in the machine'.

Let us now revert to the general topic of concepts. If we apply Ryle's principle of dispositional analysis to concepts we obtain the general formula which, as we saw, is defended by Bennett, namely that to have the concept F is to be able to do ϕ; ϕ representing a class of linguistic activities. This class is not very rigidly defined; but it is claimed that in practice it is in most cases clear from the context what can and what cannot be done; and that in any case a certain degree of indeterminacy is to the good, for it makes for flexibility and encourages a creative use of language.

But this will not do at all. We cannot pretend that concepts are explicable in terms of linguistic skills and then refuse to be more specific about the linguistic performances that display such skills. To give one or two examples in one's own language is not enough. As pointed out earlier, the problem arises of explaining the connection between the linguistic skills of speakers using *different* languages; for we must allow that despite the differences in their respective languages the speakers concerned can in principle have the same concepts.

But quite apart from this, there is always the problem of deciding when a given linguistic performance, or a series of such performances, constitutes a sufficient ground from which to infer that a person does in fact have the concept F – especially if we concede, as we must, that it is not possible to list in advance all the sentences in which a given concept can be meaningfully applied.

At this point it will probably again be said that in practice this problem does not present unsurmountable difficulties; that

we make our decisions on pragmatic grounds and that successful communicative contact is the best test of correctness of such
decisions. But the point is that we normally assume that a display of a particular linguistic skill, or skills, is accompanied by
an understanding of what is being said and an assumption that
what is being said is intelligible and reproducible by different
speakers from different points of view. We equally assume an
understanding of the possibility of one's being mistaken and
being put right by others. However, the understanding of the
possibility of intersubjective intelligibility and the possibility of
error are not themselves 'linguistic skills'. It is conceivable that
someone should possess the required linguistic skills without
understanding these possibilities as *possibilities*. Yet such an
understanding seems to be essential to an understanding of concepts *qua* concepts. It follows that the ability to give a satisfactory
linguistic performance, while it may be a necessary condition, is
not also a sufficient condition of 'having concepts'. It is possible
that someone should perform correctly on every occasion and
yet lack the real understanding of the meaning of correctness.
Similarly it is conceivable that someone should always be able
to tell the right time without understanding the meaning of time.
But if so, we can hardly maintain that having concepts is equivalent to having – rather than just *involves* having – certain
linguistic abilities.

4.   It is at this point that the relevance of a phenomenological
analysis of experiences becomes apparent. It would hardly be
possible for anyone to have the concept of time without being
capable of experiencing the passage of time. No temporal order
concepts are intelligible *qua* temporal order concepts without
temporal experiences. We should hesitate to say of a computer
that it has a concept of correctness simply on the grounds that
it accepts certain answers and rejects others. Again if someone
can be said to have a concept of fear, then this is surely not simply
because he is able to describe instances of fear behaviour, but
because he is able to have and conceive the relevant experience.
Sometimes it is possible to conceive, but not to have the relevant
experience. But unless we can refer to possible experiences, to the
ability to have and conceive certain experiences, we cannot
intelligibly discuss the question what it is to *have* concepts.

A different kind of ability, then, is brought here into focus:

the ability of having and conceiving the possibility of certain experiences; and it is maintained that the structure of experiences can be explored in a phenomenological reflexion. What is needed, it is insisted, is a careful phenomenological analysis of *modes* of experiencing.

It is necessary at this point to draw a distinction between the phenomenological method as a method and what has become customary to refer to as 'phenomenology'. Phenomenology is more than just a method; it is a philosophical attitude whereby experiences are made the *main topic* of philosophical concern. Phenomenology regards experiences as the *main philosophical theme*, just as Linguistic Analysis regards language as the *main philosophical theme*. While both these attitudes must be rejected as one-sided, the methods in question can frequently be employed with advantage.

But let us return to concepts. It seems clear from what has been said that to have concepts does not merely involve the ability to perform linguistically in some ways, but also the ability to have certain kinds of experiences and to conceive others. It presupposes an understanding of generality, i.e. the ability to see things as 'examples', the ability to see the universal in the singular, and to address oneself to both the singular and the universal in various acts of reflection. Evidently, if we are going to speak in terms of abilities, we shall have to do so in a fairly wide sense. A linguistic analysis will have to be supplemented with a phenomenological analysis of the basic modes of experiencing (or 'modes of consciousness', as they are also frequently called) characteristic of conceptual thought. It is not possible to 'have' concepts and not to have the capacity for such modes of experiencing (or 'modes of consciousness').

This is indeed one of the main premises of Husserl's own approach. He sees concepts as types of meanings, and conceptual meanings *qua* meanings, according to him, are intelligible only in the context of certain *acts of meaning*. Of course, he is anxious that this should not be interpreted in a psychological sense. Meanings are not mental states, or some kind of mental particulars forming part of the psychological content of such states. He would reject the idea of meanings as 'mental objects'. Meanings, he claims, are 'ideal-identical unities' which must not on any account be confused with the psychological contents of acts. At the same time, meanings do not exist *per se*, i.e. irrespective of the possibilities of acts. To every meaning there corresponds an act-type or act-character; in other words, a mode of consciousness. Meanings, including conceptual meanings, are intelligible only in relation to certain possible modes of consciousness. Consequently Husserl regards a phenomenological clarification of the basic modes of consciousness as his main philosophical task.[11]

In short, his reply to Bennett and Ryle would be that the intelligibility of a 'concept-exercising language' depends on the possibility of certain modes of experiencing or modes of consciousness, and that it is here that a philosophical inquiry should begin.

But while thus redirecting philosophical attention towards experiences, in particular towards what he calls 'logical' and 'cognitive' experiences, Husserl does not abandon the basic view that concepts can be properly discussed only in the context of the question of what it is to *have* concepts. Of course, he would reject any purely linguistic interpretation of 'having concepts'. His position is that concepts are types of meaning and meanings are not simply kinds of linguistic skill. They presuppose certain *acts of meaning*. In particular, references to conceptual meanings presuppose the ability of apprehending meanings as ideal unities in acts of reflexion. There are (he would argue) no conceptual meanings *per se* in abstraction from such acts. It is not meaningful to speak of concepts as if they existed *per se*. Concepts are intelligible only in the context of certain acts in which they can be 'had'.

But this unremarkable sounding theory conceals a philosophical noose in which Husserl soon became ensnared. Briefly, the problem he faced was one of reconciling the *objectivity* of meanings with the *subjectivity* of acts. This is, roughly, how he reasoned. The meaning of 'triangle' or the meanings of sentences expressing geometrical theorems about triangles, are clearly not logically dependent upon any particular act or acts as psychological events in my or any other person's consciousness. If we can speak of logical dependence here, then it is only between meanings and certain act-*types*. This, however, is a *transcendental fact* and can be understood only from the standpoint of a *transcendental consciousness*. Meanings and act-types,

---

[11] See *Logical Investigations*, trans. J. N. Findlay (London: Routledge & Kegan Paul, 1970), Vol. I, p. 386.

Husserl argued, are *transcendental correlates* and a philosophical understanding of the world should be based on an understanding of this necessary transcendental correlation.

The end-product of Husserl's analysis is thus a picture of a transcendental symmetry between meanings and act-types. But quite clearly this does not help us over the main difficulty, for the awkward fact remains that we think in concrete acts and not in act-types as such, just as we sit on concrete chairs and not on chair-types as such; and concrete acts in their full-blooded historical particularity cannot be accommodated within Husserl's transcendental model.

The problem, briefly, is this: that Husserl's model while providing, in a sense, a transcendental interpretation of what it is to 'have' concepts, or rather conceptual meanings, cannot enlighten us about the vital relation between the psychological and the transcendental sense of 'having'. The result is that the relationship between acts and conceptual meanings remains clouded in ambiguity which Husserl seems incapable of removing.

5.   It seems pretty clear from what has been said so far that a purely phenomenological treatment of concepts is just as inadequate and can cause just as much philosophical confusion as a purely linguistic treatment of concepts. It seems equally obvious that there is no justification for regarding either of the two methods of approach as being more fundamental than the other. They are directed to two different but structurally interlinked aspects of the same problem – the aspect of language and the aspect of experiences – and we cannot afford to neglect either of these two aspects if we do not wish to misunderstand the problem and its philosophical implications.

But now a new problem seems to be confronting us. We have considered concepts from both points of view under the general topic of what it is to *have* concepts. The linguistic analyst, as we saw, insists that to have concepts is to have certain linguistic abilities, while the phenomenologist underlines the importance of certain modes of experiencing. But why should we automatically assume that the topic of concepts reduces to the topic of what it is to have concepts and then proceed to interpret concepts in terms of certain capacities? Concepts are not simply subjective interpretive patterns; they are embedded in the objective structure of the world. While it may be perfectly true that the intelligibility of concepts *qua* concepts presupposes a capacity to perform linguistically in some ways and also the capacity to address oneself to certain meanings in certain acts, it is equally true that we need the idea of embeddedness of concepts in the world and that this idea cannot be explained in terms of 'capacities'.

At this point the following word of protest is likely to be heard. Concepts – it will be said – are neither entities nor names of entities. They are not necessarily exemplified by concrete particulars in the real world. Nor is it necessary that all concepts should be applicable to such particulars. From the fact that someone has a given concept nothing can be inferred about the existence of the corresponding 'exemplifying instances'. My having the concept of a winged horse does not imply the existence of winged horses. In short, the possibility of a concept does not depend on its being non-empty.

But is this always the case? Take, for example, the concept of the ego. One could hardly have the concept of the ego without there being an ego. Or take the very concept of existence. It would hardly be possible for anyone to have the concept of existence without anything existing. Whereas it is quite possible to have the concept of a winged horse without there being winged horses, one cannot have the concept of existence without some concepts at least being non-empty. Or consider the concept of truth. Obviously one could not coherently maintain both that someone 'has' the concept of truth and that nothing whatever is true. It follows that in some cases at least the existence of exemplifying instances is a necessary presupposition of the concept being intelligible; that it is part of the meaning of the concept concerned that there *should* be such instances.

It is of course concepts such as these that are philosophically most interesting. Their 'embeddedness' in the world is a feature of their meaning. These concepts cannot be adequately analysed either in linguistic or in phenomenological terms, but require a more complex *structural* analysis in which the structural interdependence of examples, use of language and experiences must be brought fully to light and philosophically elucidated.

Index of Names